In *Just* ... res more t... ng creatio... on the map, including her famous ... ach Pie and Brandied Banana Butterscotch Pie, as well as savory renditions like the Fig + Pig Quiche and Roasted Brussels Sprouts + Cherry Tart. Maya-Camille also tells the stories of heroes outside the kitchen, luminaries who strive for social justice and equity, and shares recipes they've inspired. Maya-Camille's bakery was launched in memory of her father, who was a criminal defense attorney and had a deep love for baking pies. Through her bakery she proves that good work and delicious decadence can go hand in hand.

Sweet and Savory Pies, Quiches, and Tarts
+ Inspirational Stories from Exceptional People

JUSTICE OF THE PIES

MAYA-CAMILLE BROUSSARD

PHOTOGRAPHS BY DAN GOLDBERG

CLARKSON POTTER/PUBLISHERS

NEW YORK

HEY, MOM.

THIS IS FOR YOU.

CONTENTS

INTRODUCTION

When people say "pie," they often tend to draw out the vowels. It's like speaking a word and drooling at the same time. Piiiiiiiiiiieeeee. I've never heard anyone say "cookie" this way.

Pies are nostalgic and timeless. Pies feel more grown-up than, say, a cupcake. But pies are also something many of us grew up with.

I most definitely grew up with pies. My father, Stephen Broussard, was a self-proclaimed "Pie Master." Early Saturday mornings, he'd tie on his apron that read "Skinny People Make Bad Cooks," throw on his toque (yes, he actually wore the iconic chef's hat while cooking at home), blast his favorite jazz albums on the stereo, and bake a quiche. He felt that making quiches made him seem cultured. For him, quiche was like *oui oui fancy*.

My family migrated north, to Chicago, from Louisiana, a state known for its culinary prowess. And there was no shortage of one-upmanship in my family's kitchens. Immediately after baking or cooking, my dad would call my aunt Sandy or my aunt Pat to taunt them about his food being better than theirs. The conversation went something like this:

"Hey, Pat, I made an apple cranberry pie last Sunday. It was pretty good. I served it with—"

"Yeah, you KNOW that I make a pretty good apple pie."

"I know, I get it. But what I'm saying is I just made one and it was pretty damn good."

"What did you put in it? Did you roll it around in cinnamon and sugar without cooking it down? I don't do it like that. I like to cook my apples first and then let them cool before I put them in my pie."

"Yeah, but, Pat, ain't nobody talking about your apple pie right now!"

My dad passed away in 2009. He suffered a seizure caused by an inoperable brain tumor. We held his funeral at Holy Family Catholic Church in Chicago, a few blocks from the Robert Brooks housing project where he grew up. More than four hundred people attended the service.

As his only child, and as an introvert, I was overwhelmed with the number of people walking up to me to hug me, shake my hand, or offer a word of condolence. I was happy to finally escape to the church's basement, where a handful of family and close friends were enjoying fried chicken, macaroni and cheese, greens, red fruit punch, and caramel cake. Miles Davis blasted on the portable speakers. Everything was just as my dad had requested.

I sat at a table by myself, happy to steal a moment alone to rub the tennis ball–size stress knot that had begun to form in my upper back, when my cousin Stefanie sauntered over and interrupted my quietude. "We should start a foundation," she said.

I looked at her out of the corner of my eyes. "And why?"

"In memory of Uncle Steve. We should bake pies and teach kids how to bake pies. It can be a family thing."

I was one week away from opening an art gallery and bar, and my dad's passing was just an added layer of stress on my spirit.

The last thing I wanted to think about was pies or quiches.

Stefanie understood and backed off. "Okay, I'm just saying—think about it."

Three years following his death, my tank was empty. I had poured all my energy into curating the gallery's experiences and managing the bar. I wasn't sure what my next move was going to be, but I definitely needed time to rethink and recuperate.

I flew to San Francisco to visit my cousins Justin and Shamieka. They had a new baby girl, Dawson, and I went to help them care for her while they managed a few work commitments.

They lived in the culturally rich Mission neighborhood, where streets were lined with family-run eateries. One day, Shamieka and I stumbled upon a bakery called Mission Pie. My skin began to tingle, and I felt a slight chill when we walked in the doors. I was supposed to be here.

I ordered a slice of pie with hot chocolate and my cousin ordered a slice of gluten-free quiche. I sat down and surveyed the place. It was small, cute, cozy, and reminded me of a few spots back home in Chicago. I noticed that there were a lot of teenagers working behind the counter. While we waited for our order, my cousin quipped, "I love this place. They hire a lot of displaced teens who are living in shelters." My head felt light, and my ears started to ring.

I flashed back to the basement of Holy Family Catholic Church and heard an echo of Stefanie's voice: "We should bake pies."

My dad's spirit had been trying to tell me all along, and now I heard him loud and clear.

I went back to the house, and I told my cousin Justin, "I think I'm going to start a bakery." My cousin, who watched *Iron Chef* as if it were a game of Monday Night Football, was on board with my impulsive decision. He immediately started throwing out ideas for savory pies and made a grocery list so that we could begin recipe testing the next day.

His enthusiasm confirmed, for me, that this was a good idea.

I am very decisive, and once I make up my mind I move with a purpose and walk with fortitude. The fatigue I felt from my first business was suddenly lifted. I was ready to tackle this new idea. I didn't know what my menu would be. I didn't know where I would operate a kitchen. I didn't even know who I would serve, or if anyone would want to eat the pies I made. I didn't even have a name.

"I have the perfect name," my aunt Sandy offered. "You should call it, The Pie Master's Daughter."

I hesitated for a minute and then replied, "I was thinking . . . maybe I could call it Justice of the Pies."

Aunt Sandy brushed my suggestion aside and exclaimed, "But you're the Pie Master's daughter!"

Justin backed up my decision on the bakery's name and it was settled: In the fall of 2014, Justice of the Pies was going to be my newest endeavor. We spent the remainder of that week cooking and baking and making daily trips to the grocery store. I felt renewed. I was really going to do this.

Once I returned to Chicago, I got my proper paperwork and licensing in place, I found a shared kitchen to work out of, and I applied to participate in a few spring markets. I didn't have everything figured out, but I did have

$7,000 and a willingness to go slow and steady. I also had a purpose.

I was not only celebrating my dad's love of pies but also reflecting on his life. He was a man who grew up with food insecurity and he was also a criminal defense attorney. So, in building the bakery, I integrated a social mission element to fight against food insecurities and give people second chances.

One of our social initiatives is the I KNEAD LOVE Workshop. Through the seminar, we provide elementary-aged children from lower income communities instruction on good nutrition, developing basic cooking skills, and encouraging creativity in the kitchen. In cultivating these life skills, we are helping children become more food secure and more self-sufficient in the kitchen.

I started the company eight years ago and, ever since, Justice of the Pies has been known not only for our delicious sweet and savory pies, quiches, and tarts but also for how we positively impact the lives of others. This cookbook will do the same. It includes recipes inspired by my personal experiences, my travels, and the meals I've shared with friends. I've also included recipes that were created to reflect the spirits of impactful people—people who, like me, live a purpose-driven life and whose mission it is to positively lift others. I like to refer to these people as "stewards" because they are agents who stand for fairness and equality. As a tribute to them, *Justice of the Pies* includes their stories, and recipes informed by their lives, histories, cultures, and missions.

In addition to helping people and continuing my dad's legacy of doing good, what I love most about serving pie is seeing the reactions on people's faces when they eat it. I am especially tickled when people walk away while taking their first bite, stop in their tracks, and then whip their bodies around to search for me in the crowds (likely at a farmers' market where I often have a pie stand). Their eyes are usually saying, "Whaaaaa . . ." I think my superpower is my highly attuned sense of smell and taste—you see, since I was a baby, I've had significant hearing loss, and when you lose one sense, the brain adapts by giving more sensory information to another. Flavors and aromas for me are distinct and I love to bring complexity to something as homey and simple as pie (or quiche or other delectable treats). In short, it gives me such an exhilaration to blow the lid off of someone's expectations of what an apple or peach pie *should* taste like. When it really gets down to it, baking pies makes me happy because it allows me a way to express my creativity while spreading joy.

Creativity is key for me. It was even noticed by Milk Bar's chef and founder, Christina Tosi, who handpicked me to star in *Bake Squad*, a friendly baking competition that streams on Netflix. I am always trying to push the envelope to create a pie that a customer can *only* get from me. Who else makes a Strawberry Basil Key Lime Pie? No one. Who else makes a Bleu Cheese Praline Pear Pie? No one. Customers have begged for my Salted Caramel Peach Pie recipe for years. In the past no one has made that pie but me . . . but now, you can make it, too.

Maya-Camille

NOTES FOR SUCCESS

Baking can sometimes feel like a daunting experience. It does not need to be. Though many of the recipes in *Justice of the Pies* have complex, layered flavors, the recipe itself may actually be quite simple—or, occasionally, it may take more time to make. Either way, the most important first step when baking is to read the entire recipe through before you start. Reading a recipe in its entirety will help you to be prepared to execute it.

Once you have read a recipe, gather all the ingredients needed to make it. This is called *mise en place*, a French phrase often used in kitchens that translates loosely to "everything in its place." It is important to prepare, arrange, and organize all the ingredients needed to carry out the instructions listed in a recipe. Setting up the components of a recipe prior to beginning will help you avoid mistakes and, hopefully, head off any frustrations that may come when navigating a new dish.

But no matter how hard you try, sometimes a recipe fails. If you find yourself exasperated because a recipe did not turn out exactly as you imagined, take a deep breath and think through what might have gone wrong: Was your baking temperature correct? Perhaps you need an oven thermometer to make sure what is displayed on the oven's controls matches the actual temperature in the oven. Do you have the right kind of butter or flour? Maybe the brand of ingredient you used changed the way a recipe turned out. Did you scorch sugar while melting it? It could be a possibility that the burner on your stovetop is too large, and you need to move your saucepan to a smaller burner. I have found that the most important lessons baking can teach you are to have patience, to try not to rush through a recipe, and to show yourself some grace when something doesn't turn out the way you imagined. It is perfectly acceptable to pick yourself up and try again. Some of my most memorable bakes involved recipes that I've had to make not once, not twice, but three or four times to get it just right. The feeling of victory that washed over me when I got it just right is worth persevering for.

Justice of the Pies is written to provide the clearest set of instructions for making each dish. The more you practice a recipe, the stronger you become in executing it. Following are additional notes that will help you get off to a formidable start as you approach each one of the pies, quiches, and tarts in these pages.

ON FLOUR

In all of my crusts, cookies, biscuits, and doughs, I typically use a high-protein (11%) unbleached all-purpose flour (with the exception of my gluten-free crust). I do not work with whole-grain flour, but I encourage you to try it out if that flour is your preference.

ON SALT

Kosher salt is less refined than iodized table salt and is coarser, too. Kosher salt seasons food more effectively than table salt and is free from off flavors and slightly bitter, metallic aftertastes. You can also find fine-grain kosher salt (which is texturally more like traditional table salt) that disperses more quickly in ingredients.

As a rule of thumb: 1 teaspoon of table salt equals 1½ to 2 teaspoons of coarse kosher salt. So, if you decided to substitute table salt in each recipe for kosher salt, cut its measurement down by half.

ON FAT

I prefer baking with European-style cultured butter because it has a higher fat content and less moisture than traditional butter, lending it a creamier and richer flavor. Because the fat content is higher, European-style butter will produce a flakier pie crust. That said, you can use traditional unsalted butter (the amount of salt in butter is inconsistent from brand to brand, so I recommend using unsalted butter in any of the recipes in this book and you will still end up with wonderfully, rich, flaky, and delicious pies).

None of my crusts, pies, or quiches contain pork lard in the dough unless it's critical to the dish. Lard and shortening do help produce a flaky crust, but I feel that flakiness can be achieved through the technique and process of chilling and handling butter correctly (and using European-style butter). Butter not only has more flavor but also browns more easily, which makes for a more aesthetically beautiful bake.

When cooking, I typically use extra-virgin olive oil and butter, but feel free to substitute vegetable or canola oil instead. You may also opt to add more oil and eliminate the butter entirely if you are aiming to make a dish vegan, which is perfectly fine.

ON SPICES

High-quality spices make all the difference in the flavor of a dish. If possible, purchase spices from a specialty store or a spice shop with high turnover. Spices lose their flavors and aromas over time and if exposed to excessive heat (don't store spices near your stove!) or light (a cool, dark pantry is best for storing spices). If in doubt, just buy a fresh jar—using freshly purchased spices is always better than using spices that have been hanging out in your cupboard for the past 2½ years.

ON MEASURING

I've written my recipes with ingredient measurements using both cups and teaspoons as well as the metric system (grams). I highly recommend purchasing a digital kitchen scale and measuring all your ingredients using the metric system, since it allows for greater accuracy when baking. Plus, instead of measuring a cupful of this and a tablespoon of that separately, if the ingredients are to be mixed together, you can simply place a bowl on the scale, zero it out (so the weight of the scale reads 0 even with the bowl on it), and then weigh each ingredient directly into the bowl, zeroing out after each addition.

SWEET PIES

BLEU CHEESE PRALINE PEAR PIE

MAKES ONE 9-INCH PIE

There are two groups of people: those who love bleu cheese and those who absolutely cannot stand it. One thing I *have* discovered, however, is that both sides love my bleu cheese praline pear pie.

Why? Because people who don't like bleu cheese are usually turned off by its pungent aroma. However, in this case, melt-in-your-mouth bleu cheese is offset by the sugared and spiced pears and the earthiness of the brown sugar and oat topping. The result is a pie that offers a sweet and salty flavor layering that most everyone appreciates—especially since it is served with a drizzle of buttery praline sauce. The most common response I've heard when others eat this pie is, "I *hate* bleu cheese, but this is the *best* pie I've ever had!"

Sure, bleu cheese may not smell amazing, but sometimes you cannot be afraid to put a little stank in your pie.

Flour, for rolling out

All-Butter Pie Dough (page 220)

5 or 6 ripe Bartlett or d'Anjou pears, peeled, cored, and sliced

¼ cup (34g) unbleached all-purpose flour

¼ cup (50g) granulated sugar

¼ cup (55g) packed light brown sugar

2 teaspoons ground ginger

1 teaspoon ground cinnamon

1 teaspoon ground nutmeg

½ teaspoon kosher salt

Brown Sugar + Oat Crumble (page 200)

⅓ cup (93g) Broussard Praline Sauce (page 202)

3 tablespoons (30g) bleu cheese crumbles

Adjust an oven rack to the middle position and preheat the oven to 350°F (175°C).

Lightly dust the counter with flour and roll out the pie dough to about 12 inches in diameter. Carefully transfer the dough to a 9-inch pie pan. Roll the overhanging dough to the edge of the pan and crimp. Place the pie shell in the refrigerator to chill for 10 minutes.

In a large bowl, stir together the pears, flour, granulated sugar, brown sugar, ginger, cinnamon, nutmeg, and salt. Let the pears macerate for about 5 minutes.

Remove the pie shell from the refrigerator. Set the pie pan on a baking sheet and scoop the pear mixture into the pie shell.

Transfer to the oven and bake until the crust is golden brown, about 1 hour 10 minutes.

While the filling is baking, it is the perfect time to make the brown sugar and oat crumble (this is also a good time to make the praline sauce if you haven't already).

Remove the pie from the oven and top it with the crumble. Make sure the topping completely covers the pie. The flour in the crumble helps to absorb and thicken any juice that may remain in the filling. Return the pie to the oven and continue to bake until the crumble topping is a light golden brown, about 35 more minutes.

Remove the pie from the oven and allow it to cool for at least 45 minutes before slicing. Once cool, slice the pie and top with the praline sauce and bleu cheese crumbles.

To store the pie, cover with plastic wrap and refrigerate for up to 7 days or freeze for up to 2 months. To thaw, remove the pie from the freezer and allow it to come to room temperature. It's best to warm a slice of pie before enjoying. Wait to drizzle with sauce and sprinkle with bleu cheese until just before serving.

SALTED CARAMEL PEACH PIE

MAKES ONE 9-INCH PIE

My mom (and my namesake), Dr. Camille Billingslea, specializes in family medicine. As I was growing up, she worked long shifts at the hospital, which meant that takeout was usually our best friend. When my mom did cook, she'd make leftover-friendly meals that we could easily reheat if she wasn't home, like spaghetti, tacos, or beans and rice.

Though she wasn't much of a baker and rarely made desserts from scratch, there was one dessert that she mastered, one that she learned from her own mother: peach cobbler.

If I found cans of peaches on the kitchen countertop, I knew a peach cobbler was in my near future. Mom would crank open the large cans, drain them, and tip the peaches into a huge pot. Butter, cinnamon, nutmeg, and brown sugar all went into the pot, which she always did "by eye," which we also call "cooking by vibration," adding ingredients to the dish until the ancestors whispered in your ear to ease up.

A dessert traditionally attributed to the Deep South, cobblers are not meant to be pretty. The ingredients are literally cobbled together into a deep dish and often served warm and topped with a scoop of vanilla ice cream.

In creating the Salted Caramel Peach Pie, I wanted to retain all the buttery, aromatic spices found in my mom's peach cobbler while adding oatmeal and flour to the filling to create a spongy, cake-like texture and give it a prepossessing appearance—no top crust required (making this a great starter pie to make). When my mom made a peach cobbler, there were never any leftovers—the dessert disappeared as quickly as it was pulled from the oven. The same always happens with this peach pie, too.

Flour, for rolling out

All-Butter Pie Dough (page 220)

4 tablespoons (½ stick/57g) unsalted butter, melted

1 large egg

½ cup (100g) granulated sugar

¼ cup (55g) packed light brown sugar

1 teaspoon kosher salt

1 teaspoon pure vanilla extract

½ teaspoon ground cinnamon

½ teaspoon ground nutmeg

½ cup (68g) unbleached all-purpose flour

½ cup (43g) rolled oats

2 cups drained canned sliced peaches

¼ cup (72g) Salted Caramel Sauce (page 208)

Adjust an oven rack to the middle position and preheat the oven to 350°F (175°C).

Lightly dust the counter with flour and roll out the pie dough to about 12 inches in diameter. Carefully transfer the dough to a 9-inch pie pan. Roll the overhanging dough to the edge of the pan and crimp. Place the pie shell in the refrigerator to chill for 10 minutes.

In a large bowl, whisk together the melted butter, egg, granulated sugar, brown sugar, salt, vanilla, cinnamon, and nutmeg until smooth, about 1 minute. Using a silicone spatula or large spoon, stir in the flour and oats.

Fold the peaches into the flour-oat mixture until well incorporated. Remove the pie shell from the refrigerator. Set the pie shell on a baking sheet and pour in the filling.

Transfer to the oven and bake until a cake tester or toothpick inserted in the center of the pie comes out dry, about 1 hour 10 minutes. (This is a perfect time to prepare the Salted Caramel Sauce if you haven't already.)

Remove the pie from the oven and allow it to cool for 15 minutes—this is a pie best served slightly warm. Slice and then drizzle with salted caramel sauce.

To store the pie, cover with plastic wrap and refrigerate for up to 7 days or freeze for up to 2 months. To thaw, remove the pie from the freezer and allow it to come to room temperature. It's best to warm a slice of pie before enjoying. Wait to drizzle with sauce until just before serving.

BONUS: Growing up, one of my favorite Southern-style restaurants in Chicago was called St. Rest No. 2 Country Kitchen. They made a peach and pear cobbler with dumplings throughout the filling. Served in a white Styrofoam cup with a fork perched on top, it was a dessert that was not commonly found in the Chicago culinary landscape. If you want to try it (and I suggest you do!), reduce the peaches to 1 cup and add 1 cup sliced pears.

KLEAVER CRUZ

THE BLACK JOY PROJECT

Kleaver Cruz was lying awake in bed despondent and with a heavy heart.

It was 2015, and his extremely small Dominican family was even smaller around the holiday table that Thanksgiving with the sudden, tragic loss of his only uncle and father figure. Earlier that year in the spring, Freddie Gray had died in police custody, sparking a revival of protests that had begun the year *prior*, after the killing of Eric Garner. On top of all this loss and pain, that summer the Dominican Republic stripped citizenship from thousands of Black Dominicans with Haitian ancestors and deported them to Haiti. Cruz had been organizing with various activist collectives in New York City and was working to amplify the issues of discrimination against Haitians—but on that morning, while he lay in bed, he found himself paralyzed with sadness. He could not change the ills committed against people of a darker hue, nor could he bring his uncle back. He closed his eyes and saw the words "Black" and "joy." He felt that the universe was telling him to take this deep sorrow and combat it with joy.

A few weeks later, Kleaver's mom urged him to take her to an art show. While there, he snapped a photo of his mother and reflected on how happy he was to be there with her—despite the angst and immense sadness they had experienced that year. Kleaver posted the photo to social media. In that moment, he committed to posting one photo a day, for the next thirty days, that illustrated Black joy. Additionally, he asserted that he would no longer watch, nor share, any videos of images of Black people being brutalized. It was too traumatizing. He had no strategy other than liberating himself from his despondency.

The response to his campaign was immense, and people asked for more. After the thirty days ended, Kleaver vowed to make this a permanent installation and thus created the Black Joy Project, an invitation to choose joy and to reject a world that marginalizes and discriminates against Black people. While the way people are treated may not change, Cruz asserts that the way in which one responds to and internalizes that treatment can be revolutionary. He is on a mission to urge those across the Black diaspora to conjure up joy as a collective to effectively free themselves from the injustices imposed upon them.

Cruz graduated from posting photos on social media to activating art installations, hosting radio shows, writing essays, moderating discussions, and conducting interviews. He's traveled to places with strong Black diasporic culture such as Cuba, Brazil, South Africa, and the Netherlands to interview others and ask "What does Black joy mean to you?" His is an ongoing quest to explore how joy is an effective tool for resistance and regeneration so that Black people can truly be free. Cruz claims that those who experience the most pain and trauma are often those who experience the deepest forms of joy. A heartbreak creates depth so that one can love even more moving forward. As a Black, queer man who witnessed and experienced the heartbreaks that Black people endure through discrimination and oppression, Kleaver asserts, "They can't steal our joy, 'cause we won't let them."

The Brandied Banana Butterscotch Pie is inspired by Cruz's work. Two of the pie's ingredients are significant to the Black diaspora history: brandy and bananas.

Brandy helped kickstart the cross-Atlantic triangle trade (also known as the Atlantic Slave Trade) and an exchange of "goods" between West Africa, the West Indies, North America, South America, and Europe—including sugar, tobacco, rum, brandy, and humans, specifically from the west coast of Africa. The Middle Passage, which was the midpart of the trading cycle, consisted of enslaved African "cargo" transported and sold in North and South America and the Caribbean in exchange for commodities like sugar and tobacco, which were sent back to Europe. The Middle Passage created the Black diaspora that exists today. Guards of Guineamen (ships that contained those abducted from the Guinea coast of Africa) were often paid in brandy.

Bananas are said to have originated in India more than 10,000 years ago, and many scientists believe that they may have been the world's first fruit. Modern-day bananas were developed in Africa around AD 650 with the crossbreeding of two varietals of wild bananas. Bananas and plantains (their starchy cousins) are embedded in the history of Black people around the world: Banana puddings of the American South, kelewele of Ghana, aloco of Senegal and Côte d'Ivoire, and tostones of Puerto Rico are all great examples of the fruit's importance to Black diaspora cuisine. The Brandied Banana Butterscotch Pie is a creamy, custard-based caramelly pie with a slight kick of ginger. Not only does it celebrate Black joy, but it is a joy to make and eat, too.

BRANDIED BANANA BUTTERSCOTCH PIE

MAKES ONE 9-INCH PIE

Gingersnap Cookie Crust (page 243)

FILLING

¾ cup (150g) granulated sugar

¼ cup (50g) heavy cream

½ cup (110g) packed light brown sugar

⅓ cup (45g) unbleached all-purpose flour

1 teaspoon kosher salt

3 cups (720g) whole milk

6 large egg yolks

2 tablespoons unsalted butter

2 teaspoons pure vanilla extract

TOPPING

Vanilla Bean Chantilly Cream (page 214)

7 tablespoons (98g) unsalted butter

4 large medium-ripe bananas, sliced at an angle into ½-inch-thick pieces

1 cup (220g) packed light brown sugar

⅓ cup (80g) heavy cream

¼ cup (53g) orange marmalade

¼ cup (60g) brandy

Adjust an oven rack to the middle position and preheat the oven to 350°F (175°C).

Bake the gingersnap crust until slightly browned, about 10 minutes. Remove it from the oven and set aside.

MAKE THE FILLING: In a nonreactive medium saucepan, stir together the granulated sugar and ¼ cup (60g) of water. Bring to a boil over medium-high heat, without stirring, but intermittently swirling the saucepan (if you stir it, the mixture could crystallize and you'll have to start over). Once the sugar mixture turns a light amber color, after about 10 minutes, turn off the heat and immediately—and slowly—pour in the heavy cream while vigorously whisking. It will hiss violently! Whisk until the froth subsides.

In a large heavy-bottomed saucepan, whisk together the light brown sugar, flour, and salt. Continue whisking while slowly pouring in 1 cup (240g) of the whole milk. Add the egg yolks and whisk until there are no visible traces of egg. Continue whisking and slowly pour in the remaining 2 cups (480g) whole milk. Add the butter, set the heat to medium-high, and continue to whisk the filling without stopping while the liquid heats up and thickens, being sure to also scrape the bottom edges of the saucepan while whisking so the egg doesn't congeal or burn. Once the mixture is thick and a spoon dragged across the bottom of the pan leaves a trail, remove the saucepan from the heat and slowly pour in the sugar/heavy cream mixture, whisking until well blended, about 10 minutes.

Place a fine-mesh sieve over a large bowl. Pour the mixture through the sieve and discard any solids. Whisk in the vanilla, then pour the filling into the baked pie shell. Refrigerate the pie for 6 hours to chill and set.

PREPARE THE TOPPING: Spoon the Chantilly cream over the chilled pie and use a large spoon, an offset spatula, or a small silicone spatula to spread the topping to the edges of the pie crust. Set the pie aside.

In a large stainless-steel skillet, melt 3 tablespoons (42g) of the butter over medium-high heat. Add the bananas and sauté until slightly browned and tender, about 30 seconds. Turn the banana slices in the skillet with a spatula and lightly brown the other side, an additional 30 seconds. Sprinkle 1 tablespoon of the brown sugar evenly over the bananas and heat until the sugar dissolves. Remove the bananas from the heat and set aside on a plate to cool completely.

When cool, arrange the bananas on top of the pie while layering the slices.

In a small saucepan set on medium heat, add the remaining 4 tablespoons (56g) butter and then stir in the remaining ¾ cup (165g) plus 3 tablespoons brown sugar until it dissolves and simmers, about 2 minutes. Slowly pour in the heavy cream while whisking vigorously—the mixture may hiss violently—and continue whisking until the sugar dissolves into the heavy cream, about 2 minutes.

Add the orange marmalade and brandy, whisking until the marmalade dissolves, about 3 minutes. Reduce the heat to low and allow the sauce to simmer until it slightly thickens, about 3 minutes. Remove the sauce from the heat and drizzle evenly over the bananas.

To store the pie, cover with plastic wrap and store in the refrigerator for up to 3 days.

BOURBON PECAN PIE

MAKES ONE 9-INCH PIE

One afternoon, I was selling pies at Renegade Craft Fair when an elderly couple walked up to my table. The husband looked at me over the top of his glasses and sneered, "Just how good is this pecan pie of yours?" I replied with a polite smile, "Well, sir, people tend to rave about it, so I think you might quite like it." After a few silent moments, he straightened and haughtily announced, "My grandmother made the best pecan pie I've ever had. I have never had a pecan pie as good as my grandmother's pie." His wife nervously tugged at his elbow and said, "Honey, leave her alone." He quickly looked at her and loudly said, "No! I'm going to buy a slice of this pie!" and then turned to me and threatened, "It better be good, or I want my money back."

My mom, who often stopped by if I was working a fair or festival, overheard this exchange. She told him, "Do you see this line that she has? Her pie is GOOD!" and then she turned toward me so that he could not see her face as she rolled her eyes.

I said, "I will not take your money until you've had your first bite." I presented a slice to him and proceeded to help others waiting in a line that was growing longer by the minute.

I was so busy that I forgot all about him until my mom pinched my arm and motioned for me to look behind me. I turned around just as the man's wife said, "Honey? Are you crying?" Her husband's face was bright red with tears streaming down his cheeks.

"It tastes just like my grandmother's pie. I almost feel like she is right here with me at this moment."

He reached out to hand me money for the slice before walking away. When I looked down at my hand, I realized that he had paid double the price for the slice. I can now honestly say that my pecan pie made a grown man cry.

Flour, for rolling out
All-Butter Pie Dough (page 220)
4 large eggs
1 cup (200g) granulated sugar
½ cup (178g) dark corn syrup
2 ounces (57g) bourbon

1 teaspoon pure vanilla extract
½ teaspoon kosher salt
1 tablespoon unbleached all-purpose flour
1½ cups (200g) pecan halves

Adjust an oven rack to the middle position and preheat the oven to 325°F (165°C).

Lightly dust the counter with flour and roll out the pie dough to about 12 inches in diameter. Carefully transfer the dough to a 9-inch pie pan. Roll the overhanging dough to the edge of the pan and crimp. Place the pie shell in the refrigerator to chill for 10 minutes.

In a large bowl, lightly whisk the eggs until they are light and frothy. Add the sugar, corn syrup, bourbon, vanilla, and salt, whisking just until the ingredients come together. Do not overmix. Sift in the flour and fold it into the batter.

Remove the pie shell from the refrigerator and set it on a baking sheet. Line the bottom of the pie shell with the pecans, spreading them evenly. Slowly and constantly pour the batter into the pie shell over the pecans. If you stop while pouring the batter, the pecans will get pushed to the side and your pie filling will have pockets without pecans. Wait a moment to let the pecans rise to the top before transferring to the oven.

Bake the pie until the center slightly jiggles, about 1 hour 5 minutes.

Remove the pie from the oven and allow it to cool for 1 to 2 hours before slicing.

To store the pie, cover with plastic wrap and refrigerate for up to 7 days or freeze for up to 2 months. To thaw, remove the pie from the freezer and allow it to come to room temperature.

RECIPE CONTINUES >>

VARIATION: CHOCOLATE + BACON BOURBON PECAN PIE

Follow the instructions for the Bourbon Pecan Pie (page 27), reducing the amount of dark corn syrup in the filling to ¼ cup (89g) and adding ¼ cup (67g) homemade Hot Fudge Sauce (page 217) or store-bought fudge sauce in the filling mixture. Add the pecans to the pie shell, then add the filling and bake and cool as instructed.

While the pie cools, make the bacon topping. Preheat the oven to 350°F (175°C) and line a baking sheet with parchment paper. Lay 4 or 5 strips of thick-cut bacon, evenly spaced, on the prepared pan and bake until the bacon is crispy, 18 to 20 minutes. Remove the pan from the oven and use tongs to transfer the bacon to a plate lined with paper towels. Once cool, chop the bacon into small bits.

Before serving, drizzle ¼ cup (67g) of warmed hot fudge sauce over the pie and top with the chopped bacon. Slice and serve.

To store, cover with plastic wrap and refrigerate for up to 7 days or freeze for up to 2 months. To thaw, remove the pie from the freezer and allow it to come to room temperature. Wait to drizzle with sauce until just before serving.

STRAWBERRY LEMONADE PIE

MAKES ONE 9-INCH PIE

Growing up in Chicago, summertime meant sticky weather, festivals, block parties every single weekend, and hours spent hanging out on the lakefront, cracking open the fire hydrant to create a makeshift water park, and eating Italian ices.

Italian ice is a frozen, tart dessert typically served in a Styrofoam cup with a straw and a spoon. It is made with simple ingredients including water, sugar, ice, chunks of fruit, and lemon rinds.

When Chicago's humidity proved to be too much to bear, one of my favorite childhood memories was driving to Taylor Street in Chicago's Little Italy to get Italian ice at Mario's Italian Lemonade. The line for Mario's was always at least three-quarters of a block long. Their all-natural Italian ice came in flavors such as cantaloupe, watermelon, pineapple, cherry, banana, and, of course, lemon. My favorite was a combination of lemon with strawberry, and that is the inspiration for this pie.

The tanginess of this pie, mixed with the brightness of strawberries, makes it an absolute hit during the summer.

4 large egg yolks

2 (14 oz/396g) cans sweetened condensed milk

Finely grated zest of 1 large lemon

¾ cup (187g) lemon juice (from 3 or 4 large lemons)

Graham Cracker Crust (page 238)

1½ cups strawberries, hulled and quartered or thinly sliced lengthwise

Adjust an oven rack to the middle position and preheat the oven to 350°F (175°C).

In a bowl, whisk together the egg yolks, sweetened condensed milk, and lemon zest until completely combined—the sweetened condensed milk will thin out. While whisking, slowly pour in the lemon juice until completely combined. The mixture will begin to thicken as the acids in the lemon juice react with the proteins in the sweetened condensed milk. Set aside for 5 minutes to thicken further.

Set the graham cracker pie shell on a baking sheet and pour in the filling.

Bake the pie until tiny bubbles emerge on the surface of the pie's filling, about 15 minutes. Remove the pie from the oven and refrigerate for at least 6 hours to chill and set.

Once the pie is completely chilled and you're ready to serve, top the pie with the strawberries. There is always an option to enjoy the pie without strawberries, too.

To store, place in a pie or cake box and refrigerate for up to 7 days or freeze for up to 2 months. Remove the pie from the freezer and allow it to thaw for 15 to 20 minutes before slicing.

BONUS: The hand-painted menu board at Mario's Italian Lemonade displayed so many potential flavor combinations. Try switching out the strawberries for fresh blueberries prepared in the same fashion as they are in Blueberry Banana Pudding Pie (page 33).

When Paige Chenault asks "How are you?" she isn't expecting the customary response, "I'm fine."

She truly wants to know just how you are *doing*. She has always had a deep desire to be known and to be seen—and reciprocally, to see others. As a preacher's kid from Oklahoma, she's always understood the value in people and the power of serving. Her parents modeled that for her, and living with an undercurrent of treating people well has remained a part of who she is. This idea of serving people led her to a career as an event planner.

After planning her own wedding, Paige fell in love with creating and managing the small, gritty details that come with event planning. She found it energizing when those details transformed how a person felt when they walked into a venue or a room. Once while on a plane, a pregnant Paige casually picked up the kids' magazine that was tucked in the back of the seat in front of her. Her eyes fell on a photo of a very young boy in Haiti who was standing shirtless in the middle of a muddy street, belly distended from hunger, and eyes sunken with sadness. This photo gripped Paige as she sat, rather comfortably, in her plush airline seat and thoughts flashed in her mind like, "How dare I? What about him?" As an expectant mom, Paige had daydreamed about the parties she'd throw for her baby girl, and that photo made her realize that not only did her privilege afford her the opportunity to shower her daughter with the best, but also her expertise and experience in producing parties meant that her daughter would have the ultimate celebrations for years to come. Paige wondered, "Who am I to think that I can do all of this for my kid, and leave the rest of the world behind?" She was capable of throwing incredible parties for people who could afford it, and while that was great and all, Paige really wanted to use her talents and skill set to serve those who could not.

While thirty thousand feet in the air, the idea for The Birthday Party Project literally fell from the sky. In 2012, after ten years as a professional event planner, Paige shifted her focus to planning birthday parties for children living with homelessness. Paige and her team of volunteers partner with various agencies (such as a shelter or transitional living facility) to bring joy and a degree of normalcy to a child while making sure that the important milestone of celebrating another year of life does not go unnoticed.

The Birthday Party Project has celebrated the personal new years of 16,000 children and has hosted 67,000 kids as guests at those birthday celebrations. Paige has organized parties in twenty cities across America and partners with brands that donate birthday cakes, greeting cards, children's clothes, and toys. Her loyal volunteers provide activities and games to keep the parties lively and memorable.

I created this Peanut Butter + Jelly Pie in Paige's honor. It's salty, nutty, fruity, and sweet and honors the kid-like wonderment and excitement that is experienced whenever an annual birthday milestone is celebrated. Peanut butter and jelly is a classic and timeless pairing that never grows old, even as we do.

PEANUT BUTTER + JELLY PIE

MAKES ONE 9-INCH PIE

Graham Cracker Crust (page 238)

1½ cups (402g), plus 2 tablespoons creamy peanut butter

8 tablespoons (½ stick/113g) unsalted butter, at room temperature

1 cup (117g) confectioners' sugar

½ teaspoon vanilla extract

½ cup (171g) grape jelly

Vanilla Bean Chantilly Cream (optional; page 214)

¼ cup (37g) peanuts (optional), chopped

Adjust an oven rack to the middle position and preheat the oven to 350°F (175°C).

Form the crust as directed in the recipe and then bake directly on the rack for 10 minutes. Remove it from the oven and set aside to cool.

In a standing mixer or a medium bowl with a hand mixer, whisk the 1½ cups of the peanut butter and the butter until well combined, about 1 minute. Add the confectioners' sugar and continue to mix until well combined, then stir in the vanilla.

Scrape the peanut butter mixture into the pie crust and use a silicone spatula to evenly spread the filling in the crust. Refrigerate the pie, uncovered, for 15 minutes.

In a small saucepan, melt the jelly over medium heat, stirring until it loosens, 3 to 5 minutes.

Remove the pie from the refrigerator. Evenly pour the jelly over the peanut butter layer. Return to the refrigerator to chill for 1 hour.

If desired, serve slices topped with Chantilly cream and sprinkled with chopped peanuts.

To store the pie, cover with plastic wrap and refrigerate for up to 7 days or freeze for up to 2 months.

BLUEBERRY BANANA PUDDING PIE

MAKES ONE 9-INCH PIE

Banana pudding is one of those dishes like potato salad or macaroni and cheese: Only certain people are allowed to bring their version to a family function. If you see a pan of untouched banana pudding on the table at a barbecue, you can be sure that someone is going to loudly ask "Who made the banana pudding?" before daring to taste a spoonful. In my family, if the answer is either Aunt Ruby or Mama Pat, then it has already received the familial blessing and is safe to eat—no questions asked.

When I first created this pie and offered it to my mom, she looked at it warily and said, "You know who makes a good banana pudding? Cousin Vivian." I dramatically threw my hands up in the air and looked at her. "Dang! Can you please give me a chance to shine?"

I did get my great-aunt Ruby's approval though—which is as good as gold. My heart soared when I learned that she *requested* that I bring some for the dessert table at the next family holiday dinner.

Clearly this pie, with its creamy texture and slightly tangy taste, shines rather brightly.

VANILLA PUDDING

¾ cup (150g) granulated sugar

3 tablespoons unbleached all-purpose flour

1 cup (240g) whole milk

2 large egg yolks

1 tablespoon unsalted butter

1 teaspoon pure vanilla extract

BLUEBERRY SWIRL

1 cup blueberries

¼ cup (50g) granulated sugar

1 tablespoon fresh lemon juice

PIE FILLING

8 ounces (223g) cream cheese, at room temperature

⅓ cup (67g) granulated sugar

2 large eggs, at room temperature

2 tablespoons sour cream

1 tablespoon unbleached all-purpose flour

½ teaspoon pure vanilla extract

2 or 3 ripe bananas, cut into chunks

ASSEMBLY

Vanilla Wafer Crust (page 242)

MAKE THE VANILLA PUDDING: In large heavy-bottomed pot (not over heat), whisk together the sugar and flour. While whisking, pour in ½ cup (120g) of the milk. Add the egg yolks and whisk until well blended. Pour the remaining ½ cup (120g) milk and whisk until well blended. Set over medium heat and add the butter, whisking until it melts. Continue whisking until the mixture thickens to a loose pudding consistency, 5 to 7 minutes, being sure to scrape the bottom of the pot as you whisk so the mixture does not scorch. Remove the pot from the heat and pour the mixture through a fine-mesh sieve into a medium bowl. Whisk in the vanilla and set the bowl aside.

MAKE THE BLUEBERRY SWIRL: In a small saucepan, combine the blueberries, sugar, and lemon juice. Bring the mixture to a boil over medium-high heat. Once the blueberries have reduced in size, remove the saucepan from the heat and allow the blueberries to cool for 20 minutes. Scrape the blueberry mixture into a blender or food processor (or purée in the pan using an immersion blender) and blend until smooth. Set the blueberry purée aside.

Adjust an oven rack to the middle position and preheat the oven to 335°F (168°C).

MAKE THE PIE FILLING: In a stand mixer fitted with the paddle attachment (or in a large bowl with a hand mixer), beat together the cream cheese and sugar at medium-high speed until it is light and fluffy. Add the eggs, one at a time, beating well after each addition. Be sure to stop the mixer and scrape down the sides and bottom of the bowl as needed with a silicone spatula. Add the sour cream and flour and mix on low speed until combined. Add the vanilla and 1 cup of the vanilla pudding and continue mixing on medium speed until combined.

RECIPE CONTINUES >>

In a blender, purée the bananas until very smooth. Measure out 1 cup (220g) of the purée and add to the cream cheese mixture. Mix on medium speed until well blended.

ASSEMBLE THE PIE: Set the vanilla wafer pie shell on a baking sheet and pour in the banana/cream cheese mixture. Drop 6 to 8 tablespoons of blueberry purée over the entire top of the pie filling. Using a wooden skewer or toothpick, swirl the purée into the filling, creating a marbled pattern.

Bake until the edges of the pie filling slightly brown, about 50 minutes. Turn off the oven, crack open the oven door, and let the pie cool in the turned-off oven for 1 hour (a slow cooldown helps prevent cracks from forming). After an hour, remove the pie from the oven and place it uncovered in the refrigerator. Refrigerate for at least 6 hours before slicing and serving.

To store the pie, cover with plastic wrap and refrigerate for up to 7 days or freeze for up to 2 months. Remove the pie from the freezer and allow it to thaw for 25 to 30 minutes before slicing.

BONUS: When I was a kid, my dad and I would make blueberry muffins from a box of Jiffy mix (you know the one) every other Saturday morning. My favorite part was licking the bowl while the muffins baked. I recommend reliving this childhood tradition here by adding slices of banana and a handful of crushed vanilla wafer cookies to some of the leftover pudding so you can enjoy a banana pudding snack while your pie bakes!

STRAWBERRY BASIL KEY LIME PIE

MAKES ONE 9-INCH PIE

My cousin Peter, who lives in the Bronzeville neighborhood of Chicago, once invited me over to his house for drinks, and when I arrived I found him in the kitchen creating mixology magic using vodka, basil, lime, and green peppers. He blended the basil and green peppers to create a purée, which was then added to the muddled limes in an ice-filled glass and stirred with vodka. I loved the cocktail so much that I woke up the next morning and immediately went to work figuring out how to transform that cocktail into a pie.

I blended some fresh green bell peppers with the basil and then added sweetened condensed milk and Key lime juice. When experimenting, sometimes I find that all of the ingredients simply just won't work. The green peppers did not really talk to me, but that basil was singing quite loudly and with perfect pitch.

The savory tartness of this pie (hello, basil, my love) is what makes it an unexpected and delicious surprise. Topping it with fresh strawberries provides a nice textural accompaniment to the custard's silkiness.

1 cup (54g) fresh basil leaves

2 tablespoons extra-virgin olive oil

1 cup (240g) Key lime juice

2 (14 oz/397g) cans sweetened condensed milk

4 large egg yolks

Graham Cracker Crust (page 238)

2 cups strawberries, hulled and quartered or thinly sliced lengthwise

Adjust an oven rack to the middle position and preheat the oven to 350°F (175°C).

In a small food processor or a blender, combine the basil leaves, olive oil, and 2 tablespoons (30g) of the Key lime juice. Using a silicone spatula, press the leaves toward the bottom to compress them, then pulse to blend the mixture. Pause the food processor or blender, add 2 more tablespoons (30g) of key lime juice, scrape down the sides of the container, and use the silicone spatula to press the mixture back down to the bottom. Blend once more until emulsified.

In a large bowl, whisk together the basil purée and sweetened condensed milk until well blended and the filling is an even light green color. Add the egg yolks and whisk until well combined. While whisking, slowly pour in the remaining ¾ cup (180g) Key lime juice and continue to whisk until the juice has completely blended with the sweetened condensed milk. The mixture will begin to thicken as the acids in the lime juice react with the proteins in the sweetened condensed milk. Allow the mixture to stand for 5 minutes to thicken even more.

Set the graham cracker pie shell on a baking sheet and pour in the filling.

Bake until tiny bubbles emerge on the surface of the pie's filling, about 15 minutes. Remove the pie from the oven. When cool, refrigerate until set and thoroughly chilled, at least 6 hours.

Before serving, top the pie with the strawberries.

Refrigerate the pie in a cake box for up to 7 days or freeze for up to 2 months. Remove the pie from the freezer and allow it to thaw for 15 to 20 minutes before slicing.

SWEET POTATO PRALINE PIE

MAKES ONE 9-INCH PIE

Sweet potatoes are one of my favorite ingredients to cook with since their versatility can be applied to sweet or savory dishes.

This pie is a nod to my paternal family's Louisiana roots. Pralines are a fudge-like confection with a creamy consistency that were originally brought to Louisiana by French settlers. They're typically made from evaporated milk, sugar, butter, and pecans—the same ingredients I use to make the custard filling. While I do love sweet potatoes, I must admit that the praline sauce is my favorite part of this pie. The creaminess combines with the saccharinity of the sweet potato custard and the buttery nuttiness of the pecans for a stunningly delicious pie. The pie keeps very well in the refrigerator for up to 7 days, or freeze for up to 2 months. To thaw, remove the pie from the freezer and let sit in the refrigerator until defrosted.

2 to 2½ pounds sweet potatoes (about 2 large)

Flour, for rolling out

All-Butter Pie Dough (page 220)

1½ cups (330g) packed light brown sugar

8 tablespoons (1 stick/113g) unsalted butter, at room temperature

2 large eggs

½ cup (117g) evaporated milk

2 teaspoon pure vanilla extract

½ teaspoon ground cinnamon

½ teaspoon ground nutmeg

½ teaspoon kosher salt

⅓ cup (93g) Broussard Praline Sauce (page 202)

½ cup (64g) chopped pecans

Vanilla Bean Chantilly Cream (optional; page 214)

Adjust a rack to the middle position and preheat the oven to 400°F (205°C).

Wrap the sweet potatoes with foil and place on a baking sheet. Bake until extremely soft and a knife inserted into their thickest part meets no resistance, about 2 hours. Remove from the oven and cool for 20 minutes.

Halve each sweet potato lengthwise and use a spoon to scoop the potato flesh into a medium bowl (discard the skins). Mash the sweet potatoes until they are creamy and smooth. Remove and discard any visible fibrous strings. Cover the bowl with plastic wrap and refrigerate for 1 hour.

Meanwhile, lightly flour the counter and roll the pie dough to a 12-inch circle. Carefully transfer the dough to a 9-inch pie pan. Roll the overhang to the edge of the pan and crimp. Refrigerate for 10 minutes.

Preheat the oven to 350°F (175°C).

In a stand mixer fitted with the paddle attachment (or in a large bowl using a hand mixer), beat together the brown sugar and butter on medium speed until creamed, 3 to 4 minutes. Add the eggs and mix until well combined. With the mixer on, slowly pour in the evaporated milk. Add the vanilla, cinnamon, nutmeg, and salt and mix to combine. Measure out 2 cups (546g) of mashed sweet potatoes, add to the bowl, and beat until the texture of the filling shows small white specks, about 1 minute.

Remove the pie shell from the refrigerator and place it on a baking sheet. Pour the filling into the pie shell and bake until the top is slightly browned and has a caramelized shine, about 1 hour 15 minutes.

Now is the perfect time to make the praline sauce.

Remove the pie from the oven and cool at room temperature for 1 hour before using a silicone or offset spatula to spread the praline sauce across its entire surface. Sprinkle the finely chopped pecans on top and add a dollop of Vanilla Bean Chantilly Cream if you'd like. You can also chill the pie in the refrigerator if you prefer a firmer, colder pie.

DARK CHOCOLATE CHERRY CRUMBLE PIE

MAKES ONE 9-INCH PIE

Growing up in the Midwest meant I had access to some of the best cherries from our neighboring state of Michigan, which is the largest producer of sour cherries in the United States. It's these tart cherries—not sweet Bing cherries—that make the best pies, and in June and July, when they are in season, you'll always find a colander full of them in my refrigerator.

I like to add almond liqueur and cinnamon to enhance the cherries' sweetness and floral warmth without upstaging the natural flavors of the fruit. This cherry pie is so sweet and sensual that it's impossible to not eat a whole pie in one sitting—either by yourself or with friends.

Flour, for rolling out

All-Butter Pie Dough (page 220)

1 cup (200g) granulated sugar

2 tablespoons unbleached all-purpose flour

4 cups pitted sour cherries, fresh or frozen

2 tablespoons (24g) almond liqueur

2 teaspoons almond extract

½ teaspoon ground cinnamon

Brown Sugar + Oat Crumble (page 200)

⅓ cup (112g) Hot Fudge Sauce, homemade (page 217) or store-bought

---

Adjust an oven rack to the middle position and preheat the oven to 350°F (175°C).

Lightly flour the countertop and roll the dough to a 12-inch circle. Carefully transfer it to a 9-inch pie pan. Roll the overhang to the edge of the pan and crimp. Refrigerate for 10 minutes.

Remove the pie shell from the refrigerator and use the tines of a fork to gently poke holes across the base. Line the pie shell with parchment paper and add pie weights or dried beans to weigh down the paper and the dough. Bake for 10 minutes, remove from the oven, and remove the weights by carefully lifting the parchment paper out of the shell. Return the shell to the oven and bake for another 10 minutes, until the crust is slightly pale yellow. Remove from the oven and set aside.

In a large heavy-bottomed saucepan, add the cherries and stir in the sugar until they're well coated. Set the pan over medium-high heat and cook, stirring constantly, until the mixture comes to a boil. Continue cooking and stirring until the cherries have visibly reduced in size, about 10 minutes. Remove from the heat.

Using a fine-mesh sieve set over a bowl, drain the cherries and place them in a large bowl (save the liquid for Cherry Balsamic Vinaigrette, page 216). Coat the cherries with the flour. Stir in the almond liqueur, almond extract, and cinnamon. Set the pie shell on a baking sheet and add the cherry mixture.

Bake until the crust is a light golden brown, about 45 minutes.

Remove the pie from the oven and top it with the crumble, ensuring it covers the entire pie. (The flour in the crumble helps absorb and thicken juices that may remain in the filling.) Return the pie to the oven and bake until the crumble top has slightly browned, about 35 minutes more.

Remove the pie from the oven and allow it to cool a minimum of 45 minutes and optimally 2 to 3 hours before slicing and serving with hot fudge sauce for an extra layer of richness and decadence.

To store the pie, cover with plastic wrap and refrigerate for up to 7 days or freeze for up to 2 months. To thaw, remove the pie from the freezer and allow it to come to room temperature.

Christopher LeMark is the founder of Coffee, Hip-Hop & Mental Health, an organization with the goal of destigmatizing therapy in Black and Brown communities.

Christopher had a difficult start to life—his mother was nineteen when she gave birth to him and by the time she turned twenty-two, she had five children and found herself overwhelmed and unable to take care of them. The children were placed in various foster homes until they were taken in by his uncle and aunt. Christopher's two older sisters ran away, and he was left to look after his two younger siblings.

His aunt would often send him to the corner store to pick up ingredients for dinner. He'd return faithfully with all her change, but the dinner was never for him. He wasn't allowed to eat dinner. Instead, he was locked in the basement from 3:30 p.m. until 2 a.m. and then he'd be given a pot of food to eat at 10 a.m.—this was all the food he'd receive from his caretakers for the day.

On occasion, older cousins came by the house to visit and leave take-out bags at the top of the basement stairs. "Come get this food," they'd whisper loudly, quickly closing the door so they wouldn't get caught by the aunt. Small moments of reprieve.

One afternoon, when Christopher was sent to the corner store to pick up some bread, he decided to steal it instead, hoping to get caught—perhaps if someone discovered what was going on back home, he could get some help. Instead, the attendant told his aunt, who yelled at him, "So, you gonna steal? So, you stealing now, huh?" She slapped him repeatedly. For the first time, Christopher fought back. Stunned at his retaliation, his aunt forcefully pushed him out of the back door and forbade him from ever coming back.

Christopher slept in an old car for a few days, then moved in with older cousins who lived in an affluent suburb of Chicago. He was placed in honors classes and dressed in expensive, preppy clothes, but he didn't fit in socially, and his difficulty adapting to this new, unfamiliar terrain was exacerbated by sexual abuse by a neighbor. He started skipping classes. When his cousins could no longer tolerate his behavior, he was sent to a series of group homes where he became a target of bullying. Fed up with being picked on, Christopher grabbed a baseball bat and began swinging. The boy he fought back against suffered injuries, and Christopher was arrested two days after his eighteenth birthday and charged with attempted murder.

At his arraignment, the presiding judge took a hard look at Christopher and said firmly, "Your charges are being reduced to aggravated battery. You've never been arrested, and you seem like a good kid. So, I'm going to give you a second chance, but I better not ever see you in this courthouse again."

Although no longer a minor, Christopher would remain a ward of the state until his twenty-first birthday. He was placed in independent housing with the rent and utilities covered and a food allowance allotted. At an age when most kids would be overjoyed with the newly granted freedom and independence, Christopher felt abandoned.

He hated his life and he hated himself.

He stumbled upon Nothing but the Gospels, a Christian bookstore, walked in, and asked the woman at the counter, "Can you hire me?" After briefly talking to him, the woman said, "I don't know you, but I feel good about you." She gave him a chance and taught him how to manage the store and count money.

At the age of twenty-one, Christopher soon landed a job at a bank—it was a job, a good job—and though he didn't know anything about banking or mortgages, he shadowed people who had more experience so he could learn as much as possible. But he was still burdened by feelings of inadequacy, and eventually he lost the job. Christopher, who had been writing and performing hip-hop for years, struggled as an artist—he was homeless often from 2001 to 2011 and survived three suicide attempts. Writing and performing, for him, was therapy, providing him an outlet and allowing him to imagine a way out of his emotional pain.

Christopher was working a dead-end job and was miserable—he was hungry, he was broke, his dreams of becoming a successful artist were lost, and he didn't know how to live. He took his lunch break to run to Starbucks because it was the only food he could afford. While in line, he realized that he only had enough money to buy one cup of coffee and a slice of iced lemon loaf cake—leaving him with not enough money to even buy lunch. He broke down crying and couldn't stop. The culmination of everything hit him like a ton of bricks.

With tears running down his face, he listened to the lyrics of Meek Mill rapping through his headphones: "Hold up, wait a minute, y'all thought I was finished?" In that moment, he knew he had to fix himself.

CONTINUES >>

Although Christopher didn't have much in the way of a salary, his job did offer excellent health benefits, so he began going to therapy.

While working through the turbulence of his personal history, he began to ask himself, "Why are we not talking about therapy more in the Black community? Why do my Black and Brown people not have access to services like this?" As he pondered all of this, he wrote down three words in his notebook: "Coffee. Hip-hop. Therapy."

To make therapy more acceptable to people in his community who too often relied on religion or weed to work through their frustrations, he hosted an event where he offered complimentary coffee and doughnuts to draw people in. He then shared his life experiences, followed by a ninety-minute discussion with the community and a group of therapists. The first event attracted 20 people. The second event bought out 180 people. The next: 300 people.

After the first few events, Christopher was overwhelmed by the number of people emailing him to say, "Yo. I heard you share your story. Real talk, I need help." Through his work with Black and Brown communities in Chicago, he is aiding in the effort to enact real change in how people view therapy. Often stigmatized as something that should be shamed, with Christopher's work, therapy is slowly becoming more accepted as a verifiable means of healthcare in his community.

This Lemon Espresso Pie acknowledges the pivotal moment in Chris's life when he recognized that he needed help—and celebrates all the work he has done to get others help, too.

LEMON ESPRESSO PIE

MAKES ONE 9-INCH PIE

2 (14 oz/397g) cans sweetened condensed milk

4 large egg yolks

¾ cup (187g) fresh lemon juice (about 4 lemons)

Grated zest of 1 lemon

Espresso Chocolate Cookie Crust variation (page 236)

¼ cup (66g) Lemon Curd (page 205)

Hot Fudge Sauce, homemade (page 217) or store-bought, warmed

Vanilla Bean Chantilly Cream (page 214)

Adjust an oven rack to the middle position and preheat the oven to 350°F (175°C).

In a large bowl, whisk together the sweetened condensed milk and egg yolks until well combined (the sweetened condensed milk will become thin). While whisking, slowly pour in the lemon juice and continue whisking until well blended. Fold in the lemon zest. The mixture will begin to thicken as the acids in the lemon juice react with the proteins in the sweetened condensed milk. Set aside for 5 minutes to thicken.

Place the espresso bean–infused cookie crust on a baking sheet and pour the filling into the crust.

Bake until tiny bubbles emerge on the surface of the pie's filling, about 15 minutes. Remove the pie from the oven and refrigerate for at least 6 hours to chill and set.

Using a silicone or offset spatula, spread the lemon curd across the entire surface of the pie and refrigerate for 1 more hour.

Before serving, pour ¼ cup (66g) of the hot fudge sauce on a plate. Place a slice of pie on the fudge and top with Chantilly cream.

Refrigerate the pie in a cake box for up to 7 days or freeze for up to 2 months. Remove the pie from the freezer and allow it to thaw for 15 to 20 minutes before slicing. Wait until just before serving to add sauce and top with Chantilly cream.

LAVENDER BLUEBERRY PIE

MAKES ONE 9-INCH PIE

My love for using dried lavender in baking runs deep. I use a food-grade lavender here and also in the Lavender Lemon Tart (page 141) and the Lavender Whoopie Pies (page 166). I even occasionally add dried lavender to my Billowy Biscuits (page 193)—they are so good with lemon curd or orange marmalade. Not only does lavender taste glorious, but it also promotes calmness and helps reduce stress. The blueberries are chock-full of antioxidants—see, this pie tastes amazing *and* is good for you, too!

Double recipe Lavender All-Butter Pie Dough (page 221)

1 cup (200g) granulated sugar

2 tablespoons unbleached all-purpose flour, plus extra for rolling

6 cups blueberries

2 tablespoons (23g) fresh lemon juice

1 tablespoon orange liqueur

1 tablespoon triple sec

1 teaspoon ground cinnamon

1 large egg

Make the pie dough, divide in half, and form each half into a 1½-inch-thick disk. Wrap the disks in plastic wrap and refrigerate for at least 1 hour.

Meanwhile, in a large heavy-bottomed saucepan, not over heat, whisk together the sugar and flour. Stir in the blueberries until they are well coated, then stir in the lemon juice. Set the pan over medium-high heat and, while stirring constantly, bring the mixture to a boil. Cook, stirring constantly, until the mixture has thickened and is reduced by half, about 15 minutes.

Remove the saucepan from the heat and set a fine-mesh sieve over a large bowl. Drain the blueberries to remove the excess liquid. Transfer the blueberries to a large bowl. Add the orange liqueur, triple sec, and cinnamon and toss to coat. Cover the bowl with plastic wrap and refrigerate for 1 hour.

Adjust an oven rack to the middle position and preheat the oven to 350°F (175°C).

Lightly dust the countertop with flour and roll out both disks of dough to about 12 inches in diameter. Carefully transfer one dough round to a 9-inch pie pan and ease it into the bottom and sides of the pan. Lightly dust the dough with flour.

Pour the filling into the pie shell and use the second rolled-out round of dough to make a lattice on top of the pie (see page 221 for instructions). Roll the overhanging edges of the pie dough to the edge of the pie pan and crimp.

In a small bowl, whisk together the egg and 1 tablespoon water. Using a pastry brush, lightly coat the lattice and crimped edges with the egg wash. Place the pie in the refrigerator to chill for 10 minutes.

Remove the pie from the refrigerator, set on a baking sheet, and bake until the lattice is golden brown, about 1 hour.

Remove the pie from the oven and cool 2 to 3 hours before slicing (if the pie is sliced while it's too warm, the filling will seep out and make for a soggy-bottomed crust).

To store the pie, cover with plastic wrap and refrigerate for up to 7 days.

PETITE S'MORES PIES

MAKES 6 INDIVIDUAL PIES

The very first time I had s'mores, I was in third grade at St. Dorothy School. My Girl Scout troop had organized a camping trip and I remember the eeriness of the dancing flames of the campfire, the lightning bugs that surrounded us in the pitch-black darkness of the woods, and the satisfaction I had in finding the perfect twig to skewer the marshmallows on. My concentration was dedicated to dividing the graham cracker in half with a clean break and bringing the marshmallows to the perfect toasted temperature to melt the chocolate.

S'mores are known for their gooey, messy, and unpretentious deliciousness, however, as a child, I was more concerned about creating the most beautiful, aesthetically presentable s'more, and not a burnt piece of goo. As an adult, it's apparent that not much has changed.

Crumb mixture for Graham Cracker Crust (page 238) not pressed into a pie pan
2 large eggs
2 large egg yolks
6 tablespoons (75g) granulated sugar
16 tablespoons (2 sticks/227g) unsalted butter

3 ounces (86g) dark chocolate
3 ounces (86g) bittersweet chocolate
¼ cup (34g) unbleached all-purpose flour
½ teaspoon kosher salt
6 Pillow-Soft Marshmallows (page 211)

Adjust an oven rack to the middle position and preheat the oven to 425°F (220°C).

Mist a 6-cavity mini-cheesecake pan with a removable bottom or six 6-ounce ramekins with cooking spray. Add ¼ cup (39g) of the graham cracker crumb mixture to each cavity or ramekin and slightly press it down with a spoon.

In a large glass or stainless-steel mixing bowl, vigorously whisk together the whole eggs, egg yolks, and sugar using a large balloon whisk or a hand mixer on high speed until the mixture is fluffy and airy, about 1 minute.

Fill a small saucepan with about 2 inches of water and bring it to a simmer. Set a shallow glass or stainless-steel bowl on the saucepan to create a double boiler (the bottom of the bowl shouldn't touch the water). Add the butter and dark and bittersweet chocolates to the bowl. Once they begin to melt, stir often until smooth. Remove the saucepan from the heat and set aside.

Using a silicone spatula, slowly fold the warm chocolate into the egg mixture until well combined.

Sift the flour and salt into the filling and gently fold in until no traces of flour are visible. Divide the filling evenly among the graham cracker-lined cups or ramekins (about ½ cup per cavity).

Transfer to the oven and bake until the centers are barely set (they will jiggle slightly if the pan is tapped) and the edges are slightly puffed and set, 8 to 10 minutes.

Remove from the oven and allow to cool for 2 minutes. Using a mini offset spatula or a paring knife, run the tool around the edges of the cup or ramekin to release the pies. Carefully wedge the spatula under the pie and slowly lift it out of its cavity. If you're using a ramekin, you may need to flip each pie over onto a small plate before turning it back to right-side up.

Top each pie with a marshmallow and use a kitchen torch to toast the marshmallow until lightly browned. If you don't have a kitchen torch, line a baking sheet with parchment paper, place the marshmallows on the sheet, and broil in the oven for about 1½ minutes before topping the pies. Eat immediately.

BIG KIKA + KIKA JR.

GORILLA RX WELLNESS

The mother-and-daughter team of Big Kika (Kika Keith) and Kika Jr. opened Gorilla Rx Wellness,

the first Black-owned, women-led dispensary in Los Angeles in 2020. The dispensary, set in the heart of South Central Los Angeles, has the largest selection of cannabis goods produced by Black-owned companies in California. The duo aren't just cannabis entrepreneurs, however—they are teachers who advocate for equity in an industry that has been widely weaponized to incriminate people of color.

When Kika Jr. developed a severe case of asthma, Big Kika turned to her mother's homemade remedy of a honey-sweetened chlorophyll-and-lemon drink to clear her respiratory issues. A few years later, when Kika Jr.'s inner-city orchestra, Sweet Strings, needed to raise money to continue its arts enrichment programming, Big Kika turned to the drink as the perfect way to help fund the group's efforts. She decided to call the drink Gorilla Life Water, and, along with a few family members, she rented a small production facility and grew the beverage brand into a regional hit on the West Coast and in Hawai'i.

What makes this story especially notable is that Big Kika started Gorilla Life while living in a homeless shelter—and the ingredients for Gorilla Life Water were all funded by her public assistance benefits. However, Gorilla Life was struggling despite her hustle. The pain of producing and manufacturing the drink without an infusion of cash from private investors to maintain operations began to strain the grassroots operation.

One day Big Kika noticed that every cannabis dispensary she passed had a long line of customers waiting to get in. She immediately recognized the demand and got the idea to infuse Gorilla Life Water with the nonpsychotropic component of cannabis called CBD (cannabidiol), revered for its anti-inflammatory benefits. She wasn't sure what modifying the drink would look like, but she knew that getting into the lucrative cannabis business could be the answer to saving—and growing—her business. Soon after, Gorilla Rx Wellness was born.

After cannabis was decriminalized in LA in 2016, the city began resentencing anyone incarcerated due to cannabis sales and possession. Historically, Black people accounted for 40 percent of the arrests even though they represented just 9 percent of the population (and even though statistically white people consume cannabis at a higher rate than any other ethnic group). As an effort to help the people and communities harmed by the war on drugs and by the criminalization of marijuana, the city introduced a "Social Equity Program" to promote equitable ownership and employment opportunities in the cannabis industry for Black and Brown people.

Although the Social Equity Program was intended to award a set number of licenses to dispensary owners of color, Big Kika noticed that the program did not provide community outreach or educational workshops on regulations, access to capital, policies, and compliance. The Social Equity Program also opened the door for nonminority dispensaries to abuse the program with predatory contract practices—such as offering "sharecropper agreements" to Black and Brown would-be minority partners of already-established white-owned dispensary brands.

This inequity sparked the creation of Life Development Group, a grassroots organization headed by Big Kika, Kika Jr., and other Social Equity Program applicants who were prospective cannabis entrepreneurs. Big Kika and Kika Jr. set out to educate potential applicants of color on the ever-changing policies, rules, and regulations involved in applying for a dispensary license. They also frequently attended city council meetings as a collective, protested, and taught others how to lobby city council members and the mayor's office.

Big Kika and her daughter wanted to share the knowledge they amassed during their own fight for inclusion and make sure that each minority cannabis entrepreneur was set up for success. They weren't concerned about creating competition in the marketplace—their goal was to be social equity advocates in the cannabis space, an industry known to shut out people of color. These are two Black women who are helping others get higher.

I created the Peaches + Herb Cobbler, which is made with pie dough that has been infused with a low dose of cannabis butter, in honor of Big Kika and Kika Jr.'s pioneering contributions for cannabis entrepreneurs of color. This mother-daughter duo is an advocate for equity and justice among Black and Brown business owners.

PEACHES + HERB COBBLER

MAKES ONE 9 × 12-INCH COBBLER; SERVES 8

8 to 10 medium peaches

8 tablespoons (1 stick/113g) unsalted butter

½ cup (110g) packed light brown sugar

1 tablespoon fresh lemon juice

¼ teaspoon kosher salt

3 tablespoons unbleached all-purpose flour

1 teaspoon ground cinnamon

½ teaspoon ground nutmeg

1 tablespoon pure vanilla extract

1 large egg

Flour, for rolling out

Double recipe All-Butter Pie Dough (page 220), divided into 2 disks

Double recipe All-Butter Pie Dough (page 220) made with Weed-Infused Butter (recipe follows)

Demerara sugar, for sprinkling

Fill a large bowl with ice and water and set aside.

Bring a medium pot of water to a boil over high heat. Blanch the peaches by submerging them in the boiling water for 45 seconds. With a slotted spoon, transfer the peaches from the boiling water to the ice water. When cooled, use a small paring knife to remove the peach skin. Halve, pit, and cut the peaches into slices ½ inch thick, placing them in a large pot as you go.

Set the pot over medium-high heat. Add the butter, brown sugar, lemon juice, salt, and ¼ cup (60g) water. Bring the mixture to a boil, stirring occasionally, until the peaches are fragrant and have softened, 25 to 30 minutes.

In a small bowl, combine the flour with 2 teaspoons of hot liquid from the peach pot and stir to make a paste. Gradually add 2 more tablespoons of hot liquid to loosen the flour mixture so it forms a slurry the consistency of thick porridge. Return the slurry to the pot of peaches and stir and simmer until the mixture thickens, 3 to 5 minutes. Stir in the cinnamon, nutmeg, and vanilla. Remove the pot from the heat and set aside.

Adjust an oven rack to the middle position and preheat the oven to 350°F (176°C).

In a small bowl, beat the egg with 1 tablespoon water and set the egg wash aside.

Lightly dust the countertop with flour. Starting with the regular pie dough (the dough that hasn't been infused with weed butter), roll out each disk into a rectangle measuring 12 × 16 inches. Carefully transfer both pieces to a 9 × 12-inch baking dish, overlapping them slightly in the middle so that they form about a 12 × 18-inch rectangle. Use your fingers to gently mold the middle seam of the dough together and then press the dough into the dish using your fingers to mend any tears, lines, holes, or cracks so there are no gaps. Roll the overhanging dough to the edge of the baking dish and allow it to drape over the edge. Add the peach filling to the bottom crust.

Roll the weed-infused dough on a floured surface into a rectangle about 12 × 16 inches, flouring the top of the dough as needed to prevent sticking. Roll the dough up and onto the rolling pin and then unroll over the top of the filling. Pinch the edges of the bottom and top crusts together to seal, and then tuck the edges of the dough inside the baking dish.

Use a pastry brush to coat the top crust with the egg wash, sprinkle Demerara sugar evenly on top, and use a paring knife to make two slits in the top crust to vent the cobbler as it bakes.

Bake until the crust is dark golden brown, 45 to 55 minutes.

Remove the cobbler from the oven and allow to cool for 10 to 15 minutes before serving. To store, cover with plastic wrap after cooling and refrigerate for up to 5 days.

BONUS: Top the cobbler with some vanilla ice cream and some Salted Caramel Sauce (page 208) or Broussard Praline Sauce (page 202) for an ultimate à la mode experience!

WEED-INFUSED BUTTER

MAKES EIGHT 2-TABLESPOON (28G) CUBES

Add 16 tablespoons of unsalted butter and 3 grams of cannabis flower to a large mason jar and seal tightly with a lid.

Place the canning jar in a large pot and add enough water to the pot to nearly submerge the jar. Bring the water to a simmer over medium heat and let the butter infuse for 1 hour, checking often to add water so the jar always stays mostly submerged. After 1 hour, use tongs to remove the jar from the pot and use a kitchen towel to open the lid to release any pressure. Tightly re-cover and carefully return the jar to the pot, making sure it is nearly submerged. Simmer for 1 hour, replenishing the water as needed.

Use tongs to remove the jar from the pot and set it on a kitchen towel (if you set the jar on a cold surface it could shatter). Let it sit until cool, 20 to 25 minutes. Place cheesecloth over a liquid cup measure and pour the butter through the cheesecloth to strain out the solids. Squeeze the cheesecloth to make sure you get all the butter out and then discard.

Pour the butter into 8 wells of an ice cube tray and refrigerate until chilled solid, about 2 hours. Remove the cubes from the tray. If using the weed butter in place of plain butter in the All-Butter Pie Dough (page 220), cut into smaller cubes as instructed before adding to the flour. Store in the refrigerator for up to 2 weeks or in the freezer for up to 6 months.

SALTED CARAMEL MOCHA CHESS PIE

MAKES ONE 9-INCH PIE

My dad and I often took road trips to Alexandria, Virginia, to visit my aunt Pat and my older cousins. After one such trip, when I was ten years old, though I was groggy and exhausted from the long drive, Aunt Pat asked me to make the mashed potatoes for the family's dinner that evening. Boxed mashed potatoes were a staple in my dad's kitchen back home, so I felt very confident about my low-lift contribution to the meal. As we gathered in the living room and started to eat, the room fell silent.

"Maya . . . Pumpkin . . . how much salt did you put in these mashed potatoes?" my aunt Sandy warily asked.

I looked up at her with puppy dog eyes and mumbled, "a half a cup."

Aunt Pat yelped, "A HALF A CUP!" and she proceeded to instruct everyone to get up and scrape the mashed potatoes from their plate and into the trash.

The instructions on the box of mashed potatoes called for ½ teaspoon of salt.

My dad joked that he should have given me a cup of coffee before allowing me to make the mashed potatoes.

This pie celebrates my love for salt and the caffeine that I clearly needed before being allowed in the kitchen to cook mashed potatoes. This rich and velvety pie has a full chocolate and coffee flavor that is highlighted with the addition of salt.

Flour, for rolling out
All-Butter Pie Dough (page 220)
1¾ cups (350g) granulated sugar
¼ cup (21g) unsweetened cocoa powder
2 tablespoons yellow cornmeal
1 tablespoon unbleached all-purpose flour
1 tablespoon ground espresso beans
¼ teaspoon kosher salt

4 large eggs
½ cup (126g) buttermilk
8 tablespoons (1 stick/113g) unsalted butter, melted
2 teaspoons pure vanilla extract
½ cup (169g) Salted Caramel Sauce (page 208)
Pinch of flaky sea salt

Adjust an oven rack to the middle position and preheat the oven to 325°F (165°C).

Lightly dust the counter with flour and roll out the pie dough to about 12 inches in diameter. Carefully transfer the dough to a 9-inch pie pan. Roll the overhanging dough to the edge of the pan and crimp. Place the pie shell in the refrigerator to chill for 10 minutes.

In a stand mixer fitted with the whisk attachment (or in large bowl and using a whisk), whisk together the sugar, cocoa powder, cornmeal, flour, ground espresso, and salt. While whisking, add the eggs, then slowly whisk in the buttermilk.

Once the mixture is well combined, add the melted butter and vanilla and continue to whisk again.

Working quickly, remove the pie shell from the refrigerator. Place the pie shell on a baking sheet and set the baking sheet on the pulled-out oven rack. Pour the filling into the pie shell. (Placing the baking sheet on the rack before filling the pie helps avoid spillage.)

Bake the pie until the center is set and the edges around the pie crust are dry and solid, 50 minutes to 1 hour. (The center may jiggle a bit, and that's perfectly fine.) Remove the pie from the oven and allow it to cool for 1 to 1½ hours.

Now is a great time to make the caramel sauce.

Before serving, top the cooled pie with the caramel sauce, sprinkle with the sea salt flakes, slice, and serve.

To store the pie, cover with plastic wrap and refrigerate for up to 7 days.

COQUITO CHESS PIE

MAKES ONE 9-INCH PIE

When I was twenty years old, my dad gifted my entire family a trip to Puerto Rico for Christmas. My dad's sisters, his niece, and two nephews joined us. I was the only one not yet of drinking age—and . . . it was *exactly* one week from my twenty-first birthday.

My dad was the type to sneak us a sip of beer when we were kids (he was an uncle before becoming a father, after all), so when we landed in San Juan, he declared that he would let me drink on this trip since I was merely days away from the legal drinking age and he could supervise me (okay, Dad, whatever).

I was all the more willing to imbibe because spending the holidays in Puerto Rico meant experiencing coquito for the very first time. Coquito means "little coconut" in Spanish, and the drink is a thick, sweet, and creamy concoction similar to eggless eggnog. It is infused with coconut, cinnamon, and Puerto Rican rum.

The richness of coquito makes it a perfect substitute for the buttermilk that is traditionally used in chess pies. With its warm spices, this pie is perfect for the winter holidays, or anytime, really.

¾ cup (225g) Coquito (opposite)

4 large eggs

2 teaspoons pure vanilla extract

1 cup (200g) granulated sugar

1 tablespoon unbleached all-purpose flour

1 tablespoon yellow cornmeal

¼ teaspoon kosher salt

8 tablespoons (1 stick/113g) unsalted butter, melted

Flour, for rolling out

All-Butter Pie Dough (page 220)

Adjust an oven rack to the middle position and preheat the oven to 335°F (168°C).

In a stand mixer fitted with the whisk attachment (or in a large mixing bowl and using a whisk), whisk together the coquito, eggs, and vanilla.

In a small bowl, whisk together the sugar, flour, cornmeal, and salt. Pour the melted butter into the bowl and mix until well incorporated. Add the sugar/melted butter mixture to the coquito mixture and whisk well until combined.

Lightly dust the counter with flour and roll out the pie dough to about 12 inches in diameter. Carefully transfer the dough to a 9-inch pie pan. Roll the overhanging dough to the edge of the pan and crimp. Place the pie shell in the refrigerator to chill for 10 minutes.

Remove the pie shell from the refrigerator. Place the pie shell on a baking sheet and place the baking sheet on the pulled-out oven rack. Pour the filling into the pie shell. (Placing the baking sheet on the rack before filling the pie helps avoid spillage.)

Bake the pie until the center is mostly set (it may jiggle a bit if the pan is tapped, and that's fine) and the edges around the pie crust are dry and solid, 50 minutes to 1 hour.

Remove the pie from the oven and allow it to cool at room temperature for 1½ hours before slicing and serving.

To store the pie, cover with plastic wrap and refrigerate for up to 7 days.

BONUS: After using ¾ cup of the Coquito (opposite) in the Coquito Pie, you can add rum (preferably Puerto Rican rum) to the rest of the coquito mixture—I like to add about 2½ ounces for every 1 cup of coquito mix—and enjoy it over ice in a rocks glass or neat in a small cordial glass.

COQUITO

MAKES 5 CUPS (1KG 205G)

1 (14 oz/383g) can sweetened condensed milk

1 (15 oz/417g) can cream of coconut

1 (15 oz/403g) can full-fat coconut milk

2 teaspoons ground cinnamon

2 teaspoons pure vanilla extract

In a blender, combine the sweetened condensed milk, cream of coconut, coconut milk, cinnamon, and vanilla. Blend until well mixed, about 30 seconds, then transfer to a pitcher or large container. This will keep in the refrigerator for up to 7 days.

SAVORY PIES

APPLE-BRAISED TURKEY POT PIE

MAKES ONE 9 × 12-INCH POT PIE; SERVES 4 TO 6

The Taste of Chicago was one of the premier summertime events of my childhood. The weeklong festival featured more than two hundred local restaurants in the heart of downtown Chicago where the streets were closed to traffic and, instead of cars, they were filled to the hilt with famished people.

Despite the many food establishments being featured at the Taste, there always seemed to be one star of the festival year after year: the smoked turkey leg.

I have vivid memories of watching people nosh on these huge turkey legs and being stopped midbite by someone inquiring, "Excuse me, where did you get that?" They were then directed to a booth that could have been a block away or a mile away, it was always "that-a-way."

This turkey pot pie is a love letter to that turkey leg. It's sweetened with apple cider and caramelized onions. It also has a bit of saltiness with the addition of the soy sauce. This is one of my favorite ways to cook and enjoy a turkey.

Quadruple recipe All-Butter Pie Dough (page 220)

Flour, for rolling out

3 tablespoons extra-virgin olive oil

2 tablespoons unsalted butter

2 large Vidalia or sweet onions, sliced

1 tablespoon granulated sugar

¾ cup (180g) apple cider

2 large turkey legs (976g)

3 cups (710g) chicken broth

½ cup (120g) apple cider vinegar

¼ cup (55g) soy sauce

1 large carrot, peeled and diced

2 celery stalks, diced

1 large Yukon Gold potato, cubed

2 tablespoons finely diced fresh ginger

2 teaspoons freshly ground black pepper

1 teaspoon kosher salt

¼ teaspoon cayenne pepper

¼ cup (34g) unbleached all-purpose flour

2 tablespoons (24g) capers

1 large egg

Make the pie dough and divide into 2 equal portions. Form one portion of the pie dough into a round disk, cover in plastic wrap, and refrigerate. Lightly dust the countertop with flour and roll the remaining portion into a 12 × 16-inch rectangle. Carefully transfer the dough to a 9 × 13-inch baking dish and gently mold the dough into the dish, leaving an overhang. Use your fingers to mend any tears, lines, holes, or cracks so that there are no gaps in the dough. Cut off a piece of the overhanging dough and roll it into a ball. Use the ball of dough to gently continue to mold the dough to the baking dish, making sure the dough is flush to the corners of the baking dish. Cover the baking dish with plastic wrap and place in the fridge.

In a heavy-bottomed pot or Dutch oven, heat the olive oil and butter over medium heat until the butter melts. Add the onions and cook, stirring occasionally, until the onions are tender and beginning to brown, 20 to 25 minutes.

Stir in the granulated sugar. The onions will begin to stick to the pan and brown—when they do, just stir so they don't burn. If the onions start to get really dry and stick a lot, add 2 tablespoons of water to the pot and stir with a spatula to work up all the browned bits. Continue to cook the onions until they are a deep golden brown, 25 to 30 minutes.

Add ½ cup (120g) of the cider and cook, stirring often, until the liquid has evaporated, 8 to 12 minutes.

Using a silicone spatula, create a well in the middle of the pot by pushing the onions to the edges. Place the turkey legs in the center of the pot and brown them on all sides, using tongs to turn them occasionally, 8 to 10 minutes total.

RECIPE CONTINUES >>

Stir in 1 cup (235g) of the chicken broth, the vinegar, soy sauce, and remaining ¼ cup (60g) cider. Bring to a boil, then cover the pot and reduce the heat to medium-low. Cook, using tongs to flip the turkey legs about every 30 minutes, until the meat is tender and pulls away from the bone, about 1 hour 45 minutes.

Remove from the heat. Remove the turkey legs from the pot and place them on a large plate to cool slightly. Using two forks, shred the turkey meat off the bone, discarding any tendons, bones, skin, and fat. Return the shredded meat to the pot. Stir in the remaining 2 cups (473g) chicken broth, the carrot, celery, potato, ginger, black pepper, salt, and cayenne. Cover the pot and increase the heat to medium-high. Cook until the vegetables are fork-tender, about 45 minutes.

In a small bowl, stir together the flour and 5 tablespoons of liquid from the pot. Stir to make a paste, then stir in an additional 5 tablespoons of broth to make a slurry. Stir the slurry into the pot and simmer until the filling thickens, about 5 minutes.

Stir in the capers and remove from the heat. Set the filling aside to cool slightly, 25 to 30 minutes.

Adjust an oven rack to the middle position and preheat the oven to 350°F (175°C).

In a small bowl, whisk together the egg and 1 tablespoon water. Set the egg wash aside.

Remove the disk of pie dough from the refrigerator and unwrap. Lightly dust the countertop with flour and roll the dough to a 12 × 16-inch rectangle. Using the rolling pin, roll the dough over onto itself and set aside.

Remove the dough-lined baking dish from the refrigerator and uncover. Pour in the filling and then unroll the rolled-out dough rectangle over the top of the pie filling. Pinch the edges of the top and bottom crust together, roll them under, and tuck inside the baking dish.

Use a pastry brush to coat the top of the dough with egg wash and then make 2 slits in the top crust with a paring knife to vent the pie as it bakes. Transfer to the oven and bake until dark golden brown, 55 to 60 minutes.

Allow the pie to cool for 10 to 15 minutes before serving.

To store, cover with plastic wrap and refrigerate for up to 5 days. To reheat, cover with foil and bake on the middle rack of the oven preheated to 350°F (175°C) until the center is warm, 25 to 30 minutes.

CHICKEN + BISCUIT POT PIE

MAKES ONE 9 × 13-INCH POT PIE; SERVES 5 TO 7

Chicken pot pie is an all-American comfort food that is as iconic as apple pie. Most chicken pot pies are encased in a double crust—one piece lines the bottom of the pie and another covers the filling. To me, combining the creaminess of the chicken filling with the flakiness of a butter crust makes it such a classic, timeless favorite.

My version takes the pot pie a step further by adding a biscuit topper to the pot pie, too—I think it's the perfect cross between a chicken pot pie and a chicken and dumpling casserole. The creamy chicken filling is chock-full of vegetables and filled with herbaceous spices, while the biscuit's crunchy exterior and super-soft interior make each bite a close-your-eyes-as-it-melts-in-your-mouth moment.

Billowy Biscuits dough (page 193)

Double recipe All-Butter Pie Dough (page 220)

Flour, for rolling out

3 tablespoons extra-virgin olive oil

2 tablespoons unsalted butter

1 large Vidalia or sweet onion, finely diced

1 tablespoon crushed garlic

¼ cup (34g) unbleached all-purpose flour

2½ cups (591g) chicken broth

2 large carrots, peeled and diced

3 celery stalks, diced

2 ears corn, kernels sliced off

1 large Yukon Gold potato, cubed

1 teaspoon dried oregano

2 sprigs fresh thyme

1 teaspoon kosher salt

1 teaspoon freshly ground black pepper

3 or 4 large boneless, skinless chicken breasts (650g to 700g), cubed

1 cup (235g) heavy cream

1 cup fresh peas

Make the biscuit dough, shape into biscuits, and set on a parchment-lined baking sheet. Cover and refrigerate until ready to bake.

Adjust an oven rack to the middle position and preheat the oven to 350°F (175°C).

Make the pie dough, but do not divide into 2 discs. Keep as one portion of dough. Lightly dust the countertop with flour and roll the dough out to a 12 × 16-inch rectangle. Carefully transfer the dough to a 9 × 13-inch baking dish. Gently mold the dough into the dish, leaving an overhang. Use your fingers to mend any tears, lines, holes, or cracks so that there are no gaps in the dough. Cut off a piece of the overhanging dough and roll it into a ball. Use the ball of dough to gently mold the dough to the baking dish, making sure the dough is flush to the corners of the baking dish. Use a paring knife to trim the excess dough. Cover the dough-lined dish with plastic wrap and place in the fridge to chill for 10 minutes.

Remove the baking dish from the refrigerator and prick the dough on the bottom with the tines of a fork. Place parchment paper inside the baking dish and pour in dried beans or pie weights. Bake until the crust is lightly golden around the edges, about 15 minutes. Remove the crust from the oven and remove the pie weights and parchment paper. Return to the oven and bake until golden brown, an additional 15 minutes. Set the parbaked crust aside.

Increase the oven temperature to 400°F (205°C) for the biscuits. If your oven has a convection option, preheat to 325°F (165°C).

RECIPE CONTINUES >>

In a heavy-bottomed pot or Dutch oven, heat the olive oil and butter over medium-high heat until the butter melts. Add the onion and cook, stirring occasionally, until very tender, about 15 minutes.

Add the garlic and continue to cook for 5 more minutes. Remove from the heat. Add the flour and stir until it coats the onion/garlic mixture. Pour in the chicken broth, stirring until there are no traces or lumps of flour. Stir in the carrots, celery, corn, and potato and set over medium-high heat. Stir in the oregano, thyme sprigs, salt, and pepper and bring to a boil. Reduce the heat to a simmer and cook until the vegetables are fork-tender, 25 to 30 minutes.

Meanwhile, place the biscuits in the oven and bake until the center of the biscuit is done, about 45 minutes.

Add the chicken to the pot and cook until it's no longer pink, about 10 minutes. Stir in the heavy cream and peas, then reduce the heat to medium-low and simmer until the filling has thickened, an additional 15 minutes. Discard the thyme sprigs.

Ladle the chicken filling into the baking dish with the parbaked crust. Transfer to the oven (it can bake at the same time as the biscuits) and bake until the crust is golden brown, about 20 minutes.

To serve, place the biscuits on top of the chicken filling in the baking dish and serve hot.

To store, cover the cooled pot pie with plastic wrap and refrigerate for up to 5 days.

ITALIAN BEEF POT PIES

MAKES FOUR 5-INCH DEEP-DISH POT PIES

While many chef-driven, award-winning restaurants call Chicago home, the most iconic foods in the City of Big Shoulders don't require reservations or dress codes to enjoy. One such food is the Italian beef sandwich.

Purported to have been created by Al Ferrari in 1938, the Italian beef sandwich from Al's #1 Italian Beef sandwich shop is a staple in Chicago's Little Italy neighborhood. Order one and you'll get a long Italian roll stacked with thin slices of seasoned roast beef that have been simmered in an au jus and topped with provolone cheese, giardiniera (mild or spicy oil-cured peppers—like a chunky relish), and roasted sweet green peppers.

When you order, you must specify how you want your beef: "dry," "wet," or "dipped." *Dry* means your roast beef is removed from the au jus with tongs and the juices are allowed to drip off before being placed on the bread roll; *wet* means your beef is immediately placed on the roll while still juicy. However, if you are a true Chicagoan, you order your beef *dipped*, meaning the whole sandwich gets submerged in the meaty au jus for an unparalleled experience.

This pot pie not only celebrates my hometown but also honors this classic sandwich in an unconventional way.

Quadruple recipe All-Butter Pie Dough (page 220)

Flour, for rolling out

3 tablespoons extra-virgin olive oil

2 tablespoons unsalted butter

1 large Vidalia or sweet onion, finely sliced

1 tablespoon crushed garlic

3 pounds (1.36kg) boneless chuck roast, fat trimmed

3 cups (710g) beef broth

1 tablespoon kosher salt

1 tablespoon granulated sugar

2 teaspoons dried basil

2 teaspoons dried oregano

2 teaspoons dried thyme

2 teaspoons onion powder

2 teaspoons freshly ground black pepper

¼ cup (15g) chopped fresh parsley

5 small pepperoncini (30g)

1 large carrot, peeled and diced

2 celery stalks, diced

½ cup (137g) mild or hot giardiniera

¼ cup (34g) unbleached all-purpose flour

1 large egg

Divide the dough into 8 portions of 6 ounces (170g) each. Set one piece on a lightly floured countertop (place the rest on a plate, cover with plastic, and refrigerate) and roll to about 7 inches in diameter. Carefully transfer to a 5-inch deep-dish ramekin. Gently mold the dough into the dish and use your fingers to mend any tears, lines, holes, or cracks so that there are no gaps in the dough. Allow the excess dough to hang over the ramekin, then roll it under to make an edge. Continue to roll the crust under all the way around the ramekin. Cover with plastic wrap and place in the fridge. Repeat with 3 more portions of dough and three more ramekins.

In a Dutch oven, heat the olive oil and butter over medium heat until the butter melts. Add the onion and cook, stirring occasionally, until tender, 15 to 20 minutes.

Add the garlic and continue to cook for 5 more minutes. Using a silicone spatula, push the onion mixture to the edges of the pot, creating a well in the center big enough to brown the chuck roast. Place the chuck roast in the center of the pot and brown on all sides, using tongs to turn the meat once a side is browned, 8 to 10 minutes total.

Pour in the beef broth. Stir in the salt, sugar, basil, oregano, thyme, onion powder, black pepper, and parsley. Add the pepperoncini. Reduce the heat to low, cover, and simmer until the meat is tender on the bottom (a fork will easily slip in, but the top side of the roast will still be tough), about 1 hour.

Flip the roast over, cover, and simmer until the roast is fork-tender all the way through and easy enough to shred, another 1 hour 45 minutes.

Remove from the heat. Using the tines of 2 forks, shred the roast directly in the pot. Discard any fat. Stir in the carrot, celery, and giardiniera and set the pot over medium-high heat. Cook the vegetables until they are fork-tender, 25 to 30 minutes.

In a small bowl, whisk together the flour and 5 tablespoons of the hot liquid from the pot. Once the mixture forms a paste, add an additional 5 tablespoons of hot liquid and continue to stir to make a slurry. Stir the slurry into the pot and allow the filling to thicken as it simmers, about 5 minutes, stirring occasionally.

Remove from the heat and allow the filling to cool slightly, 25 to 30 minutes.

Adjust an oven rack to the middle position and preheat the oven to 350°F (175°C).

Lightly dust the countertop with flour and roll out the 4 remaining portions of dough until each is about 7 inches in diameter. In a small bowl, whisk together the egg with 1 tablespoon of water and set the egg wash aside.

Remove the ramekins from the fridge and take off the plastic wrap. Add 1½ cups of the slightly cooled filling to each ramekin. Cover each ramekin with a round of rolled-out dough, pinching the edges of the top and bottom crust together to seal (and tucking the lip of the dough inside the ramekin). Repeat with the remaining ramekins and rolled rounds of the top dough.

Using a pastry brush, brush the egg wash on top of the crust, then use a small paring knife to make 2 slits in the top of the crust to vent the pot pies as they bake.

Place the ramekins on a baking sheet, then place the sheet in the oven and bake until the crust becomes dark golden brown, 30 to 45 minutes.

Remove the ramekins from the oven and set aside to cool for 10 to 15 minutes before serving.

To store, cover with plastic wrap and refrigerate for 3 to 5 days. To reheat, cover with aluminum foil and bake on the middle rack of the oven set at 350°F (175°C) until the center is warm, 25 to 30 minutes.

LEMON CHICKEN + LEEK POT PIE

MAKES 4 TO 6 SERVINGS

One thing people are always surprised to learn about me is that I spent a significant portion of my childhood and teenage years being grounded. The reasons for my punishments were hilarious and, in my opinion, quite ridiculous.

One time I was grounded for walking to the corner store for honeybuns instead of going straight home after my bestie, Keisha, and I got permission to take the "L" train (the elevated subway in Chicago) back home to the Hyde Park neighborhood from Evanston, a suburb just north of the city. I rationalized that if we could take public transportation to a whole other town outside of Chicago, then a quick trip a half block from my house to grab snacks wouldn't hurt, right?

My dad was not here for my logic. My punishment for my honeybun craving got my weekly allowance slashed down to a mere $2 a day: $1 for lunch in the school cafeteria and $1 for the bus ride home.

Now, my high school's cafeteria food was gross. On one side of the room, the cafeteria ladies served daily specials. Think mystery meat and mashed potatoes. No ma'am, Pam.

On the other side, a popular food chain sold tacos and burritos. Most of us dared not touch them after seeing a box labeled "Grade E Meat" being poured into a catering pan (if you were spotted eating a taco, a classmate was bound to tease you for eating "kangaroo meat").

The safest, and most popular, option was also the most affordable: the "Sandwich Line." Here you could grab a sandwich with a pickle for $5 or a bowl of soup for $.95 and, for an extra $.30, your soup could come in a bread bowl. The "Sandwich Line" was the holy grail of the lunch options because it was good *and* also the cheapest option. As a teen on a fiscal lockdown, this line was my saving grace—I may not have been

Goat Cheese + Chive Biscuits (page 196), unbaked

3 tablespoons extra-virgin olive oil

2 tablespoons unsalted butter

1 large Vidalia or sweet onion, finely diced

1 tablespoon crushed garlic

¼ cup (34g) unbleached all-purpose flour

2 cups (475g) chicken broth

Scant ½ cup (110g) dry white wine

3 celery stalks, diced

1 large Yukon Gold potato, peeled and cubed

2 large leeks, finely sliced

1 teaspoon ground cumin

1 teaspoon ground sage

1 teaspoon kosher salt

1 teaspoon ground white pepper

Grated zest of 1 lemon

3 or 4 large boneless, skinless chicken breasts (650g to 700g), cubed

1 cup (235g) heavy cream

2 cups (144g) shaved Parmesan cheese

Make the dough for the biscuits up through shaping and set them on the lined baking sheet. Refrigerate them 1 hour. Do not brush with egg wash.

In a heavy-bottomed pot or Dutch oven, heat the olive oil and butter over medium heat until the butter melts. Add the onion and cook, stirring occasionally, until tender, about 15 minutes. Add the garlic and continue to cook for 5 more minutes. Remove from the heat. Add the flour and stir until the onion/garlic mixture is well coated. Pour in the chicken broth and white wine and stir until there are no traces of flour.

Stir in the celery, potato, and leeks. Return the pot to medium-high heat. Stir in the cumin, sage, salt, white pepper, and lemon zest. Bring to a boil, then reduce the heat to a simmer and cook until the vegetables are fork-tender, about 30 minutes.

Meanwhile, adjust an oven rack to the middle position and preheat the oven to 400°F (205°C) for the biscuits. If your oven has a convection option, preheat to 325°F (165°C).

Transfer the biscuits to the oven and bake them until they are fully baked, about 30 minutes.

Meanwhile, add the chicken pieces to the vegetables, stir, and cook until the chicken is no longer pink, about 10 minutes. Stir in the heavy cream, reduce the heat to medium-low, and simmer the chicken/vegetable mixture until the filling thickens, about 15 minutes. Remove from the heat and stir in the Parmesan cheese.

To serve, ladle about 2 cups of filling into a bowl or large mug. Top with a biscuit and serve.

To store, cover with plastic wrap and refrigerate for up to 5 days.

able to afford a sandwich, but I would order a bowl of soup, my favorite being the creamy lemon chicken soup. (And I always seemed to find a quarter under the floor mat of my dad's purple minivan so I could splurge for the bread bowl.) I was balling on a budget.

The most impressive takeaway from that whole experience is that I never tired of eating that same meal—a bowl of lemony chicken soup—day in and day out for nearly a month. This Lemon Chicken + Leek Pot Pie brings me right back—it's filled with herbs like sage, cumin, and chives that work together harmoniously. The addition of lemon zest adds a slightly tangy brightness. And just like that comforting bowl of soup, this pot pie—topped with flaky and tender biscuits made with goat cheese (a grown-up upgrade from the bread bowl)—is like receiving a hug of nostalgia that we all need from time to time.

Tanya and her sister call themselves "struggle kids," raised in a family of activists, organizers, and *comadres*.

Her dad, Walter "Slim" Coleman, is a Methodist pastor and a former member of the Black Panther Party who worked very closely with Chairman Fred Hampton in the Rainbow Coalition to bring attention to the police brutality, redlining, and gentrification in lower-income neighborhoods. Her mom, Emma Lozano, is also a pastor and an internationally recognized immigration activist and founder of illegal immigration advocacy group Centro Sin Fronteras. Her uncle, Rudy Lozano, a labor activist and community organizer, was pivotal in mobilizing the Latino community and advocating for Black and Brown unity. Tanya has followed in their footsteps, using her proclivity for sports and fitness to lessen the morbidity gap among Black, Brown, and white residents of Chicago.

In Chicago, there is a twenty-year gap in life expectancy between those who live in affluent neighborhoods and those in communities predominantly occupied by people of color. A white person living in a well-to-do neighborhood might live to be eighty years old, whereas a Black person living in a blighted neighborhood has only a sixty-year life expectancy. This gap is one of the largest disparities in the nation. Tanya, who went to college to play basketball and has been active and sports-minded her whole life, wanted to do something to close that gap.

After college, she became a fitness instructor. She was disheartened that most of the instructors in the studios she knew were persons of color while the majority of the clients were moneyed and white. She was moved to create an inclusive space where she could offer classes for those who could not afford pricey memberships in glossy, high-end fitness studios.

With her best friend, Seobia Rivers, Tanya cofounded Healthy Hood Chicago, a nonprofit organization that provides fitness, wellness, and lifestyle guidance to those living in lower-income neighborhoods. She converted a floor of her parents' church into a space where she could offer free or low-cost Zumba classes, wellness workshops, and mental health services. Her volunteers even cultivated and maintained a community garden in the church's backyard.

Tanya also created an arm of the organization called Youth Health Service Corps. The motto behind the corps is "Five plus one equals twenty," meaning if she could teach students how to identify the five diseases that lead to premature deaths (asthma, cancer, diabetes, HIV/AIDS, and hypertension) and help them discover one lifestyle change to combat those diseases, then they could add twenty years to their lives.

The Youth Health Service Corps partnered with nurses from Rush Hospital on Chicago's West Side and together they visited more than twenty Chicago public schools to teach school-aged children how to conduct prescreenings or to recognize signs of health abnormalities.

But this wasn't enough. While the workshops were effective in teaching youths how to identify signs of certain diseases, Tanya noticed that there was still a lack of basic resources in the community—and this was a major culprit in the morbidity gap she so desperately wanted to close. Inspired by the Black Panther Party's community survival initiatives such as the Free Breakfast for Children program, together with her father she created "Survival Days," during which time Healthy Hood Chicago would provide hot meals, free groceries, flu shots, HIV tests, and other essentials to lower-income communities in Chicago.

Tanya recognizes that health is wealth, and by continuing her family's legacy of activism, she hopes to enhance the lives and lengthen the life spans of Black and Latino families.

Inspired by Tanya's work with Healthy Hood Chicago, I've taken a "hood snack," Pizza Puffs, and converted it into something healthier. Traditionally, Pizza Puffs are handheld, deep-fried pastries that are stuffed with meat, mozzarella cheese, and pizza sauce commonly found at local fast-food establishments in Chicago's South and West neighborhoods. My Open-Faced Pizza Puffs feature puff pastry and fresh basil. Rather than loading it up with cholesterol-heavy cheese and deep-frying it, I use a bit of grated Parmesan to deliver a hint of cheesy goodness. It's a delicious tribute to the work Tanya is doing.

OPEN-FACED PIZZA PUFFS

MAKES 8 INDIVIDUAL PUFFS

2 tablespoons extra-virgin olive oil

2 tablespoons unsalted butter

½ large Vidalia or other sweet onion, diced

½ pound (220g) ground beef or ground turkey

4 garlic cloves, crushed

¼ cup (67g) tomato paste

½ teaspoon kosher salt

½ teaspoon dried sage

½ teaspoon dried marjoram

½ teaspoon dried oregano

½ teaspoon smoked paprika

½ teaspoon dried red pepper flakes

¼ teaspoon freshly ground black pepper

1 sprig fresh rosemary

1 sprig fresh thyme

2 tablespoons finely chopped fresh parsley

Flour, for rolling out

Puff Pastry, homemade (page 232) or store-bought

1 large egg

½ cup (227g) fresh basil leaves

¼ cup (30g) grated or shaved Parmesan cheese, for garnish

In a large Dutch oven or heavy-bottomed pot, heat the olive oil and butter over medium heat until the butter melts. Add the onion and cook, stirring occasionally, until tender, 15 to 20 minutes.

Add the ground meat, breaking it up with a spatula or fork and cooking until browned, about 15 minutes.

Add the garlic and continue to cook until fragrant, about 5 more minutes. Stir in the tomato paste and mix until the meat is fully coated. Stir in the salt, sage, marjoram, oregano, paprika, pepper flakes, black pepper, and ¼ cup (60g) of water. Add the rosemary and thyme sprigs. Reduce the heat to low and simmer, stirring occasionally, until the water evaporates, 5 to 8 minutes.

Remove from the heat. Discard the rosemary and thyme stems, stir in the parsley, and set aside.

Adjust an oven rack to the middle position and preheat the oven to 425°F (220°C). Line two baking sheets with parchment paper.

Lightly dust the countertop with flour and roll out the puff pastry into a rough 18 × 9-inch rectangle ⅛ inch thick. Using a pastry cutter, cut the puff pastry in half lengthwise to make two 18 × 4½ inch strips. Cut the pastry strips crosswise into 4½-inch squares for a total of 8 squares. Place 4 squares of puff pastry on each of the prepared baking sheets

In a small bowl, whisk together the egg and 1 tablespoon of water. Using a pastry brush, brush the egg wash on top of the pastry. Place 2 or 3 fresh basil leaves on each square of pastry.

Spoon 2 tablespoons of the meat filling on top of the basil.

Bake until the pastry is puffed and golden brown, 10 to 12 minutes. Remove the baking sheets from the oven and garnish each pastry with a pinch of Parmesan. Serve immediately.

SEAFOOD POT PIES

MAKES 4 TO 6 INDIVIDUAL POT PIES

Every year for Christmas, we went to my great-aunt Ruby's house. She typically served honey-baked ham, roast beef, rutabaga, candied sweet potatoes, greens, macaroni and cheese, cornbread dressing, dinner rolls, and a dessert table piled high with lemon pound cake, sweet potato pie, German chocolate cake, banana pudding, and fruit Jell-O molds.

It was a dinner spread that you'd expect to see on most Southern-inspired tables. Yet, every once in a while, she'd throw all of us for a loop. One time, she served a lobster-stuffed sirloin. Another time, she had an egg noodle casserole immersed in a white sauce. I have no idea what the name of the dish was or what was in it—all I remember is that it was freaking delicious.

My favorite atypical holiday dish of all time was a seafood-packed dressing made with mounds of seafood that she bought in New Orleans, packed in a cooler with dry ice, and brought with her on the Amtrak home to Chicago.

My God!

I have *never* in my life had anything as delicious as that dressing. It was like a smooth R & B song playing on my tongue and I often find myself trying to chase the memory of that recipe with my own rendition.

This Seafood Pot Pie is my best remix of Aunt Ruby's delectable dressing. It's creamy, mildly spicy, and has a slight licorice flavor from the fennel and Pernod.

Billowy Biscuits dough (page 193)
3 tablespoons coconut oil
2 tablespoons unsalted butter
1 large Vidalia or sweet onion, diced
1 tablespoon crushed garlic
½ cup (68g) unbleached all-purpose flour
2 cups (430g) bottled clam juice
½ cup thinly sliced fennel
2 ears corn, kernels sliced off
1 large carrot, peeled and diced
2 celery stalks, diced
2 sprigs fresh thyme
2½ teaspoons Cajun seasoning
2 teaspoons kosher salt
1½ teaspoons Old Bay seasoning

1 teaspoon freshly ground black pepper
¼ teaspoon cayenne pepper
¾ cup roasted red peppers, diced
1 cup (236g) dry white wine
1 cup (235g) heavy cream
1½ tablespoons Pernod
¼ cup (10g) roughly chopped fresh parsley
11 ounces (317g) langoustine tails
8 ounces (226g) lump crabmeat
9 ounces (264g) shrimp, peeled, deveined and tails removed
10 ounces (283g) bay scallops
1 cup fresh peas

Make the biscuit dough, shape as directed, and place on a parchment-lined baking sheet. Cover and refrigerate until ready to bake.

In a heavy-bottomed pot or Dutch oven, heat the coconut oil and butter over medium heat until the butter melts. Add the onion and cook, stirring occasionally, until very tender, about 15 minutes.

Add the garlic and continue to cook for 5 more minutes. Remove from the heat and use a silicone spatula to mix in the flour, stirring until the onion/garlic mixture is fully coated. Pour in the clam juice, stirring until there are no traces of flour.

Stir in the fennel, corn, carrot, and celery and return the pot to medium-high heat. Add the thyme, Cajun seasoning, salt, Old Bay, black pepper, and cayenne. Bring the mixture to a boil, then reduce to a simmer and cook until the vegetables are fork-tender, 25 to 30 minutes.

Meanwhile, adjust an oven rack to the middle position and preheat the oven to 400°F (205°C) for the biscuits. If your oven has a convection option, preheat to 325°F (165°C).

Stir the roasted red peppers, white wine, heavy cream, Pernod, and parsley into the pot with the vegetables and cook until the filling thickens, stirring occasionally, for an additional 20 minutes.

While the filling simmers, slide the biscuits into the oven and bake until they are lightly browned and the center is dry. See the Billowy Biscuits recipe (page 193) for oven temperatures and baking times.

To the thickened filling, add the langoustine tails, crab, shrimp, scallops, and peas. Cook until the shrimp are pink, 15 to 20 minutes. Remove from the heat. Discard the thyme sprigs.

Place 2 biscuits in a bowl. Ladle 2 cups of filling on top and serve.

To store, cover the filling with plastic wrap and refrigerate for up to 5 days. Store the leftover biscuits in an airtight container (see Bonus).

BONUS: It is best to enjoy the biscuits straightaway while they're soft and tender, though you can store them overnight in an airtight plastic bag. Leftover biscuits can be used for an amazingly quick strawberry shortcake: Cut 3 cups of strawberries into quarters and toss with ⅓ cup sugar. Set it aside to macerate and get juicy. Halve the biscuits and layer with a large spoonful of strawberries and a big dollop of Vanilla Bean Chantilly Cream (page 214).

BRAZILIAN FISH POT PIE

MAKES ONE 9 × 13-INCH POT PIE; SERVES 6 TO 8

When I travel, I am always interested to learn how cuisines from various countries have been influenced by the African diaspora.

I've noticed that many coastal cities often show the strongest evidence of influence, which makes sense since these cities are usually where enslaved Africans were transported to and sold. Since fishing was also important to commerce and survival in these places, it's not uncommon to see fish dishes with strong African influences like poisson yassa in Dakar, Senegal; shrimp and grits from the Gullah Geechee community in South Carolina's Low Country; and flying fish and cou cou of Barbados.

Brazil, however, imported more enslaved Africans than any other country, and African influences like feijoada are ingrained in its cuisine. Another example is moqueca, a coastal fish stew made with a sweet coconut milk, refogado (a Portuguese blend of aromatic spices), spicy chili peppers, and palm oil (brought from Africa). This pot pie is inspired by moqueca and derives its sweetness from caramelized onions in addition to the coconut, and gets extra heat from red pepper flakes.

Quadruple recipe All-Butter Pie Dough (page 220)

Flour, for rolling out

MARINATED FISH

1 cup (230g) distilled white vinegar

6 tablespoons (90g) crushed garlic

1 tablespoon freshly ground black pepper

1 tablespoon ground coriander

1 tablespoon ground cumin

1 tablespoon red pepper flakes

2 teaspoons granulated sugar

1½ teaspoons ground turmeric

1½ teaspoons kosher salt

3 pounds (1.36kg) skinless white fish fillets, such as cod, whiting, haddock, or similar

FILLING

3 tablespoons extra-virgin olive oil

2 tablespoons unsalted butter

3 large sweet onions, diced

1½ teaspoons kosher salt

3 tablespoons granulated sugar

¼ cup (55g) apple cider (or Mexican Coca-Cola)

½ cup (68g) unbleached all-purpose flour

4½ cups (1.06kg) bottled clam juice

2 large green bell peppers, finely diced

2 large red bell peppers, finely diced

1 medium jalapeño, seeded and finely diced

1 tablespoon freshly ground black pepper

2 teaspoons red pepper flakes

1½ teaspoons ground coriander

1½ teaspoons ground cumin

1½ teaspoons ground turmeric

3½ cups (612g) cooked long-grain rice (brown or white)

1 large egg

MAKE THE PIE DOUGH and divide into 2 equal portions. Form one portion of the dough into a round disk, cover in plastic wrap, and refrigerate. Lightly dust the countertop with flour and roll out the remaining portion to a 12 × 16-inch rectangle. Carefully transfer the dough to a 9 × 13-inch baking dish and gently mold the dough into the dish, leaving an overhang. Use your fingers to mend any tears, lines, holes, or cracks so that there are no gaps in the dough. Cut off a small piece of the overhanging dough and roll it into a ball. Use the ball of dough to gently continue to mold the dough to the baking dish, making sure the dough is flush to the corners of the baking dish. Cover the baking dish with plastic wrap and place in the fridge.

MARINATE THE FISH: In a medium bowl, whisk together the vinegar, garlic, black pepper, coriander, cumin, pepper flakes, sugar, turmeric, and salt. Place the marinade in a large zip-top plastic bag. Add the fish fillets to the bag, seal it, and place in the refrigerator for 1 hour.

MAKE THE FILLING: In a heavy-bottomed pot or Dutch oven, heat the olive oil and butter over medium heat until the butter melts. Add the onion and cook, stirring occasionally, until they are tender and begin to brown, about 20 minutes.

RECIPE CONTINUES >>

Add the salt and 1½ tablespoons of the sugar. Allow the onions to stick to the pan to brown but stir them before they can burn. If the onions start to dry out, add 2 tablespoons of water to the pot and stir. Scrape up the browned bits on the bottom of the pan and mix them into the onions. Allow the onions to continue cooking until they are a deep golden brown, stirring constantly, 25 to 30 minutes.

Add the apple cider to the onions and cook until the liquid has evaporated, 7 to 10 minutes. Remove from the heat. Add the flour to the onions and stir until the onions are coated. Add the clam juice and stir until there are no traces of flour visible. Return the pot to medium-high heat and add the bell peppers, jalapeño, black pepper, pepper flakes, coriander, cumin, turmeric, and the remaining 1½ tablespoons sugar. Bring to a boil, then reduce the heat to a simmer and cook, stirring occasionally, until the filling thickens and the vegetables become slightly tender, 10 to 15 minutes.

Remove the fish from the marinade (discard the marinade) and add it to the pot, gently stirring to coat in the liquid. Cook, using a metal spatula to break up the fish fillets into smaller chunks, until the fish cooks through and becomes flaky, 10 to 15 minutes. Add the cooked rice and stir until combined. Remove from the heat and allow the mixture to cool to room temperature.

Meanwhile, adjust an oven rack to the middle position and preheat the oven to 365°F (185°C).

In a small bowl, whisk together the egg with 1 tablespoon of water. Set the egg wash aside.

Remove the disk of pie dough from the refrigerator and unwrap. Lightly dust the countertop with flour and roll the dough into a 12 × 16-inch rectangle. Set aside.

Remove the dough-lined baking dish from the refrigerator. Uncover and spoon in the fish filling. Using the rolling pin, roll the rolled-out dough over onto itself and then unroll it over the top of the filling. Pinch the edges of the top and bottom crust together, roll them under, and tuck inside the baking dish.

Use a pastry brush to coat the top of the dough with egg wash and then make 2 slits in the top crust with a paring knife to vent the pie as it bakes. Transfer to the oven and bake until dark golden brown, 55 to 60 minutes.

Allow the pie to cool for 10 to 15 minutes before serving.

To store, cover with plastic wrap after baked and cooled and refrigerate for up to 5 days. To reheat, cover with foil and bake on the middle rack of the oven preheated to 350°F (175°C) until the center is warm, 25 to 30 minutes.

COCONUT CURRY CHICKEN POT PIE

MAKES ONE 9 × 13-INCH POT PIE; SERVES 6 TO 8

During the filming of the series *Bake Squad* for Netflix, the cast often took lunch breaks in our trailers while video conferencing our producers. One day, Max, my wrangler (the person who handles the cast on a television or movie set), brought me a container filled with coconut curry and white rice. After a long morning of baking and being surrounded by chocolate and sugar, the savory aromas were a welcome change and it smelled divine. My producer, Arielle, had an identical container in front of her and as we chatted on our screens, we each took a bite and then just stared at each other. Arielle finally broke it: "Oh my gosh—that is so good."

With my mouth full of the slightly sweet filling with the perfect kick of heat, I nodded vigorously and said, "Who you telling? I'm about to make this into a pie." I wasn't lying. And here it is.

Quadruple recipe All-Butter Pie Dough (page 220)

Flour, for rolling out

3 tablespoons coconut oil

2 tablespoons unsalted butter

½ large Vidalia or sweet onion, diced

1 stalk lemongrass, tough outer layer removed, inner stalk diced

1 shallot, halved and diced

3 tablespoons finely chopped fresh ginger

1 tablespoon crushed garlic

5 tablespoons (42g) unbleached all-purpose flour

1 cup (236g) chicken broth

1 cup (225g) canned full-fat coconut milk

1 tablespoon light brown sugar

2 teaspoons Thai green curry paste

1½ teaspoons garam masala

1 teaspoon ground cumin

1 teaspoon curry powder

1 teaspoon kosher salt

½ teaspoon ground turmeric

3 or 4 large skinless, boneless chicken breasts (650g to 700g), cubed

¼ cup (60g) fish sauce

2 tablespoons (5g) chopped fresh cilantro

Grated zest and juice of 1 lime

1 large egg

Make the pie dough and divide into 2 equal portions. Form one portion of the dough into a round disk, cover in plastic wrap, and refrigerate. Lightly dust the countertop with flour and roll the remaining portion out to a 12 × 16-inch rectangle. Carefully transfer the dough to a 9 × 13-inch baking dish and gently mold the dough into the dish, leaving an overhang. Use your fingers to mend any tears, lines, holes, or cracks so that there are no gaps in the dough. Cut off a small piece of overhanging dough and roll it into a ball. Use the ball of dough to gently continue to mold the dough to the baking dish, making sure the dough is flush to the corners of the baking dish. Cover the baking dish with plastic wrap and place in the fridge.

In a heavy-bottomed pot or Dutch oven, heat the coconut oil and butter over medium-high heat until the butter melts. Add the onion and cook, stirring occasionally, until very tender, about 15 minutes.

Add the lemongrass, shallot, ginger, and garlic and cook until slightly browned, 10 more minutes. Remove from the heat. Stir in the flour and mix until the vegetables are fully coated. Pour in the chicken broth and coconut milk and stir until no traces of flour are visible. Stir in the brown sugar, curry paste, garam masala, cumin, curry powder, salt, and turmeric.

Return the pot to medium-high heat and add the chicken. Stir, simmering until the chicken is no longer pink, about 10 minutes. Stir in the fish sauce, cilantro, lime zest, and lime juice. Reduce the heat to medium-low, cover the pot, and simmer until the mixture thickens slightly, 15 to 20 minutes.

RECIPE CONTINUES >>

Remove from the heat and set the filling aside to cool slightly, 25 to 30 minutes.

Adjust an oven rack to the middle position and preheat the oven to 350°F (175°C).

In a small bowl, whisk together the egg with 1 tablespoon of water. Set the egg wash aside.

Remove the disk of pie dough from the refrigerator and unwrap. Lightly dust the countertop with flour and roll the dough to a 12 × 16-inch rectangle. Using the rolling pin, roll the dough over on itself; set aside.

Remove the dough-lined baking dish from the refrigerator and uncover. Pour the slightly cooled filling into the crust, then roll the rolled-up dough over the top of the filling. Pinch the edges of the top and bottom crust together, roll them under, and tuck inside the baking dish.

Use a pastry brush to coat the top of the dough with egg wash and then make 2 slits in the top crust with a paring knife to vent the pie as it bakes. Transfer to the oven and bake until dark golden brown, 55 to 60 minutes.

Allow the pie to cool for 10 to 15 minutes before serving.

To store, cover with plastic wrap and refrigerate for up to 5 days. To reheat, cover with foil and bake on the middle rack of the oven preheated to 350°F (175°C) until the center is warm, 25 to 30 minutes.

SALMON WELLINGTON

MAKES 5 TO 7 SERVINGS

Chicago is sometimes referred to as "Up South" because of the large Black American population that migrated there from the South in search of better jobs and an easier way of life. My family came to Chicago from various Southern cities such as Lake Charles (Louisiana), Anderson (South Carolina), Macon (Georgia), and Birmingham (Alabama). People who came North brought their food and culture with them, one of the most significant, at least in Black neighborhoods, being the Friday night (or Sunday afternoon) fish fry.

Fried catfish was often served with a heaping mound of cheddar-topped baked spaghetti and a side salad, a pairing attributed to Memphis. While my dad never mastered frying catfish, he did love to fry "sammy patties," which were essentially salmon croquettes formed into round patties, coated in a cracker or bread crumb crust, and panfried. My dad served them with linguine (his favorite type of noodle) and a generous glass of red wine or red Kool-Aid for me. ("Red" defined the Kool-Aid flavor—whether it was watermelon, cherry, or strawberry flavored . . . it was *red* Kool-Aid.)

This Salmon Wellington is inspired by the salmon croquette recipe I developed and redeveloped over the years based on my dad's version. It does involve some time and patience, so my recommendation is to make it over two days (on day 1 you bake the salmon, make the filling, and then chill it overnight to firm up; on day 2 you make and bake the Wellington). It is definitely worth the wait!

2 pounds (910g) skinless salmon fillets

½ red onion, diced

½ red bell pepper, diced

⅓ cup sun-dried tomatoes, chopped

3 tablespoons finely minced fresh parsley

1½ teaspoons freshly ground black pepper

1½ teaspoons Cajun seasoning

1½ teaspoons garlic powder

1½ teaspoons Old Bay seasoning

1½ teaspoons Worcestershire sauce

Grated zest and juice of 1 large lemon

½ cup (40g) finely crushed saltine crackers

2 or 3 large eggs, plus 2 for the egg wash

Flour, for rolling out

1 pound (1 piece) Puff Pastry, homemade (page 232) or store-bought

2 tablespoons heavy cream

DAY 1

Adjust an oven rack to the middle position and preheat the oven to 350°F (175°C). Line a baking sheet with foil.

Place the salmon fillets on the baking sheet and bake until medium-well, 15 to 20 minutes.

Remove the baking sheet from the oven and set aside for the salmon to cool completely.

Once cooled, use a spatula to transfer the salmon to a large bowl. With a fork, slightly break up the larger chunks of salmon into smaller chunks (if you notice any bones, remove them). Add the red onion, bell pepper, sun-dried tomatoes, parsley, black pepper, Cajun seasoning, garlic powder, Old Bay, Worcestershire sauce, lemon zest, and lemon juice. Stir with a silicone spatula or a large spoon until well combined. Add the cracker crumbs and mix well, then taste to ensure it's seasoned to your preference (you may want to add a pinch of Old Bay or pepper).

Add 2 of the eggs to the mixture and use your hands to massage the egg into the salmon filling. Squeeze portions of the salmon filling to see if the filling holds together. If the filling falls apart, mix in a third egg.

Place a 20 × 12-inch-long piece of plastic wrap on your work surface. Squeeze handfuls of salmon filling to remove any excess liquid and place them on the plastic wrap. Repeat this until all the salmon filling is on the plastic wrap in one long row. Now shape the filling into a rectangular log that is 16 inches long and with a 3½-inch diameter. Lift the edges of the plastic wrap and wrap up the salmon. You may need to use additional plastic wrap to make sure the salmon log is fully covered.

RECIPE CONTINUES >>

Place the salmon log on a baking sheet and refrigerate overnight. (If you absolutely must make the dish the same day, place the salmon log in the freezer for 3 hours.)

DAY 2

Lightly dust the countertop with flour and roll out the puff pastry to an 18 × 13-inch rectangle. Remove the salmon from the refrigerator, open the plastic wrap, and use the edges of the plastic wrap to carefully pick up the log and flip it over onto the center of the puff pastry rectangle with the top facing down. Fold the long sides of the puff pastry up over the top of the salmon log. Using a paring knife, trim away any excess pastry so the two edges just meet—you don't want any pastry overlap. Fill a small bowl with water and use your fingertips to dab a little water on the top edges of the dough and use your fingers to pinch the two sides together. At each short end, trim away the excess dough, wet the dough with your fingertips, and pinch the dough together until there are no gaps.

Flip the entire Wellington over onto a baking sheet so that the seam side is down and the smooth side is facing up.

In a small bowl, whisk together the remaining 2 eggs and heavy cream. Using a pastry brush, coat the dough with the egg wash. Place the Wellington in the refrigerator for 30 minutes. Remove the Wellington from the refrigerator and apply a second coat of egg wash and return to the refrigerator to chill for an additional 30 minutes.

Adjust an oven rack to the middle position and preheat the oven to 365°F (185°C).

Bake the Wellington until it is golden brown, 50 minutes to 1 hour.

Remove the Wellington from the oven and set aside to cool for 10 to 15 minutes before cutting crosswise into 3-inch slices for serving.

To store, cover the remaining Wellington with plastic wrap and refrigerate for up to 5 days.

BONUS: To make salmon croquettes, or "sammy patties" as my dad called them, make the filling as directed, then cover the bowl with plastic wrap and refrigerate for 1 hour. Fill a large skillet with ½ inch vegetable oil and set over medium-high heat. While the oil is heating, take ¼-cup mounds of the mixture and form them into patties 1½ inches thick. Place the patties in the skillet and fry until they are golden brown, about 3 minutes on each side. Remove the patties from the oil with a spatula and place them on a plate lined with paper towels. Enjoy with a squeeze of lemon and some hot sauce—or make some spaghetti to have on the side.

SHEPHERD'S PIE

MAKES ONE 9 × 13-INCH POT PIE; SERVES 6 TO 8

My dad may have been renowned for his pies and quiches, but when it came to dinner, there were just three meals that he kept in rotation: frozen Swedish meatballs with instant mashed potatoes, salmon croquettes with spaghetti, and Hamburger Helper. If he decided to get especially creative, he would top the Hamburger Helper casserole with mashed potatoes—and this was my dad's version of shepherd's pie on a budget. Bless his heart.

This shepherd's pie is a comforting dish made rich with the addition of a dark ale in the filling. A traditional shepherd's pie is made with lamb. Technically, using beef changes the name of this dish to a *cottage pie*, but I won't tell the pie authorities if you don't. Yukon Gold potatoes are perfect for this dish: They have a naturally buttery taste, they have a nice, creamy texture when mashed (without becoming "gluey"), and they brown nicely in the oven for that all-important slightly textured top crust.

¼ cup (38g) vegetable oil

1 large Vidalia or sweet onion, diced

1 tablespoon crushed garlic

3 pounds (1.36kg) ground turkey or ground beef

6 tablespoons (51g) unbleached all-purpose flour

1 (29 oz/822g) can tomato purée

1 cup (234g) beef broth

1 cup (234g) dark ale

2 large carrots, peeled and diced

2 ears corn, kernels sliced off

2 tablespoons (30g) Worcestershire sauce

1 tablespoon dried rosemary

1 tablespoon dried thyme

1 tablespoon kosher salt

1 teaspoon freshly ground black pepper

1 cup fresh peas

Buttery Mashed Potatoes (page 212)

In a heavy-bottomed pot or Dutch oven, heat the vegetable oil over medium-high heat until very hot (if bubbles form on the end of a wooden spoon dipped in the oil, then it's hot enough), about 3 minutes. Add the onion and cook, stirring occasionally, until tender, about 15 minutes.

Add the garlic and continue to cook for 5 more minutes. Add the ground meat and brown it, using a wooden spoon to break it up, and stir occasionally, until it is completely cooked through, 15 to 20 minutes.

Remove from the heat. Stir in the flour and tomato purée and mix until no traces of flour are visible. Pour in the beef broth and dark ale and stir the mixture until well combined. Add the carrots, corn, Worcestershire sauce, rosemary, thyme, salt, and pepper. Stir and then bring to a boil over medium-high heat. Reduce the heat to a simmer and continue to cook until the vegetables are fork-tender, 25 to 30 minutes.

Remove from the heat. Stir in the peas and set aside.

Adjust an oven rack to the middle position and preheat the oven to 350°F (175°C).

Pour the ground meat filling into a 3-inch-deep 9 × 13-inch baking dish. Using a silicone spatula or a large spoon, spread the mashed potatoes over the filling and into the corners of the baking dish.

Transfer to the oven and bake until the mashed potatoes have browned slightly, 25 to 30 minutes.

To store, cover with plastic wrap and refrigerate for up to 5 days. To reheat, cover with foil and bake on the middle rack of the oven preheated to 350°F (175°C) until the center is warm, 25 to 30 minutes.

BONUS: Depending on the size of your baking dish, you may have a bit of meat filling left over. If you find that you do, you can butter and toast large brioche rolls and then scoop the remaining meat filling onto a roll for an elevated sloppy joe!

VEGETARIAN CHILI POT PIE

MAKES ONE 9 × 13-INCH POT PIE; SERVES 6 TO 8

It's no secret that in Chicago the winters are *harsh*. So, you can be pretty sure that a hearty, comforting, hot bowl of chili is going to be served for supper at least a few times a month. At my Catholic high school, we had to wear uniforms—a plaid skirt with a V-neck sweater vest and black or brown shoes—and most of us wore the same outer layers (the sweater vest and skirt) every day for the entire week before it would get dry-cleaned. This may sound disgusting (and let's be honest, it probably was), but we always wore layers beneath the skirts and a shirt beneath the vest, so the top layers stayed fairly clean. One thing that couldn't be helped, though, is how the fabric of our uniform seemed to just drink up the fragrance of food.

Sitting in homeroom in the morning, you could just easily *smell* what everyone ate the night before or that morning—be it pancakes with syrup for breakfast, or fried fish or meatloaf for dinner. But the most unmistakable smell was that of chili.

A classmate could walk into class, survey the room while sniffing the air, and loudly probe, "WHOSE MAMA MADE CHILI LAST NIGHT?" The whole class would erupt in laughter. We teased (in a nice way!) whoever we thought was the culprit of the aromas of onions and chili powder. Someone would finally raise their hand and fess up while laughing with pride, "My mom made it . . . and it was good, too!"

Growing up in a city with punishing windchills, chili was a staple in many of our homes. And whenever I put together this vegetarian pot pie made with its blend of colorful peppers, hearty beans, and warm spices with cornbread baked on the top instead of pie dough, I go right back to my childhood. That memory carries with it perhaps the most important lesson I learned back then: Always close your bedroom door before cooking dinner!

3 tablespoons extra-virgin olive oil

2 tablespoons unsalted butter

1 large Vidalia or sweet onion, diced

1 tablespoon crushed garlic

1 large green bell pepper, diced

1 large orange or yellow bell pepper, diced

1 large red bell pepper, diced

2 ears corn, kernels sliced off

3 (15.5 oz/439g) cans black beans, drained

1 (29 oz/822g) can kidney beans, drained

1 (29 oz/822g) can tomato purée

2 tablespoons packed light brown sugar

2 tablespoons chopped fresh cilantro

1 tablespoon plus 1 teaspoon dark chili powder

1 tablespoon port sherry

2 teaspoons smoked paprika

1 teaspoon ground cumin

1 teaspoon dried oregano

1 teaspoon ground white pepper

¼ teaspoon cayenne pepper

2 bay leaves

Buttermilk Cornbread batter (page 209)

In a heavy-bottomed pot or Dutch oven, heat the olive oil and butter over medium-high heat until the butter melts. Add the onion and cook, stirring occasionally, until tender, about 15 minutes.

Add the garlic and continue to cook for 5 more minutes. Add the bell peppers and cook, stirring frequently, until the vegetables are very tender and slightly caramelized, 20 to 25 minutes.

Stir in the corn, black beans, kidney beans, and tomato purée. Stir in the brown sugar, cilantro, chili powder, port sherry, smoked paprika, cumin, oregano, white pepper, cayenne, and bay leaves. Bring to a boil, reduce the heat, and simmer for 30 minutes.

Remove from the heat and let cool slightly, 20 to 25 minutes.

This is a good time to make the cornbread batter.

Adjust an oven rack to the middle position and preheat the oven to 350°F (175°C).

Discard the bay leaves. Transfer the chili to a large baking dish that is 9 × 13 or can hold at least 3 quarts and spoon the cornbread batter on top of the chili. Using a silicone spatula or a large spoon, spread the batter to the corners of the baking dish.

Bake until the center of the cornbread is dry, about 1 hour 15 minutes.

To store, cover with plastic wrap and refrigerate for up to 5 days. To reheat, cover with foil and bake on the middle rack of the oven preheated to 350°F (175°C) until the center is warm, 25 to 30 minutes.

CLAUDIA GORDON

DISABILITY RIGHTS ADVOCATE

There once was a woman who was often seen walking tall and gracefully down the paths and roads of Cascade, Jamaica.

She didn't speak and never bothered anyone. Whenever the local children saw her, they'd quickly run and hide behind a tree or a house, and when the woman came near, they'd emerge from their hiding places and launch stones at her while taunting, "Dummy! Dummy! Dummy!" before running away.

Claudia Gordon, a local of the village, didn't understand why her peers engaged in that activity. All she knew was that this person was ostracized as a "dummy" and was considered different from everyone else in her small, rural village.

When Claudia was eight years old, she began to experience immense pain in her ears. Her mother was working in the United States, so Claudia's aunt Mildred took her to a small clinic where a very basic diagnoses was provided: She was going deaf. For a while, Claudia did not know that she was deaf because she would read people's lips and imagine that she was hearing their voices, too. But when the children began to mock her, she realized she was being treated just like the woman who was ostracized. That woman, like Claudia, was deaf.

People in her town who used to smile and greet her now only stared. Healers would try to perform rituals to rid her of her deafness. Although Claudia was considered the brightest student in her class and earned the highest marks, the teachers and principal decided that she was no longer "qualified" to attend school. Claudia was labeled as "deaf and dumb," and instead of learning with the other children, she stayed home to do domestic chores. While well liked in her community, people didn't know how to treat her. They'd sometimes stare and other times ignore her completely. Claudia began to feel that she didn't belong and often felt invisible.

When Claudia was eleven, she moved to the Bronx in New York City to live with her mom. She attended the Lexington School and Center for the Deaf in Queens and learned ASL (American Sign Language). She was thrilled to be receiving an education again. She excelled academically, participated in sports, and earned the honor of being valedictorian of both her junior high school and high school graduating classes. While in high school, she decided she wanted to be an attorney. Some shrugged off her ambition as wishful thinking, assuming that her deafness would present itself as an insurmountable obstacle. She understood then that their cynicism dictated neither her worth nor her capacity.

Upon graduating from Howard University in 1995

with a BA in political science, Claudia entered American University's Washington College of Law. While there, she received the prestigious Skadden Fellowship for law graduates working in public interest fields. The fellowship allowed her to work at the National Association of the Deaf Law and Advocacy Center, which handles cases of discrimination and provides technical assistance on behalf of deaf and hard of hearing individuals in America.

Her experience made her realize that landing a job within the federal government would allow her to effect greater change, like enforcing laws such as the Americans with Disabilities Act of 1990 and the Rehabilitation Act of 1973. By advocating for their rights, Claudia felt she could help alleviate the discrimination that people with disabilities faced.

Claudia served as a consultant for the National Council on Disability and as a senior policy advisor for the Department of Homeland Security in the Office of Civil Rights and Civil Liberties. She is an ardent supporter of the National Black Deaf Advocates and countless other disability rights organizations.

As a member of the Obama administration, Claudia took on a variety of roles, including as chief of staff for the US Department of Labor's Office of Federal Contract Compliance Programs (OFCCP) and associate director for the White House Office of Public Engagement. At OFCCP, a worker protection agency, she enforced the civil rights of American workers who either work for or seek employment with companies that benefit from government contracts. At the White House, she served as the liaison to the disability community and advised on disability policies.

The common denominator in all she does is to use compliance and advocacy as vehicles for breaking down barriers for individuals with disabilities plus cultivate environments that are inclusive and equitable for all.

Patties are a traditional and iconic food of Jamaica made from flavorful fillings enclosed in a flaky crust. These Cauliflower Patties were inspired by Claudia's West Indian roots. I used Jamaican curry to tint and flavor the dough and Scotch bonnet peppers to give the filling heat. On the outside, these patties may look like any other Jamaican meat patties—which are often served tucked into coco bread and washed down with some Kola Champagne—but on the inside, the filling exceeds the expectation of what a traditional meat-filled pattie is supposed to look and taste like with its plant-based ingredients.

CAULIFLOWER PATTIES

MAKES EIGHTEEN 3-INCH PATTIES

2 tablespoons olive oil

½ large onion, finely diced

1 large head cauliflower (1¾ lb), cored and chopped into small florets (about 7 cups)

1 Scotch bonnet or habanero chile, finely diced (optional)

2 garlic cloves, minced (about 1 teaspoon)

1 teaspoon smoked paprika

1 teaspoon Jamaican curry powder

1 teaspoon dried thyme

1 teaspoon ground white pepper

½ teaspoon ground allspice

½ teaspoon chili powder

½ teaspoon kosher salt, plus more as needed

⅓ cup (84g) full-fat coconut milk

¼ cup (59g) bread crumbs

3 scallions, both white and green parts, chopped

2 tablespoons finely chopped fresh parsley

Double recipe Curry Dough (page 228)

Flour, for rolling out

2 large eggs, lightly beaten

In a heavy-bottomed pot or Dutch oven, combine the olive oil and onion and cook over medium-high heat, stirring occasionally, until tender, 15 to 20 minutes.

Add the cauliflower and Scotch bonnet chile (if using) and cook, stirring occasionally, until fork-tender, 15 to 20 minutes.

Stir in the garlic, smoked paprika, curry, thyme, white pepper, allspice, chili powder, salt, and coconut milk. Cook until fragrant, stirring occasionally, about 30 minutes, or until the cauliflower florets are pliable. Remove from the heat and cool completely, 1 to 1½ hours.

Stir the bread crumbs, scallions, and parsley into the cooled cauliflower mixture.

Line two baking sheets with parchment paper and set aside.

Divide the curry dough into 18 equal portions (about 3¼ oz/90g each). Set one piece on a lightly floured countertop (place the rest on a plate and cover with plastic) and roll to about 6 inches in diameter. Repeat with a few more pieces of dough. Add 3 tablespoons of cauliflower filling in the center of each disk.

In a small bowl, mix the beaten eggs with 2 tablespoons of water. Using a pastry brush, apply the egg wash around the edges of the dough. Fold the dough in half to encase the filling and, using a fork or your fingers, firmly press the edges together to seal. Place the filled patties on the prepared baking sheet, spacing them 1 inch apart. Repeat this process with the remaining dough and filling, placing 9 patties on each pan. Brush the top of the patties with the egg wash and refrigerate for 20 to 30 minutes (or up to 6 hours).

Adjust the oven racks to the upper-middle and lower-middle positions and preheat the oven to 400°F (205°C). Bake the patties until yellow-golden brown, 35 to 40 minutes. Remove from the oven and cool for 10 minutes before serving.

BONUS: Freeze the shaped, unbaked patties in a sealed plastic bag for up to 60 days. The patties can be baked straight from the freezer—just allow for an extra 10 minutes of baking time. The cauliflower can be replaced with cubed sweet potatoes, carrots, tofu, or any other vegetable you'd like to experiment with.

STEAK + ALE POT PIES

MAKES FOUR 5-INCH DEEP-DISH POT PIES

Simmering beef in beer is a classic technique that helps break down the tough fibers in the meat while helping it develop a rich, caramel-like flavor.

Unlike Shepherd's Pie (page 85), which calls for ground lamb or ground beef, this pot pie calls for a chuck roast. This tougher cut has outstanding marbling, which makes the roast tender and juicy when slowly braised. Marbling—the white striations of fat—also adds a lot of flavor to the beef, while the acid in red wine vinegar further tenderizes the beef and imparts a savory depth of flavor in each bite.

Caramelized onions, portobello mushrooms, and *especially* the steak sauce and Worcestershire sauce round out this pot pie with their touches of sweetness and umami.

Quadruple recipe All-Butter Pie Dough (page 220)

Flour, for rolling out

3 tablespoons extra virgin olive oil

2 tablespoons unsalted butter

1 large Vidalia or sweet onion, diced

1 tablespoon crushed garlic

3 pounds (1.36kg) boneless chuck roast, fat trimmed

1 cup (233g) beef broth

1⅔ cups (330g) dark ale

3 sprigs fresh thyme

2 sprigs fresh rosemary

2 teaspoons kosher salt

1 teaspoon freshly ground black pepper

1¾ cups sliced chestnut mushrooms

3 Roma (plum) tomatoes, diced

2 celery stalks, diced

1 large carrot, diced

¼ cup (67g) tomato paste

¼ cup (10g) chopped fresh parsley

1 tablespoon balsamic vinegar

1 tablespoon steak sauce

1 tablespoon Worcestershire sauce

2 tablespoons unbleached all-purpose flour

1 large egg

Make the dough and divide it into 8 portions of 6 ounces (170g) each. Set one piece on a lightly floured countertop (place the rest on a plate, cover with plastic, and refrigerate) and roll to about 7 inches in diameter. Carefully transfer to a 5-inch deep-dish ramekin. Gently mold the dough into the dish and use your fingers to mend any tears, lines, holes, or cracks so that there are no gaps in the dough. Allow the excess dough to hang over the ramekin, then roll it under to make an edge. Continue to roll the crust under all the way around the ramekin. Cover with plastic wrap and place in the fridge. Repeat with 3 more portions of dough and ramekins.

In a heavy-bottomed pot or Dutch oven, heat the olive oil and butter over medium-high heat until the butter melts. Add the onion and cook, stirring occasionally, until very tender, 15 to 20 minutes.

Add the garlic and continue to cook for 5 more minutes. Using a silicone spatula, create a well in the middle of the pot by pushing the onion to the edges. Place the chuck roast in the center and brown all sides of the roast, using tongs to turn the meat, 8 to 10 minutes total.

Pour in the beef broth and dark ale. Stir in the thyme sprigs, rosemary sprigs, salt, and pepper and bring to a boil, then reduce the heat to medium-low, cover the pot, and simmer until the meat starts to become tender, about 1 hour.

Remove the lid and use the tongs to carefully turn the roast over. Replace the lid and simmer until the meat is very tender and easily pulls apart, about 1 hour 45 minutes.

RECIPE CONTINUES >>

Using 2 forks, shred the beef directly in the pot. Discard any fat. Stir in the mushrooms, tomatoes, celery, carrot, tomato paste, balsamic vinegar, steak sauce, and Worcestershire sauce. Increase the heat to medium-high and cook until the vegetables are fork-tender, 25 to 30 minutes.

In a small bowl, stir together the flour and 5 tablespoons of the cooking liquid from the pot. Stir and, once it is well blended, add an additional 5 tablespoons of cooking liquid and continue to stir to make a slurry. Return the slurry to the pot and stir. Allow the filling to thicken, about 5 minutes. Discard the rosemary and thyme sprigs and stir in the chopped parsley.

Remove from the heat to cool slightly, 25 to 30 minutes.

Adjust an oven rack to the middle position and preheat the oven to 350°F (175°C).

Lightly dust the countertop with flour and roll out the 4 remaining portions of dough until each is about 7 inches in diameter.

In a small bowl, whisk together the egg with 1 tablespoon of water. Set the egg wash aside.

Remove the ramekins from the fridge and uncover. Add 1½ cups of the slightly cooled filling to each ramekin. Cover the ramekins with a round of rolled-out dough, pinching the edges of the bottom and top crust together (and tucking the lip of the crust inside the baking dish). Repeat with the remaining ramekins and rolled-out rounds of dough.

Using a pastry brush, brush the egg wash on top of the dough, then use a small paring knife to make 2 slits in the top of the crust to vent the pot pies as they bake.

Place the ramekins on a baking sheet, then place the sheet in the oven and bake until the crust becomes dark golden brown, 30 to 45 minutes.

Remove the ramekins from the oven and set aside to cool for 10 to 15 minutes before serving.

To store, cover with plastic wrap and refrigerate for up to 5 days. To reheat, cover with foil and bake on the middle rack of the oven preheated to 350°F (175°C) until the center is warm, 25 to 30 minutes.

SWEET POTATO + LENTIL POT PIE

MAKES 4 TO 6 SERVINGS

Sweet potatoes and lentils always remind me of when I was sick and my mom used to get me soup from this Lebanese restaurant called The Nile in Hyde Park, where I grew up on the south side of the city. It's one of the more diverse neighborhoods in Chicago, and the variety of restaurants there reflects the population, especially on 57th Street, where you would find a Jewish deli next to a Korean restaurant next to a Thai spot that was next to The Nile.

Whenever I was sick with a cold, my mom might pick up soup from any one of those places, but the red lentil soup was my favorite. Sipping on it was soothing to my soul. This Sweet Potato + Lentil Pot Pie pays tribute to The Nile's perfect combination of spice and acid and at the same time incorporates some other flavors I love, like curry powder in the filling and sweet potato biscuits perched on top. Like the Chicken + Biscuit Pot Pie (page 63) or the Vegetarian Chili Pot Pie (page 86), this pot pie is more like a savory cobbler than a traditional two-crusted pot pie. To make this vegan and gluten-free, use rice flour instead of all-purpose flour and serve with Sweet Potato Cornbread (page 207) made with vegan butter and plant-based eggs.

Sweet Potato Biscuits dough (page 198)
¼ cup (38g) vegetable oil
1 large Vidalia or sweet onion, diced
2 tablespoons finely diced fresh ginger
1 tablespoon crushed garlic
4 cups (946g) vegetable broth
1 pound sweet potato, cut into 1½-inch cubes
2 tablespoons (30g) tomato paste
2 teaspoons chili powder
1 teaspoon ground turmeric

½ teaspoon curry powder
¼ teaspoon kosher salt
⅛ teaspoon cayenne pepper
1 (15 oz/425g) bag red lentils
¼ cup (60g) fish sauce
1 cup (240g) canned full-fat coconut milk
3 plum tomatoes, cored and diced
5 ounces kale leaves, tough stems removed, and leaves roughly chopped
Chopped fresh parsley, for serving
Lime wedges, for serving

Make the biscuit dough, shape into biscuits, and set them on a parchment-lined baking sheet. Cover and refrigerate until ready to use.

In a heavy-bottomed pot or Dutch oven, heat the vegetable oil over medium-high heat until hot, about 3 minutes. Add the onion and cook, stirring occasionally, until tender, about 15 minutes.

Add the ginger and garlic and cook until the garlic is slightly tender, about 5 more minutes, stirring occasionally. Add the vegetable broth, 2 cups of water, and sweet potatoes. Cover the pot and bring everything to a boil, then reduce the heat to medium-low and cook until the sweet potatoes are tender, 15 to 20 minutes. Stir in the tomato paste, chili powder, turmeric, curry powder, salt, and cayenne.

While the sweet potatoes are cooking, fill a small saucepan with 3 cups of water and bring it to a boil. Add the lentils and simmer until the lentils are tender, stirring occasionally, 15 to 20 minutes. Remove the saucepan from the heat and drain the lentils in a sieve or colander.

Add the drained lentils and fish sauce to the sweet potato mixture. Cover and cook until the lentils partially dissolve and develop a creamy texture, an additional 30 minutes or so. Once the lentils are completely tender, remove the lid and stir in the coconut milk, tomatoes, and kale. Cover, reduce the heat to medium-low, and simmer until the tomatoes have slightly cooked down, about 20 minutes.

Meanwhile, adjust an oven rack to the middle position and preheat the oven to 425°F (218°C) for the biscuits.

RECIPE CONTINUES >>

Take the sweet potato biscuits out of the refrigerator and transfer to the oven. Bake the sweet potato biscuits until they are golden brown and fully cooked through, 12 to 14 minutes. Remove the biscuits from the oven and allow them to cool slightly.

Remove the lentil mixture from the heat and uncover to let the filling cool slightly. To serve, ladle into bowls or mugs and top each with chopped parsley and a biscuit (or two!). Serve with a lime wedge or two on the side.

To store, cover with plastic wrap and refrigerate for up to 5 days. To reheat, cover with foil and bake on the middle rack of the oven preheated to 350°F (175°C) until the center is warm, 25 to 30 minutes.

VARIATION: SWEET POTATO + LENTIL PIE TOPPED WITH SWEET POTATO CORNBREAD

Make the sweet potato and lentil filling as directed and pour the filling into a 9 × 13-inch baking dish. Make the batter for Sweet Potato Cornbread (page 207). Preheat the oven to 350°F (175°C). Spoon the cornbread batter on op of the lentil filling. Using a silicone spatula or a large spoon, spread the batter to the corners of the baking dish. Bake until the center of the cornbread is dry, about 1 hour 15 minutes.

BONUS: You can top your Sweet Potato + Lentil Pie with just one Sweet Potato Biscuit, but I can never resist grabbing two! Sometimes I like to smear a touch of butter and drizzle honey on my extra biscuit for a sweet finish.

QUICHES

OUR LADY OF QUICHE CUSTARD

MAKES 1¼ CUPS (ENOUGH FOR ONE 9-INCH QUICHE)

On Saturday mornings, my dad had a ritual: He'd wake up early, put on Miles Davis or Tito Puente and an apron, and get a quiche in the oven, then he'd start to clean. With one hand he'd run the vacuum, and with his other one he'd scream into the phone, arguing with my aunt Sandy over who made the best quiche.

The argument didn't end on Saturday. On Sunday mornings, with jazz music now blaring through the car's stereo, my dad and aunt would continue the same argument during the entire drive to Holy Family Catholic Church. This happened Every. Single. Weekend.

I couldn't really wear headphones properly because their shape interfered with my hearing aids, so I could never totally tune them out. The minute I heard my dad begin with, "So, I made this quiche today . . . ," I would ram the back of my head into the pillow or car seat and would cut my eyes and kiss my teeth as hard as I could.

And then when I became an adult it all became clear—because I started to eat quiche. The fluffy, eggy custard offset the buttery, flaky crust, and a variety of fillings as creative as you could think of. Quiche finally made so much sense to me!

It's not only delicious but also a perfect any-time-of-the-day meal that can be eaten warm or cold in the morning or at midnight. And, with a good custard base, you can improvise to your heart's content.

This quiche custard has yet to fail me so I'm sharing it with you, to use in the recipes that follow or for dreaming up your own filling combinations. It makes enough custard for one 9-inch quiche, but it can be easily scaled up for a deep-dish quiche or a deep-dish pie plate (see Batch It Up, opposite).

5 large eggs (263g)
1 tablespoon unbleached all-purpose flour (or gluten-free flour)
½ teaspoon dried basil
½ teaspoon dark chili powder
1 garlic clove, crushed
½ teaspoon onion powder
½ teaspoon dried oregano
½ teaspoon smoked paprika
½ teaspoon dried thyme
½ teaspoon kosher salt
½ teaspoon freshly ground black pepper
¼ teaspoon cayenne pepper
1 cup (240g) whole milk

In a large bowl, whisk together the eggs, flour, basil, chili powder, garlic, onion powder, oregano, smoked paprika, thyme, salt, black pepper, and cayenne. While whisking, pour in the whole milk. Continue to whisk until the batter becomes light and airy, about 1 minute.

Refrigerate in an airtight container for up to 7 days.

BONUS: For the times when you just don't have time to make pie crust, you can turn this quiche base into a frittata. Preheat the oven to 350°F (175°C). Pour the custard in a well-oiled ovenproof skillet and cook on the stovetop over medium heat until the edges of the eggs begin to dry and set, about 10 minutes. Transfer the pan to the oven until the center is set, 15 to 20 minutes. One of my favorite quick frittata fillings includes spinach and sun-dried tomatoes with a healthy sprinkle of feta or Parmesan cheese—but really any of the quiche fillings on pages 102 to 127 would make a great frittata filling, too.

BATCH IT UP

	DEEP DISH 9-inch Pie Plate	DEEP DISH 10-inch Pie Plate
	1½ × base recipe	2 × base recipe
EGGS	7 whole plus 1 egg yolk	10
FLOUR	1½ tablespoons	2 tablespoons
DRIED BASIL	¾ teaspoon	1 teaspoon
DARK CHILI POWDER	¾ teaspoon	1 teaspoon
GARLIC	2 cloves	3 cloves
ONION POWDER	¾ teaspoon	1 teaspoon
DRIED OREGANO	¾ teaspoon	1 teaspoon
SMOKED PAPRIKA	¾ teaspoon	1 teaspoon
DRIED THYME	¾ teaspoon	1 teaspoon
KOSHER SALT	¾ teaspoon	1 teaspoon
FRESHLY GROUND BLACK PEPPER	¾ teaspoon	1 teaspoon
CAYENNE PEPPER	⅓ teaspoon	½ teaspoon
WHOLE MILK	1½ cups	2 cups

TOMATO + BASIL QUICHE

MAKES ONE 9-INCH QUICHE

My grandma Billingslea had a small strip of land between her garage on the side of the house and the alleyway—this was her garden, where she grew tomatoes, cucumbers, mustard greens, turnip greens, collard greens, kale, Swiss chard, and green peppers. Impressive, right? As a little girl I loved to pick a tomato off a vine, sprinkle some salt on it, and take a bite, letting the sweet flavors of the sun-kissed tomato burst in my mouth and be heightened by the salt.

This is the experience that I channeled for this tomato quiche. I prefer whole grape and cherry tomatoes because they are sweeter and have less water content than plum or beefsteak tomatoes, which can sometimes leach so much liquid that they prevent the quiche custard from setting fully. Small whole tomatoes provide for a more even bake and gift the eater with a warm and juicy explosion of flavor in each forkful.

Flour, for rolling out
All-Butter Pie Dough (page 220)
½ cup cherry tomatoes
½ cup grape tomatoes

½ cup (41g) grated extra-sharp cheddar cheese
Leaves from 2 sprigs fresh basil, chopped
Our Lady of Quiche Custard (page 100)

Adjust an oven rack to the middle position and preheat the oven to 350°F (175°C).

Lightly dust the countertop with flour and roll out the dough to about 12 inches in diameter. Carefully transfer the dough to a 9-inch pie pan. Roll the overhanging dough to the edge of the pan and crimp.

Place the tomatoes in the pie shell, taking care to evenly distribute them across the bottom. Sprinkle the cheddar and basil over the tomatoes and place the pie pan on a baking sheet. Pour the custard into the pie crust.

Transfer to the oven and bake until the crust is golden brown, the edges of the custard are puffed, and the center is dry, 25 to 30 minutes. Remove the quiche from the oven and set aside to cool slightly, about 10 minutes, before slicing and serving. Or cool completely and serve at room temperature.

To store, cover the cooled quiche with plastic wrap and refrigerate for up to 7 days. To reheat: Set the rack to the middle and preheat the oven to 350°F (175°C). Cover the slices with aluminum foil and heat until their centers are warm, 20 to 25 minutes.

LAUREN BUSH LAUREN

FEED PROJECTS

During her sophomore year at Princeton University, where she was studying anthropology, Lauren was invited by the World Food Programme to be its Student Ambassador.

Her very first trip as an ambassador was to Guatemala. While there, she visited a therapeutic feeding center where she saw children who were ill and lacked the energy and vibrancy that young children typically display. As she was leaving the center, she came across a young boy who looked to be around three or four years old. He was actually seven, but he was so chronically malnourished that he was literally wasting away. He soon died of hunger. This experience deeply touched Lauren and helped shaped her view on and mission for food access.

Extreme hunger affects 795 million people worldwide. Through her experience as a student ambassador, Lauren developed a strong belief that people—no matter where they are born—deserve the right to live to their full human potential. At the core of that is getting the proper food and nutrition they need.

As a member of a well-known, wealthy family (she's the granddaughter of former president George H. W. Bush and is married to Ralph Lauren's son), Lauren was advised by a family friend to go and make money—and then give it away. But she was not interested in making money for the sake of being able to give money away. She was interested in creating a company with a culture centered around giving back. She admired philanthropic giving, but she was more interested in social entrepreneurship.

In 2007, Lauren founded FEED, which works with organizations such as No Kid Hungry and Feeding America to provide meals for school-aged children in need. While there are many issues that persist throughout the world, hunger is at the core of what it means to be human. When children are properly nourished, their attendance at school doubles and their overall academic performance improves. The school meal programs incentivize parents to send their children to school; and the more education children receive, the less chance there is for them to live in poverty.

Lauren created the first FEED bag, a utilitarian tote, as a tangible way for her peers to get involved in her efforts to address world hunger. Each FEED bag is stamped with the number of meals that the bag supports: The purchase of one bag can provide up to 185 meals.

What Lauren started with just a tote bag has since grown into an impact-driven lifestyle brand that also sells clothing and housewares made by artisans worldwide. This allows the organization to not only provide meals for children but also support and sustain the livelihoods of their artisan partners and their families. Since its founding, the brand's efforts have been massive—they have provided more than 120 million school meals worldwide.

The meals that FEED provides to children are rich in the nutrients important for health and growth. So, in honor of the impactful efforts of FEED and Lauren's passion in building consumers' conscious buying practices, this Ginger Carrot + Asparagus Quiche is filled with nutrients. In addition to being delicious, the quiche is rich in high-quality protein (eggs), calcium (milk, cheese), the antioxidant beta-carotene (carrots, asparagus), important B vitamins (asparagus, cheese), and immune-boosting zinc (milk, cheese). Not to be overlooked is the presence of fat, which is extremely important to the growth and development of young children—and also makes many of the other nutrients more available to the body.

GINGER CARROT + ASPARAGUS QUICHE

MAKES ONE 9-INCH QUICHE

GLAZED CARROTS

1 tablespoon packed light brown sugar

1 tablespoon unsalted butter, melted

½ tablespoon olive oil

½ teaspoon kosher salt

½ teaspoon freshly ground black pepper

3 tri-color petite carrots, peeled, stemmed, and halved lengthwise

ROASTED ASPARAGUS

7 small asparagus spears, tough ends trimmed

½ tablespoon olive oil

½ teaspoon kosher salt

½ teaspoon freshly ground black pepper

FILLING AND CRUST

Flour, for rolling out

All-Butter Pie Dough (page 220)

2 cups (141g) grated aged Gouda cheese

Our Lady of Quiche Custard (page 100)

CARROT-GINGER PURÉE

3 medium carrots, peeled, stemmed, and cut into pieces ½ inch thick (about 2 cups)

2 tablespoons extra-virgin olive oil

1 tablespoon unsalted butter

½ medium Vidalia onion, diced

1 garlic clove, finely diced

1 tablespoon grated fresh ginger

½ teaspoon ground coriander

½ teaspoon ground cumin

2 teaspoons kosher salt

½ teaspoon freshly ground black pepper

1 tablespoon fresh lemon juice

2 cups (473g) chicken broth or vegetable broth

MAKE THE GLAZED CARROTS: Adjust an oven rack to the middle position and preheat the oven to 425°F (220°C). Line a sheet pan with foil.

In a medium bowl, whisk together the brown sugar, melted butter, olive oil, salt, and pepper. Toss the carrots in the brown sugar mixture to coat and turn them onto the lined pan. Roast until slightly browned and caramelized, about 10 minutes. Remove the pan from the oven and use a fork or tongs to flip the carrots over. Return the carrots to the oven and bake until the carrots are caramelized, an additional 10 minutes. Remove the carrots from the oven and set aside. Leave the oven on for the asparagus.

ROAST THE ASPARAGUS: Arrange the asparagus on a baking sheet and coat with the olive oil. Sprinkle with the salt and pepper and roast in the oven until slightly tender, about 5 minutes. Remove from the oven and set aside.

Leave the oven on and reduce the temperature to 350°F (175°C).

PREPARE THE FILLING AND CRUST: Lightly dust the countertop with flour and roll out the dough to about 12 inches in diameter. Carefully transfer the dough to a 9-inch pie pan and fit it in against the sides and bottom. Roll any overhanging dough to the edge of the pie pan and crimp the edge.

Scatter the Gouda into the quiche shell, taking care to evenly distribute it across the bottom. Pour the custard into the quiche shell. Layer the carrots and asparagus on top of the custard. The cheese will serve as a shelf for the vegetables so that they don't sink in the custard.

Bake until the crust is golden brown, the edges of the custard are puffed, and the center is dry, 25 to 30 minutes. Remove the quiche from the oven and set aside to cool slightly, about 10 minutes, before slicing and serving.

MAKE THE CARROT-GINGER PURÉE: Toss the carrots in olive oil to coat, and arrange them in an even, single layer on a baking sheet. Bake until slightly caramelized and browned around the edges, 25 to 30 minutes. Remove from the oven and set aside. Place a medium saucepan over medium-high heat. Place the butter in the saucepan and melt, then add the onions, garlic, and ginger. Cook until the onions are translucent, 7 to 10 minutes. Stir in the coriander, cumin, salt, and pepper, and cook, stirring frequently, until fragrant, about 3 minutes. Add in the broth and carrots. Bring the mixture to a boil, then lower the heat to medium-low and allow the mixture to simmer for the flavors to meld, about 15 minutes. Remove from the heat and cool slightly, about 10 minutes. Pour the carrots, broth, and lemon juice into a blender (or use a handheld immersion blender) and purée until smooth.

Serve each slice of quiche with a drizzle of the warm carrot-ginger purée or garnish the plate with a smear of purée.

Cover any leftover quiche with plastic wrap and refrigerate for up to 7 days. To reheat: Set the rack to the middle and preheat the oven to 350°F (175°C). Cover the slices with aluminum foil and heat until their centers are warm, 20 to 25 minutes.

SMOKED SALMON QUICHE

MAKES ONE 9-INCH QUICHE

I love a charcuterie board—but if there isn't smoked salmon on it, don't even bother. Nibbling on a cracker stacked with smoked salmon and a thin slice of hard cheese, while sipping on a glass of white wine, is the epitome of life's small (yet great) joys, and I bring that spirit together in this quiche.

There are generally two versions of smoked salmon: lox, which is cold-smoked and thinly sliced, and hot-smoked salmon, which is sold as a fillet (and if it's glazed, it's sometimes called candied salmon). I use lox here because the thin slices are ideal for layering in a quiche. The dill adds a light flavor enhancement that complements the fish.

When building the quiche, float slices of the smoked salmon gingerly on top of the quiche so they do not fully submerge into the custard while baking.

Flour, for rolling out
All-Butter Pie Dough (page 220)
12 ounces (340g) smoked lox-style salmon, sliced (plus 1.5 ounces/42g [optional] for garnish)

½ cup (52g) freshly grated Manchego cheese
2 sprigs fresh dill, fronds removed and roughly chopped, plus more (optional) for garnish
Our Lady of Quiche Custard (page 100)

Adjust an oven rack to the middle position and preheat the oven to 350°F (175°C).

Lightly dust the countertop with flour and roll out the dough to about 12 inches in diameter. Carefully transfer the dough to a 9-inch pie pan. Roll the overhanging dough to the edge of the pan and crimp.

Arrange half of the smoked salmon slices (6 ounces/170g) evenly across the bottom of the pie shell. Evenly sprinkle in the Manchego cheese and then sprinkle with half the dill. Place the pie shell on a baking sheet and pour in the custard.

Transfer to the oven and bake until a light film forms on top of the quiche's custard, about 15 minutes. Gently remove the baking sheet from the oven and evenly distribute the remaining salmon slices (6 ounces/170g) and remaining dill on top of the quiche. Return the baking sheet to the oven until the center is dry, 15 to 20 minutes longer.

Remove the quiche from the oven and set aside to cool slightly, about 10 minutes, before slicing and serving, or serve at room temperature. If desired, garnish with 1.5 ounces of smoked salmon and dill.

To store, cover with plastic wrap and refrigerate for up to 7 days. To reheat: Set the rack to the middle and preheat the oven to 350°F (175°C). Cover the slices with aluminum foil and heat until their centers are warm, 20 to 25 minutes.

CHILI-ROASTED SWEET POTATO + GOAT CHEESE QUICHE

MAKES ONE 9-INCH QUICHE

At Justice of the Pies, we use a lot of sweet potatoes. Whether we're making Sweet Potato Biscuits (page 198) or Sweet Potato Praline Pie (page 38), this is one vegetable that we always have in abundance. Oftentimes we have so many sweet potatoes left over from our day's prep that we look for unique ways to use up the leftovers. One time, we made rosemary- and chili-rubbed sweet potatoes as a breakfast side. They were absolutely delicious with their slightly caramelized crust from the vegetable's natural sweetness when roasted and the hint of heat from the chili. Immediately my bakers and I knew the egg + sweet/spicy/herby combination of the potatoes needed to go into a quiche!

I think this combination is so perfect because the creaminess of the goat cheese and the heat of the chili powder make for an immaculately balanced flavor.

1 pound sweet potatoes, cut into 1-inch cubes

1 tablespoon olive oil

2 teaspoons dark chili powder

½ teaspoon dried rosemary

¼ teaspoon kosher salt

Flour, for rolling out

All-Butter Pie Dough (page 220)

1½ ounces (45g) goat cheese

Our Lady of Quiche Custard (page 100)

Adjust an oven rack to the middle position and preheat the oven to 350°F (175°C).

Place the sweet potatoes in a large bowl and add the olive oil, 1 teaspoon of the chili powder, the rosemary, and salt. Rub the seasonings onto the sweet potatoes until all the cubes are well coated.

Place the sweet potatoes on a baking sheet and spread them out evenly. Bake until they are fork-tender, 15 to 20 minutes. Remove the baking sheet from the oven and set aside to cool slightly.

Lightly dust the countertop with flour and roll out the pie dough to about 12 inches in diameter. Carefully transfer the dough to a 9-inch pie pan. Roll the overhanging dough to the edge of the pan and crimp.

Sprinkle the sweet potatoes across the bottom of the pie shell. Add small dollops of goat cheese over the sweet potatoes. Place the pie on a baking sheet and slowly pour in the custard. Sprinkle the remaining 1 teaspoon of chili powder on top of the custard.

Transfer to the oven and bake until the crust is golden brown and the center is dry, 25 to 30 minutes. Allow the quiche to cool slightly, about 10 minutes, before slicing and serving, or serve at room temperature.

To store, cover with plastic wrap and refrigerate for up to 7 days. To reheat: Set the rack to the middle and preheat the oven to 350°F (175°C). Cover the slices with aluminum foil and heat until their centers are warm, 20 to 25 minutes.

BONUS: Roasted sweet potatoes rubbed in chili powder, rosemary, and olive oil also make a lovely side dish that works as an alternative to hash browns or a side of mashed potatoes. I love serving them as an accompaniment to Brussels sprouts, cabbage, or kale, as I find the sweetness complements the bitter undertones in those veggies.

DRAGGED THROUGH THE GARDEN QUICHE

MAKES ONE 9-INCH QUICHE

In Chicago, the all-beef frankfurter is King. We eat hot dogs with diced onions, bright green sweet pickle relish, piquant and pickled sport peppers, yellow mustard, a dill pickle, slices or wedges of tomato, sprinkled with celery salt, and stuffed into a poppy seed bun—and never ever with ketchup. This Chicago-style quiche packs all of this nostalgia into each slice, and it can't help but remind me of hot summer evenings in Chicago, me playing with my neighbor's daughters or my imaginary friends, chasing the green, fluorescent tails of lightning bugs (*never fireflies*) and listening to my dad and his friends talking sports and telling dirty jokes while drinking hard-earned end-of-week beers.

Flour, for rolling out

All-Butter Pie Dough (page 220)

1 cup (194g) sliced hot dogs (preferably all-beef) or smoked sausage (such as andouille sausage), cut 1½ inches thick

¼ cup finely chopped sweet onion, such as Vidalia

2 tablespoons roughly chopped pickled sport peppers

½ cup grape tomatoes, halved

2 tablespoons sweet pickle relish

½ teaspoon celery salt

½ teaspoon mustard powder

Our Lady of Quiche Custard (page 100)

Dill pickle spears, for serving

Adjust an oven rack to the middle position and preheat the oven to 350°F (175°C).

Lightly dust the countertop with flour and roll out the pie dough to about 12 inches in diameter. Carefully transfer the dough to a 9-inch pie pan. Roll the overhanging dough to the edge of the pan and crimp.

Place the pie shell on a baking sheet and add the sliced hot dogs (or smoked sausage), onion, sport peppers, and tomatoes, distributing them all as evenly as possible. Whisk the pickle relish, celery salt, and mustard into the custard and immediately pour into the crust.

Carefully transfer the baking sheet to the oven and bake until the crust is golden and the center is set, 35 to 40 minutes. Remove from the oven and let the quiche cool slightly, about 10 minutes, before slicing, or cool completely before serving. Serve with pickle spears on the side.

To store, cover with plastic wrap and refrigerate for up to 7 days. To reheat: Set the rack to the middle position and preheat the oven to 350°F (175°C). Cover slices with aluminum foil and heat until their centers are warm, 20 to 25 minutes.

SPINACH, FETA + BACON QUICHE

MAKES ONE 9-INCH QUICHE

There is a restaurant in Chicago called the Greek Isle—for us, this was an I-finally-have-a-little-extra-money-to-spend type of restaurant or a we've-got-company-in-from-out-of-town type of restaurant. So, my dad got especially excited to go there, and was extra annoying once we arrived.

He'd stare at the waiters with trays of food, and feign deep sadness with dramatic, melancholic sighs when he realized the food was another table's. And once our dishes arrived, he'd yell "OPA!" really loudly. Thankfully he didn't smash any plates. As an introvert, I rebelled against his exuberance by refusing to eat at the Greek Isle unless he'd calm the hell down. Breaking news: He never calmed down and I never gave in.

Once he had to bribe me with twenty dollars just so that I would take one bite of food. For a large portion of my childhood, I could not even fathom the idea of eating Mediterranean food because it reminded me of his excessive happiness around attending the Greek Isle. Fortunately I grew out of that. (Mediterranean food is so delicious.)

When I was considering the kind of quiche that I would make in honor of my dad, I came up with this one. The spinach and feta are a nod to the ingredients used in a classic Greek spanakopita. His spirit probably yells, "OPA!" every time I make it.

Flour, for rolling out

All-Butter Pie Dough (page 220)

Our Lady of Quiche Custard (page 100)

3 cups spinach

½ cup (70g) feta cheese crumbles

About 1 tablespoon sliced pitted Kalamata olives

10 slices thick-cut bacon (8½ oz/250g)

Adjust an oven rack to the middle position and preheat the oven to 375°F (190°C).

Lightly dust the countertop with flour and roll out the pie dough to about 12 inches in diameter. Carefully transfer the dough to a 9-inch pie pan. Roll the overhanging dough to the edge of the pan and crimp.

Place the pie shell on a baking sheet and slowly pour in the custard. Mound the spinach on top of the custard, being careful not to submerge it—it should rise like a gently sloping hill from the custard. Sprinkle the feta and olives over the spinach. Evenly cover the spinach with slices of bacon, laying the slices next to one another. The bacon should sit on top of the spinach without being submerged in the custard. This will allow the bacon to crisp while baking.

Carefully transfer the baking sheet to the oven and bake until the crust is golden brown, the bacon is crispy, and the center is set, 30 to 35 minutes. Remove from the oven and allow it to cool slightly. Serve warm or at room temperature.

To store, cover with plastic wrap and refrigerate for up to 7 days. To reheat: Set the rack to the middle position and preheat the oven to 350°F (175°C). Cover slices with aluminum foil and heat until their centers are warm, 20 to 25 minutes.

FIG + PIG QUICHE

MAKES ONE 9-INCH QUICHE

Flour, for rolling out
All-Butter Pie Dough (page 220)
1 cup dried figs, stemmed and sliced

2 ounces (52g) Parmesan cheese, shaved with a vegetable peeler (about ½ cup)
Our Lady of Quiche Custard (page 100)
10 slices thick-cut bacon (8½ oz/250g)

This fig quiche, made with dried figs and Parmesan cheese, brings me back to being four or five years old when I was a fanatic for fig cookies. They were the solution to all of my problems. Just tripped and slightly scraped my knee? Comfort me with fig cookies. LeVar Burton sharing books on *Reading Rainbow*? I had to watch while eating fig cookies. One night, I hid a package under my bed, my plan to retrieve them when the lights were turned off so I could enjoy them in the dark, undisturbed.

No sooner had I stashed my treasure than my bedroom door flung open, my mom standing there, arms crossed, scolding.

"Did you take fig cookies from the kitchen?" I was called out.

"Answer me!" she said.

I slowly shook my head no.

"What's under the bed then?"

I reached under the bed and pulled out my contraband.

"Didn't I tell you that you couldn't have fig cookies?"

If I confessed to knowing that I was not allowed the cookies, I'd lose plausible deniability about what I actually could or couldn't hear. Enter: the blank stare.

"Go grab the TV and put it in the other room," she ordered.

I sulked over to the small wardrobe dresser that doubled as a console for our small, 13-inch TV that had a handle on top, and I carried it to the next room. No explanation was needed. I fully understood that my fig cookie heist cost me the pleasure of watching Saturday morning cartoons.

But you know what? I love figs so much, I'd do it all over again. If your love of figs equals my own, then you will love this quiche. The sweetness of the dried figs offers a nice balance to the saltiness of the bacon.

Adjust an oven rack to the middle position and preheat the oven to 350°F (175°C).

Lightly dust the countertop with flour and roll out the pie dough to about 12 inches in diameter. Carefully transfer the dough to a 9-inch pie pan. Roll the overhanging dough to the edge of the pan and crimp.

Place the figs and Parmesan in the bottom of the pie shell, reserving a few slices of figs for the top of the quiche.

Place the quiche on a baking sheet and slowly pour in the custard.

Carefully transfer the baking sheet to the oven and bake until a light film forms on top of the quiche's custard, about 15 minutes.

Gently remove the quiche from the oven. Layer the bacon slices and the reserved sliced figs on top of the quiche. Return the baking sheet to the oven and bake until the crust is golden brown and the center is set, 20 to 25 minutes longer.

Remove from the oven and allow to cool slightly. Serve warm or at room temperature.

To store, cover with plastic wrap and refrigerate for up to 7 days. To reheat: Set the rack to the middle position and preheat the oven to 350°F (175°C). Cover slices with aluminum foil and heat until their centers are warm, 20 to 25 minutes.

LAKE CHARLES QUICHE

MAKES ONE 9-INCH QUICHE

Gumbo, made with a dark, rich roux, is one of my family's prized dishes. My grandfather Elmo and his siblings moved to Chicago from New Iberia and Lake Charles, Louisiana, during the Great Migration north (see page 81) and brought with them an aggregation of Creole family recipes. Every Thanksgiving, my dad and I went to my great-aunt Nettie's, who lived on Chicago's West Side, or my great-aunt Irene's, who was on the South Side. No matter where we landed, the spread would always be the same: cornbread dressing, collard greens, macaroni and cheese, candied yams, and gumbo. In all the years that we spent Thanksgiving at their houses, we never had turkey. The star dish was always a big pot of gumbo—with seafood, chicken, sausage, and enough crab legs so everyone got one (two if you were lucky)—that remained on the stovetop throughout the meal. In this quiche, the custardy filling stands in for the roux, but the rest of the gumbo is there, from the shrimp to the andouille sausage and Cajun seasoning—I add jumbo lump crabmeat to the filling, too, so anyone who eats it feels extra lucky with every bite.

BONUS: If I have any crab topping left over, I'll make a simple, buttery grilled cheese with sharp cheddar and dunk the sandwich halves into the topping. The topping is also a perfect dipping sauce for some lightly salted tortilla chips.

Flour, for rolling out

All-Butter Pie Dough (page 220)

FILLING

10 large shrimp (120g), peeled, deveined, and tails removed

½ cup (97g) ¼-inch-thick andouille sausage slices

½ cup (80g) jumbo lump crabmeat

2 ounces (52g) Parmesan cheese, shaved with a vegetable peeler (about ½ cup)

Our Lady of Quiche Custard (page 100)

TOPPING

2 tablespoons unsalted butter

2 tablespoons all-purpose flour

⅓ cup (18g) diced scallions

10 sprigs fresh parsley (9g), leaves finely chopped

1 tablespoon tomato paste

¼ cup (60g) port wine

2 cups (470g) heavy cream

2 teaspoons Cajun seasoning

½ teaspoon freshly ground black pepper

¼ teaspoon cayenne pepper

2 cups (320g) jumbo lump crabmeat

Adjust an oven rack to the middle position and preheat the oven to 350°F (175°C).

Lightly dust the countertop with flour and roll out the pie dough to about 12 inches in diameter. Carefully transfer the dough to a 9-inch pie pan. Roll the overhanging dough to the edge of the pan and crimp.

MAKE THE FILLING: In a medium bowl, mix together the shrimp, andouille sausage, crabmeat, and Parmesan. Spoon the mixture into the pie shell, distributing it across the bottom. Place the pan on a baking sheet and slowly pour in the custard.

Carefully transfer the baking sheet to the oven and bake until the crust is golden brown and the center is set, 45 to 50 minutes. Remove from the oven and set aside to cool slightly.

MAKE THE TOPPING: In a large heavy-bottomed pot, melt the butter over low heat. Once melted, remove from the heat and use a silicone spatula to stir in the flour until there are no traces of flour visible. Stir in the scallions, parsley, and tomato paste. Whisk in the port wine and increase the heat to medium-high. While whisking, slowly pour in the heavy cream and stir until the tomato paste has completely dissolved.

Stir in the Cajun seasoning, black pepper, and cayenne. Add the crabmeat and stir until well combined. Reduce the heat to medium-low and simmer the mixture until it thickens slightly, about 10 minutes, stirring every few minutes. Remove the pot from the heat.

Serve each slice of quiche covered with ¼ cup of the warm crab topping.

To store, cover the quiche with plastic wrap and refrigerate for up to 7 days. Store the topping in a separate air-tight container. To reheat: Set the rack to the middle position and preheat the oven to 350°F (175°C). Cover slices with aluminum foil and heat until warmed through, 20 to 25 minutes. Reheat the topping in a saucepan set over medium heat for 5 minutes until warmed.

DEEP-DISH CHILAQUILES QUICHE

MAKES ONE 9-INCH DEEP-DISH QUICHE

Justice of the Pies is a social mission–based bakery, and our signature workshop is called the *I Knead Love Workshop*, through which we teach kids in the fifth through eighth grades how to make a savory quiche and a sweet pie. Besides going home with a homemade meal and sweet treat, the children learn kitchen skills, nutritional basics, and how to cook creatively in the kitchen. The workshops are a part of our bakery's initiative to fight against food insecurities by helping kids become more self-reliant and independent. We often work with nonprofit organizations that have existing programs in place for children who reside in lower income communities most affected by food apartheid.

One cohort of kids we worked with was from Gage Park on the southwest side of Chicago, a predominantly Latino and Black neighborhood. Given that the majority of the children in this group were very familiar with Mexican cuisine, we wanted to demonstrate a way to translate a classic (and beloved) Mexican dish, such as chilaquiles, into a quiche.

Here, I combine the rich custard of a quiche with the traditional Mexican breakfast of chilaquiles—tortilla chips coated in green or red salsa, queso fresco, sliced onions or avocados, and *crema*—to make a deep-dish quiche that can accommodate all the other chilaquiles components, too, like salsa, black beans, and pulled chicken.

Flour, for rolling out

Double recipe All-Butter Pie Dough (page 220)

9 (156g) tostadas amarillos (crispy yellow corn tortillas) or 3 cups tortilla chips

1 cup (150g) crumbled queso fresco

1 cup (118g) shredded Chihuahua or Cotija cheese

Triple recipe Our Lady of Quiche Custard (page 100)

1 cup homemade salsa (recipe follows) or your favorite brand of store-bought

1½ cups Savory Black Beans (recipe follows)

½ cup (60g) crumbled Cotija cheese

10 sprigs fresh cilantro (9g), leaves and thin stems only, finely chopped

Lightly dust the countertop with flour and roll out the pie dough to about 16 inches in diameter. Carefully transfer the dough to a 3-inch-deep 9-inch tart pan with a removable bottom. Gently mold the dough into the tart pan, leaving an overhang. Use your fingers to mend any tears, lines, holes, or cracks in the dough so that there are no gaps in the dough. Cut off a piece of the overhanging dough and roll it into a ball. Use the ball of dough to gently continue to mold the dough to the tart pan, making sure the dough is flush to the corners and grooves of the tart pan. Trim the overhanging dough in one of two ways: Use a paring knife and trim off the dough following the edge of the tart pan. Or use the rolling pin and gently roll it on top of the tart pan's edge. (You can use the excess dough to patch cracks or add to create thicker sides if needed.)

Cover the tart shell with plastic wrap and refrigerate for 30 minutes.

Adjust an oven rack to the middle position and preheat the oven to 350°F (175°C).

Remove the tart pan from the fridge and uncover. Gently break one tostada in half and set it in the tart shell (if using chips, add 1 cup to the tart shell and arrange in a single layer). Top the tostada (or chips) with some queso fresco and Chihuahua cheese. Repeat the layering until the last tostada (or layer of chips) is in the tart pan.

Place the tart pan on a baking sheet. Slowly pour the custard into the tart shell. Use a whisk or a spoon to gently push the top tostada (or layer of chips) into the custard to coat it and then release the tostada so that it can float back to the top. It is fine if the last tostada is not completely immersed in the custard (but it should be coated so it doesn't burn).

Transfer the baking sheet to the oven and bake until the center is dry, about 1 hour.

RECIPE CONTINUES >>

Remove the quiche from the oven and allow it to cool for 15 to 20 minutes. Turn a large bowl upside down and place the tart pan on top of the bowl. Gently push the rim of the tart pan downward toward the countertop to release the quiche from the sides of the pan. Lift the quiche by the base of the tart pan, remove the metal round from the base, and slide the quiche onto a serving plate or cake stand.

Serve with salsa and black beans. Sprinkle with a few pinches of Cotija and a pinch of cilantro.

To store, cover the quiche with plastic wrap and refrigerate for up to 7 days. To reheat: Set the rack to the middle position and preheat the oven to 350°F (175°C). Cover slices with aluminum foil and heat until their centers are warm, 20 to 25 minutes.

BONUS: When I have a lot of leftover tostadas, salsa, and black beans, I will use everything to make some loaded nachos with a good sharp cheddar cheese, sour cream, sliced jalapeño, and diced scallions.

ROASTED SALSA

MAKES APPROXIMATELY 2 CUPS

4 medium vine-ripened tomatoes

4 small tomatillos, husked, rinsed, and stem removed

1 large sweet onion, halved

1 medium jalapeño, halved and seeded

⅓ cup (97g) chipotle chiles in adobo

1 tablespoon minced garlic

2 teaspoons kosher salt

2 teaspoons freshly ground black pepper

2 tablespoons olive oil

2 tablespoons fresh lime juice

10 sprigs cilantro (9g), leaves and fine stems only, finely chopped

Adjust an oven rack to the middle position and preheat the oven to 375°F (190°C).

Arrange the tomatoes, tomatillos, onion halves, and jalapeño on a sheet pan or in a cast-iron skillet. Roast the vegetables until they are charred, 50 to 60 minutes. Remove the pan from the oven to cool slightly.

Using tongs, lift the charred vegetables out of the pan (leaving the excess liquid behind) and transfer to a blender (or to a bowl if using an immersion blender). Add the chipotle chiles, minced garlic, salt, and black pepper and blend until the vegetables are puréed.

In a large pot, heat the olive oil over medium-high heat. Pour the puréed vegetables into the pot, bring to a boil, then reduce the heat and simmer until the salsa thickens, about 10 minutes. Stir in the lime juice and chopped cilantro. Remove from the heat and set aside.

SAVORY BLACK BEANS

MAKES 1½ CUPS

2 tablespoons extra-virgin olive oil

1 medium vine-ripened tomato, diced

½ large sweet onion, finely diced

2 tablespoons finely minced jalapeño

2 (15 oz/425g) cans black beans, drained and rinsed

1 teaspoon chili powder

1 teaspoon ground cumin

1 teaspoon dried oregano

1 teaspoon finely minced garlic

1 teaspoon smoked paprika

2 teaspoons kosher salt

In a medium saucepan, heat the olive oil over medium-high heat. Stir in the diced tomato, onion, and jalapeños and allow the vegetables to simmer until the onions are translucent, 8 to 10 minutes.

Stir in the beans, chili powder, cumin, oregano, garlic, smoked paprika, and salt. Bring to a boil, then reduce the heat to low and allow it to simmer, 10 to 12 minutes.

FULLY LOADED QUICHE

MAKES ONE 9-INCH DEEP-DISH QUICHE

My brother, Mazi, and I both went through a baked potato phase when we were teenagers. It was literally all we would eat for dinner for a couple of years. We were not being deprived of other delicious meals; we just chose to eat baked potatoes. We were weird.

I would mash up an extra-large baked potato with a fork, then deftly dress it with the perfect balance of butter, salt, pepper, sour cream, and cheese—you know where I'm going with this. In this quiche I combine Yukon Gold potatoes, which have a buttery, sweet flavor, and creamy, smooth texture (an ideal pairing with the quiche custard), with sweet onions and cheddar-Jack cheese for a "fully loaded" quiche that gets topped with a cooling dab of sour cream and a pinch of scallions. A slice of this is so satisfying. You will need a deep-dish tart pan for this quiche.

Flour, for rolling out

Double recipe All-Butter Pie Dough (page 220)

2 large Yukon Gold potatoes

2 tablespoons extra-virgin olive oil

1 teaspoon Cajun seasoning

2 teaspoons minced garlic

1 teaspoon smoked paprika

1 teaspoon kosher salt

1 teaspoon freshly ground black pepper

2 tablespoons unsalted butter

1 large sweet onion, chopped

2 cups (225g) grated sharp cheddar cheese

⅓ cup sliced scallions, plus more for serving

Double recipe Our Lady of Quiche Custard (page 100)

Sour cream, for serving

Lightly dust the countertop with flour and roll out the dough to about 16 inches in diameter. Carefully transfer the dough to a 3-inch-deep 9-inch tart pan with a removable bottom. Gently press the dough into the tart pan and up the sides, leaving an overhang. Use your fingers to mend the seams of the dough so that there are no gaps. Trim the overhanging dough in one of two ways: Use a paring knife and trim off the dough following the edge of the tart pan. Or use a rolling pin and gently roll it over the tart pan's edge. (You can use the excess dough to patch cracks or add to create thicker sides if needed.)

Cover the tart shell with plastic wrap and refrigerate for 30 minutes.

Adjust an oven rack to the middle position and preheat the oven to 350°F (175°C).

Using a mandoline or a chef's knife, cut the potatoes into ⅛-inch-thick slices and place them in a medium bowl. Add 1 tablespoon of the olive oil, the Cajun seasoning, garlic, smoked paprika, salt, and pepper and use your hands to massage the oil and spices onto the slices, ensuring everything is evenly coated.

Heat a large skillet over medium-high heat. Add the remaining 1 tablespoon of olive oil and the butter to the skillet. Once the butter has melted, add the onion and stir to coat. Add the potatoes, cover with a lid, and stir every few minutes to move the potato slices from the bottom to the top. Cook until the potatoes are firm yet nearly fork-tender, 15 to 20 minutes.

Remove the potatoes from the heat and set aside.

Remove the tart shell from the fridge and uncover. Set the tart pan on a baking sheet. Place half of the potatoes into the tart shell and top with 1 cup of the cheddar. Top with the remaining potatoes and then with the remaining cheese.

Whisk the scallions into the prepared custard, then slowly pour it into the tart shell. Carefully transfer to the oven and bake until the center is set and dry, about 1 hour.

Remove the quiche from the oven and allow it to cool for 15 to 20 minutes. Turn a large bowl upside down and place the tart pan on top of the bowl. Gently push the tart pan down toward the countertop to release the sides of the tart pan. Remove the metal base and slide the quiche onto a serving plate or cake stand.

Serve with sour cream and sprinkle with scallions.

To store, cover the quiche with plastic wrap and refrigerate for up to 7 days. To reheat: Set the rack to the middle position and preheat the oven to 350°F (175°C). Cover slices with aluminum foil and heat until their centers are warm, 20 to 25 minutes.

TARTS

CHERRY AMARETTO TART

MAKES ONE 9-INCH TART

Whenever I make this tart, I am transported back to my college days when I attended Howard University and drank amaretto sours at Republic Gardens, where my sorority sister Arlene hooked me and our other sorority sisters up with cocktails. As a broke twenty-one-year-old college student, I eagerly slurped on and savored the almond sweetness of the amaretto sour. This tart—rich with a chocolate crust, an amaretto-infused cream filling, and sweet cherry topping—is the kind that makes you close your eyes in bliss after the first bite.

Chocolate Cookie Crust (page 236)

FILLING

4 ounces (113g) cream cheese, at room temperature

4 ounces (113g) mascarpone cheese, at room temperature

2½ tablespoons granulated sugar

1 large egg, at room temperature

1 tablespoon sour cream

½ teaspoon almond extract

½ tablespoon unbleached all-purpose flour

TOPPING

6 cups (3¼ pounds/1.5kg) frozen or fresh pitted and stemmed dark cherries

1 cup (200g) granulated sugar

Juice of ½ lemon

2 tablespoons amaretto (almond liqueur)

Adjust an oven rack to the middle position and preheat the oven to 335°F (168°C).

Prepare the chocolate cookie crust as directed, pressing the crumbs into a 9-inch tart pan with a removable bottom. Set aside.

MAKE THE FILLING: In a small bowl, use a hand mixer or silicone spatula to cream together the cream cheese and mascarpone cheese until well blended. Stir in the sugar until just combined (do not overmix), then whisk in the egg until well blended. Stir in the sour cream and almond extract. Sift in the flour and fold it into the filling.

Place the tart pan on a baking sheet, set the baking sheet on a pulled-out oven rack, and pour the filling into the tart crust.

Bake until the center is set, about 45 minutes.

Turn the oven off and crack open the oven door. Allow the tart to remain in the oven as it cools, about 1 hour. Transfer the tart to the refrigerator, uncovered, and allow it to chill for 2 to 4 hours.

MEANWHILE, MAKE THE TOPPING: In a medium saucepan, combine the cherries, sugar, and lemon juice. Bring to a rolling boil over medium heat. Cook the cherries until they reduce in volume, 30 to 35 minutes.

Remove the pot from the heat. Drain the cherries in a fine-mesh sieve set over a bowl. (Reserve the juice for another time, like using it to make Cherry Balsamic Vinaigrette, page 216.)

Place the cherries in a bowl, pour in the amaretto, and stir. Cover with plastic wrap and refrigerate until chilled.

Remove the tart from the refrigerator. To remove the tart from the pan, place the tart pan on top of an upturned bowl and gently press down on the outer ring to release the tart crust from the pan. Top with the amaretto-infused cherries.

To store, cover with plastic wrap and refrigerate for up to 3 days.

CHOCOLATE PEAR TART

MAKES ONE 10-INCH TART

Ever since I could remember, my dad would receive a box of one dozen pears every winter holiday as a gift from a client. Each pear was wrapped in gold foil and arrived ripe and sweet. I'd stand over him at the dining room table and watch him unbox these delicate, yellow-green treats.

Without saying a word, he'd look at my craving eyes and simply nod his head as if to say, "Go ahead." I'd quickly grab one out of the carton's shredded packing paper, gingerly peel the foil back, and bite into it, the juice running down my chin. With my mouth full, I would yell, "Thank you!"

Caramelized pears layered in an ultrarich chocolate filling takes me back to those wintry nights when that special package would arrive at our doorstep and to when I first discovered that food could be gifted. The caramelized pears layered in a gooey chocolate filling are in themselves a present worth devouring.

Flour, for rolling out

Pâte Sucrée (page 225)

10 tablespoons (5 oz/140g) unsalted butter

¼ cup (55g) lightly packed light brown sugar

3 d'Anjou pears, peeled and cut into ½-inch-thick slices

3 tablespoons Dutch process cocoa powder

1 cup (200g) granulated sugar

1 large egg

¼ cup (34g) unbleached all-purpose flour

1 teaspoon pure vanilla extract

Vanilla Bean Chantilly Cream (page 214)

Chocolate shavings, for serving

Lightly dust the countertop with flour and roll out the pâte sucrée to 12 to 13 inches in diameter. Carefully transfer the dough to a 2-inch-deep 10-inch tart pan. Gently mold the dough into the tart pan, leaving an overhang. Use your fingers to mend any tears, lines, holes, or cracks so that there are no gaps in the dough. Make sure the dough is flush to the corners and grooves of the tart pan. Trim the overhanging dough in one of two ways: Use a paring knife and trim off the dough following the edge of the tart pan. Or use the rolling pin and gently roll it on top of the tart pan's edge. (You can use the excess dough to patch cracks or add to create thicker sides if needed.) Cover the tart pan with plastic wrap and refrigerate for 30 minutes.

Meanwhile, in a medium saucepan, melt 4 tablespoons of the butter over medium-high heat. Stir in the brown sugar and add the pear slices. Using a silicone spatula, stir the pears and flip the slices over so that all the pear slices are covered in the buttery brown sugar mixture. Allow the pears to simmer and caramelize in the buttery brown sugar while stirring every few minutes. Once the pears are soft and pliable, after about 30 minutes, remove the saucepan from the heat. Set aside.

Adjust an oven rack to the middle position and preheat the oven to 390°F (198°C).

Remove the chilled tart shell from the refrigerator, discard the plastic wrap, and prick the bottom of the dough all over with the tines of a fork. Place parchment paper inside the tart pan and add dried beans or pie weights to weight the paper and dough down. Bake until the crust is lightly golden around the edges, about 15 minutes. Remove the crust from the oven and remove the paper and pie weights. Leave the oven on.

Meanwhile, in a separate saucepan, melt the remaining 6 tablespoons butter over medium heat. Stir in the cocoa powder until it dissolves. Remove from the heat and stir in the granulated sugar until well combined. Whisk in the egg until it is well blended with the chocolate mixture. Whisk in the flour until no traces are visible. Stir in the vanilla and set aside until the crust comes out of the oven.

Evenly distribute the pears across the bottom of the tart crust and pour the chocolate filling over the pears into the tart crust. Tap the tart pan against a countertop a few times to make sure that there are no air gaps between the pear slices.

Set the tart pan on a baking sheet and return the tart to the oven to bake until the center is barely set, 18 to 22 minutes.

Allow the tart to sit at room temperature for 15 to 20 minutes to set further. To remove the tart from the pan, place the tart pan on top of an upturned bowl and gently press down on the outer ring to release the tart crust from the pan. Place the tart (still on the bottom of the pan) on a serving plate.

Top the tart with the Chantilly cream and chocolate shavings.

To store, cover with plastic wrap and refrigerate for up to 3 days.

JULIA TURSHEN + GRACE BONNEY

EQUITY AT THE TABLE (EATT) AND DESIGN*SPONGE

Julia first became familiar with the interior design blog *Design*Sponge* when a freelance writer for the blog interviewed her about her work as a cookbook author.

The blog was founded by Grace Bonney, whom Julia didn't personally know—but had admired. In early 2013, Grace wrote a short and sweet coming-out post on *Design*Sponge*. One night, after a late dinner with friends, Julia was home alone and a tad bit tipsy. She read Grace's post, was instantly intrigued, and sent Grace an email. In the email, Julia asked Grace out and mentioned that if Grace wanted to know more about Julia, then Grace could click on the link to her *Design*Sponge* interview. A week after emailing back and forth, Julia met up with Grace and Grace's dog, Hope, for an alfresco dinner. Four months to the day after that dinner, Grace and Julia were married.

The two felt closely aligned despite having different upbringings. Julia grew up in New York City. Her family, Ashkenazi Jewish refugees, came to America from Eastern Europe, and while her mom was very grateful to be safe and secure in America, she felt an intergenerational anxiety and karmic responsibility to help others feel secure as well. Thus, Julia had been instilled with a sense of giving from a very young age—she often volunteered with the group God's Love We Deliver. But her awareness of issues related to race and class was something that developed later in life.

Grace grew up in Virginia Beach, Virginia. Having initially worked in the record industry and then public relations, Grace founded the interior design blog *Design*Sponge* at the age of twenty-three. *Design*Sponge* reached two million readers a day, and the content was read by and showcased a diverse audience, but those who worked for the brand were still predominantly white. When a Black writer and designer, Tina Shoulders, pointed out these issues, Grace was defensive. But through that calling in, Grace began unpacking layers of privilege and better understanding the changes that needed to happen personally and professionally.

Over the next four months, *Design*Sponge* quietly changed its content. Every article written for the blog was about a person of color from the creative community. People took notice. This move did not just modify *Design*Sponge*'s reach, but it also changed the way Grace lived.

Julia witnessed this shift in Grace and actively found ways to hold herself accountable as well. In 2017, Julia released *Feed the Resistance: Recipes + Ideas for Getting Involved*, a cookbook filled with recipes from a diverse range of celebrated chefs of color. The book serves as a handbook for community activism, and the recipes were designed to foster a sense of community. The sales from the book were donated to the ACLU (American Civil Liberties Union). Shortly after, Julia created Equity at the Table (EATT), a digital directory of women, persons of color, and gender nonconforming individuals in or around the food industry. In creating the database, Julia was responding to the gender and racial discriminations that plague the hospitality industry and especially food media.

Grace closed *Design*Sponge* in 2019 and focused on a new book, *Collective Wisdom: Lessons, Inspiration, and Advice from Women over 50*, a follow-up to Grace's 2016 *New York Times* bestseller, *In the Company of Women: Inspiration and Advice from over 100 Makers, Artists, and Entrepreneurs*. Both books featured women from all ages, races, backgrounds, and industries—a true testament to Grace's active work of encouraging diverse representation in media.

Grace and Julia moved to the Hudson Valley, where they continue to be active parts of community support groups. Both Grace and Julia work frequently to make their experience and fields of expertise more transparent for people from marginalized communities and have a shared commitment to use their access and privilege to support queer, people of color, and disabled creatives in their fields.

The Charo Galette that follows is a nod to Julia's Jewish heritage and Grace's Southern American roots in a mash-up of charoset (an apple-walnut dish typically served at Passover seder) and a classic American apple pie. The flaky, aromatic apple galette is drizzled with a sweet red wine reduction and topped with candied walnuts for a nutty crunch. This reimagined galette celebrates Julia and Grace's ongoing desire to promote diversity and embrace otherness.

CHARO GALETTE TART

MAKES ONE 18 × 13-INCH GALETTE

GALETTE

Flour, for rolling the dough

1 sheet Puff Pastry (page 232)

4 Granny Smith apples (1¼ lb total), peeled, cored, and cut into slices ¼ inch thick

1 tablespoon fresh lemon juice

½ cup (110g) packed light brown sugar

2 tablespoons unbleached all-purpose flour

1 teaspoon ground allspice

1 teaspoon ground cinnamon

1 large egg, lightly beaten

RED WINE GLAZE

½ cup (59g) confectioners' sugar

½ teaspoon ground cinnamon

1 cup (215g) sweet red wine

CANDIED WALNUTS

2 tablespoons light brown sugar

½ teaspoon ground cinnamon

½ teaspoon kosher salt

1 large egg white

½ teaspoon vanilla extract

2 cups (219g) walnuts, chopped

Adjust an oven rack to the middle position and preheat the oven to 350°F (175°C). Line a 17.25 × 12.5-inch baking sheet with parchment paper.

MAKE THE GALETTE: Lightly dust the countertop with flour and roll out the puff pastry to a 17 × 23-inch rectangle. Transfer the pastry to the prepared pan, letting the excess length of the pastry hang over the two short sides of the pan.

In a large bowl, combine the apple slices, lemon juice, brown sugar, flour, allspice, and cinnamon. Gently toss to coat the apples. Allow the mixture to macerate for about 5 minutes. Leaving a 2-inch border around the pastry's edge, arrange the apple slices on top of the pastry, slightly overlapping one slice over the next until five equal rows have been created. Fold the 2-inch border nearest to you in toward the center, and over the apples. Repeat until all the borders are folded in toward the fruit.

In a small bowl, whisk together the egg and 1 tablespoon of water. Using a pastry brush, coat the edges of the dough with the egg wash.

Bake the galette until the pastry is golden brown and the fruit is tender, 50 to 55 minutes.

WHILE THE GALETTE BAKES, MAKE THE RED WINE GLAZE: In a small saucepan, combine the sugar, cinnamon, and 2 tablespoons of the wine and whisk over medium heat until the sugar dissolves. Stir in the remaining wine and whisk until the mixture loosens. Let the mixture come to a boil, 8 to 10 minutes, then reduce the heat to low and let the mixture simmer until it reduces to half its volume and thickens slightly, 10 to 12 minutes. Remove from the heat and set aside.

Remove the galette from the oven and set aside, letting the galette cool on the pan. (Leave the oven on.)

WHILE THE GALETTE COOLS, MAKE THE CANDIED WALNUTS: Line a baking sheet with parchment paper. In a small bowl, whisk together the brown sugar, cinnamon, and salt. In a medium bowl, whisk together the egg white and vanilla. Add the walnuts to the egg white mixture and toss until evenly coated. Add the brown sugar mixture and use a silicone spatula to stir until the walnuts are completely coated. Spread the walnuts evenly on the prepared baking sheet.

Bake the walnuts until fragrant, 10 to 15 minutes. Remove from the oven and use a silicone spatula to flip the walnuts over. Return to the oven and bake until browned, about 5 minutes longer. Set aside.

Pour ¼ cup of the red wine glaze on top of the galette and sprinkle all over with ½ cup of the candied walnuts. Add more glaze and walnuts if desired and serve immediately.

HEIRLOOM TOMATO TART

MAKES ONE 10-INCH TART

Heirloom tomatoes have been carefully bred by farmers for generations. Seeds were removed from the best tomato plants and passed down year after year; hence, the name *heirloom*. Heirloom tomatoes are open-pollinated naturally by insects, bees, birds, and the wind, and unlike other, commercially produced, tomatoes, the heirlooms are often oddly shaped and are often named for their colors: Purple Cherokee, Amana Orange, Brandywine, Black Cherry, Green Zebra, and Gold Medal to name just a few.

Pairing these sweet, flavorful tomatoes with a creamy, cheesy, and herb-packed filling makes this tart a seasonal darling.

Flour, for rolling out

All-Butter Pie Dough (page 220)

16 ounces (454g) ricotta cheese

2 tablespoons crushed garlic

1 large egg

1 cup (54g) fresh basil leaves, plus more for serving

1 teaspoon dried oregano

1 teaspoon dried thyme

1 teaspoon kosher salt, plus more for finishing

1 teaspoon ground white pepper

4 ounces (120g) Parmesan cheese, shaved with a vegetable peeler (about 1 cup)

1 pound heirloom tomatoes, cored and cut into ¼-inch-thick slices

3½ ounces (100g) mozzarella cheese, cut into ¼-inch-thick slices (about 6 slices)

Lightly flour the countertop and roll the dough to 12 to 13 inches in diameter. Carefully transfer it to a 2-inch-deep 10-inch tart pan with a removable bottom. Gently mold the dough into the tart pan, leaving an overhang. Use your fingers to mend any tears or holes. Make sure the dough is flush to the corners and grooves of the pan. Trim the overhanging dough using either a paring knife to trim off the dough following the pan edge or using the rolling pin to gently roll it off the pan's edge. (You can use the excess dough to patch cracks or create thicker sides if needed.) Cover the pan with plastic wrap and refrigerate 30 minutes.

Adjust a rack to the middle position and preheat the oven to 350°F (175°C).

Once the tart shell is chilled, prick the bottom all over with a fork. Line the dough with parchment paper and add dried beans or pie weights to weight the dough down. Bake until the crust is lightly golden around the edges, about 15 minutes. Remove from the oven and remove the weights by carefully lifting the parchment paper out of the shell.

In a blender or food processor, combine the ricotta, garlic, egg, basil, oregano, thyme, salt, and white pepper until the basil is puréed, about 30 seconds. Transfer to a medium bowl and stir in the Parmesan.

Place the pan on a baking sheet. Pour in the filling and smooth with a silicone or offset spatula. Layer the tomato slices on top, tucking in a portion of each slice so that it's submerged while the rest remains visible. After layering 4 or 5 slices of tomatoes, add a slice of mozzarella. Repeat this layering pattern around the perimeter of the tart until it is covered with tomatoes and mozzarella. Bake until the filling is set and the perimeter of the filling is puffed and dry, about 30 minutes.

Remove the tart from the oven and cool until the liquid from the mozzarella solidifies, about 20 minutes. To remove the tart from the tart pan, place an upturned bowl over the pan and turn over to release the crust from the sides of the pan. Sprinkle with basil and a pinch of salt and enjoy the tart warm. To store, cover with plastic wrap and refrigerate for up to 5 days.

BUTTERSCOTCH TART

MAKES ONE 9-INCH TART

My grandma Billingslea attended St. James AME Church on the far South Side of Chicago. Her family was one of the first to become members of this African Methodist Episcopalian church. My grandmother passed when I was relatively young, so my memories of visiting the church regularly are quite vague. However, I do recall that we often went to see my aunt Marsha sing in the choir with her angelic, soprano voice. I also remember watching the elders march down the aisles with collection plates and being so excited to contribute my crumpled dollar bill to the offering.

After the choir selections and the offering, my attention waned and I'd start to fidget. My grandma would tell me to lie down on the pew, which was covered with a bright red, wool-like cushion. To cool and soothe me, she'd flick a paper fan with the face of Martin Luther King Jr. printed on one side and the contact information for a funeral home printed on the other side. Directives to take a nap never worked. There was only one thing that would get me to settle down: candy.

Grandma Billingslea's pocketbook was filled with magical things: mints, toothpicks, a coin purse, tissue. I'd reach in and know just what I wanted: a gold cellophane-wrapped butterscotch candy. The small, buttery, and salty confection was all that I needed to sit still while the preacher carried on and someone caught the Holy Ghost.

This butterscotch tart, made with a cookie-like pâte sucrée crust and a perfectly caramelized filling, is what I make in honor of my grandma Billingslea, who always knew just what I needed to settle down and chill.

Flour, for rolling out
Pâte Sucrée (page 225)
12 tablespoons (1½ sticks/170g) unsalted butter

8 tablespoons (140g) half-and-half
1 cup (220g) packed light brown sugar
½ cup (68g) unbleached all-purpose flour

Adjust an oven rack to the middle position and preheat the oven to 390°F (198°C).

Lightly dust the countertop with flour and roll out the pâte sucrée to 12 to 13 inches in diameter. Carefully transfer the dough to a 1-inch-deep 9-inch tart pan with a removable bottom. Gently mold the dough into the tart pan, leaving an overhang. Use your fingers to mend any tears, lines, holes, or cracks so that there are no gaps in the dough. Make sure the dough is flush to the corners and grooves of the tart pan. Trim the overhanging dough in one of two ways: Use a paring knife and trim off the dough following the edge of the tart pan. Or use the rolling pin and gently roll it on top of the tart pan's edge. (You can use the excess dough to patch cracks or add to create thicker sides if needed.)

Cover the tart pan with plastic wrap and refrigerate for 30 minutes.

Remove the pan from the refrigerator and discard the plastic. Prick the bottom of the tart shell with the tines of a fork. Line the tart shell with parchment paper and add pie weights or dried beans to weight down the paper and the dough.

Transfer to the oven and bake until the crust is lightly golden around the edges, about 15 minutes. Remove the pie weights and parchment paper. Return to the oven and bake the crust until it is a golden brown, about 10 minutes longer. Set aside.

In a medium saucepan, combine the butter and 3 tablespoons of the half-and-half and set over medium-low heat. Once the butter has melted, stir in the brown sugar until dissolved. Allow the mixture to come to a slight boil, 3 to 4 minutes.

Meanwhile, in a small bowl, combine the flour and 3 tablespoons of the half-and-half and stir to make a paste. Add the remaining 2 tablespoons half-and-half to loosen the paste into a slurry. Once the slurry is smooth (no lumps!), whisk it into the brown sugar/butter mixture in the saucepan. Allow the filling to simmer and thicken, 1 to 2 minutes. Remove from the heat and pour the filling into the tart shell.

Set the tart in the fridge to chill for at least 4 to 6 hours.

To remove the tart from the pan, place a small bowl upside down on the counter. Set the tart pan on the bowl and gently work the sides down until the tart is released. Place the tart (still on the bottom of the pan) on a serving plate.

To store the tart, cover with plastic wrap and refrigerate for up to 5 days.

LAVENDER LEMON TART

MAKES ONE 9-INCH TART

Lavender thrives in the sunlight but can wilt in the rain or in excessive humidity. Planting lavender under lemon trees allows the plants to receive sunlight while also being protected from the rain and moisture since the leaves of citrus trees act as a canopy. So, when I began thinking about another citrusy dessert to add to the Justice of the Pies menu in 2014, I leaned into lavender and lemon. If they work seamlessly together in nature, then they should pair beautifully together when baked.

Lavender Shortbread Crust (page 241)

1 cup (200g) granulated sugar

3 tablespoons unbleached all-purpose flour.

3 large eggs

½ cup (119g) fresh lemon juice

Vanilla Bean Chantilly Cream (page 214), for serving

Dried lavender flowers, for garnish (optional)

Prepare the dough as directed with the addition of 2 tablespoons of dried lavender flowers, and fit into a 9-inch tart pan with a removable bottom. Leave the oven on at 350°F (170°C).

In a large bowl, whisk together the sugar and flour. Add the eggs and whisk until well combined, about 1 minute. Pour in the lemon juice and whisk until blended.

Place the tart shell on a baking sheet, place the baking sheet on a pulled-out oven rack, and pour the filling into the tart shell. (Placing the baking sheet on the rack before filling the pie helps avoid spillage.)

Bake until the tart is set and jiggles slightly in the center, 22 to 25 minutes. Remove the tart from the oven and allow it to cool at room temperature for 1 hour, then refrigerate the tart uncovered to chill for up to 2 hours.

To remove the tart from the pan, place a small bowl upside down on the counter. Set the tart pan on the bowl and gently work the sides down until the tart is released. Place the tart (still on the bottom of the pan) on a serving plate. Serve with the Chantilly cream and sprinkle with lavender, if using.

To store the tart, cover with plastic wrap and refrigerate for up to 7 days or freeze for up to 2 months.

HUMMINGBIRD TARTE TATIN

MAKES ONE 10-INCH TART

It is often believed that the hummingbird cake originated in the American South; however, it's actually from Jamaica, where it was called Doctor Bird Cake. The cake is named for an indigenous hummingbird known as doctor bird, red-billed streamertail, or scissor-tail. In an effort to encourage more Americans to visit the island, Jamaica sent out a press kit in 1968 that included several of the country's more popular recipes, including the Doctor Bird Cake. The tropical flavors resonated with cooks in the American South and, soon after, the cake began popping up at various state and county fairs.

Inspired by that Jamaican cake, the Hummingbird Tarte Tatin captures all the brightness of the fruit and the warmth of the cinnamon and molasses-y brown sugar. The fruit is caramelized in butter and sugar before being topped with a super-flaky pastry crust and baked. This rustic treat can be made in a skillet or in a cake pan.

BONUS: Slice the leftover pineapple into spears and refrigerate in an airtight container for snacking or making another tarte Tatin.

Flour, for rolling out

1 sheet (1 pound) all-butter Puff Pastry, homemade (page 232) or store-bought

1 whole pineapple

6 tablespoons (¾ stick/85g) unsalted butter

¾ cup (165g) packed light brown sugar

1 teaspoon ground cinnamon

¼ teaspoon kosher salt

2 bananas, halved lengthwise

2 tablespoons dark rum

1 teaspoon pure vanilla extract

Vanilla ice cream, for serving (optional)

Adjust an oven rack to the middle position and preheat the oven to 400°F (205°C).

Lightly dust the countertop with flour and roll out the pastry until it is 12 × 13 inches and ¼ inch thick. Set aside.

Using a chef's knife, cut off the top and bottom of the pineapple. Set the pineapple upright and remove the skin by slicing from the top to the bottom, following the curve of the fruit. Cut the pineapple lengthwise into quarters and then lay each wedge on its side and slice out the core. Cut one wedge of the pineapple lengthwise into four ½-inch-thick slices. (Save the other 3 wedges for another use. See Bonus.) Set everything aside.

Set a 10-inch cast-iron skillet over medium heat. Add the butter and, once melted, stir in the brown sugar, cinnamon, and salt, whisking until the brown sugar dissolves. Allow the mixture to simmer without stirring, swirling occasionally, until the mixture begins to bubble slightly and turns an amber color, about 4 minutes.

Using a fork, place the banana halves and pineapple slices in the sugar mixture, flipping each slice to fully coat both sides. Arrange the fruit by alternating layers (first a banana half and then a pineapple slice) until all areas around the diameter of the skillet are covered. Add the rum and vanilla and continue to let the mixture simmer until most of the liquid has evaporated, about 5 minutes.

Remove from the heat. Place the pastry round over the banana and pineapple slices in the skillet, tucking the overhanging pastry into the mixture.

Bake until the pastry is golden brown and puffed, 25 to 30 minutes.

Remove the skillet from the oven and allow the tarte Tatin to rest for 5 minutes. Set a large plate over the skillet (the plate must be larger than the skillet to catch all the fruit and caramelized sugar) and, holding the skillet with one hand and the bottom of the plate with the other, flip the skillet over in one swift motion so the tarte is inverted onto the plate. Slowly lift the skillet. Slice and serve warm with vanilla ice cream, if using.

The tart is best served immediately.

BLEU CHEESE + CARAMELIZED ONION TART

MAKES ONE 9-INCH TART

Bleu cheese and caramelized onions are a perfect paring. The duo creates a sweet and savory effect that is pure bliss on the tongue. To properly caramelize onions, you slowly brown them until they are melt-in-your-mouth soft and slightly sweet. This requires patience and know-how. While some people may like to add a bit of granulated sugar or Mexican Coca-Cola (made with natural sugar and not high fructose corn syrup) to their onions to accelerate the caramelization process, one of my favorite caramelizing accelerants to use is tangy-sweet apple cider. The apple cider adds a bit of earthiness and tanginess to the onions, too.

Flour, for rolling out

All-Butter Pie Dough (page 220)

6 tablespoons (81g) extra-virgin olive oil

4 tablespoons (½ stick/57g) unsalted butter

6 large sweet onions, sliced

3 tablespoons granulated sugar

1 tablespoon kosher salt, plus more for finishing

2 teaspoons freshly ground black pepper, plus more for finishing

½ cup (110g) apple cider (or Mexican Coca-Cola)

6 ounces (170g) bleu cheese crumbles

1 cup (128g) bread crumbs

Lightly dust the countertop with flour and roll out the dough to about 12 inches in diameter. Carefully transfer the dough to a 2-inch-deep 9-inch tart pan with a removable bottom. Gently mold the dough to the tart pan, leaving an overhang. Use your fingers to mend any tears, lines, holes, of cracks so that there are no gaps in the dough. Cut off a piece of the overhanging dough and roll it into a ball. Use the ball of dough to gently continue to mold the dough to the tart pan. Make sure the dough is flush to the corners and grooves of the tart pan. Trim the overhanging dough in one of two ways: Use a paring knife to trim off the dough following the edge of the tart pan. Or use the rolling pin and gently roll it on top of the tart pan's edge. (You can use the excess dough to patch cracks or add to create thicker sides if needed.)

In a heavy-bottomed pot or Dutch oven, heat the olive oil and butter over medium heat. Once the butter melts, add the onions and cook, stirring occasionally, until they are tender and beginning to brown, 20 to 25 minutes.

Meanwhile, preheat the oven to 350°F (175°C).

Stir the sugar, salt, and pepper into the onions. Allow the onions to stick to the pan to brown, but stir occasionally so they don't burn. If the onions start to dry out and stick too much, stir in 2 tablespoons of water. (Using a metal spatula is recommended for scraping up the browned bits on the bottom of the pan.) Cook the onions, stirring every so often, until they are a deep golden brown, 25 to 30 minutes.

Meanwhile, prick the bottom of the tart shell with the tines of a fork. Place a large sheet of parchment paper inside the tart shell so it drapes over the sides and add dried beans or pie weights. Bake until the crust is lightly golden around the edges, about 15 minutes. Remove the crust from the oven and remove the pie weights and parchment paper. Return to the oven and bake until the crust is a golden brown, about 15 minutes longer. Set aside. Leave the oven on.

Add the cider to the onions and cook until the liquid evaporates, 8 to 12 minutes. Remove from the heat and stir in half of the bleu cheese.

Spread the bread crumbs evenly across the bottom of the tart shell. Top with the caramelized onions, spreading them evenly with a silicone or offset spatula. Sprinkle with the remaining bleu cheese.

Place the tart on a baking sheet, transfer to the oven, and bake until the cheese has melted and is slightly browned, 15 to 20 minutes. Remove from the oven and allow the tart to cool slightly until it sets, 15 to 20 minutes. Finish it with a pinch of salt and pepper before serving.

To remove the tart from the pan, place the tart pan on top of an upturned bowl and gently press down on the outer ring to release the tart crust from the pan. Place the tart (still on the bottom of the pan) on a serving plate.

To store the tart, cover with plastic wrap and refrigerate for up to 5 days.

JORDAN MARIE BRINGS THREE WHITE HORSES DANIEL

LAKOTA ACTIVIST + RUNNER

Jordan comes from a long line of runners.

Her grandfather, Nyal Three White Horses, was a member of the Kul Wicasa nation of the Lower Brulé Sioux Tribe in South Dakota. He didn't have access to transportation to get to school, so when his tribe's reservation was forcibly removed from the neighboring town where he attended school, he had to walk for miles to get there—and rather than slowly trek across long stretches of the plains, he ran.

Running became a lifelong practice for Nyal Three White Horses, and Jordan was ten years old when she first ran with her lala (grandfather in Lakota). Running with him allowed her to connect with her lala in a deeper way, and she adored being next to him in the open spaces of the prairie.

She continued to run as a student athlete throughout elementary school, high school, and college. In 2017, she created the Rising Hearts Coalition, an indigenous-led group designed to elevate awareness of indigenous issues while also building collaborative partnerships to accomplish equitable and just treatment of her people. Through the coalition, Jordan participated in protests at Standing Rock, a grassroots movement that objected to the construction of the Dakota Access Pipeline because of its direct threat to ancient burial grounds, culturally historic sites, and the reservation's water supply. Jordan also heavily invested in native youth initiatives and MMIWG (Missing and Murdered Indigenous Women and Girls).

When she ran the San Diego Half Marathon she combined her two passions, activism and running, to bring awareness to the fact that Indigenous women are three and a half times more likely to disappear and die due to domestic violence and sexual assault. Jordan wanted to use her body to honor the 5,596 women whose disappearances were ignored by law enforcement agencies the first year she ran (2016). She wanted to use her miles to inspire people to take action. As she ran the 26.2-mile race, she prayed for and recited the names of 26 missing Indigenous women.

Even though she wore #MMIWG on her bib during the San Diego Marathon, which sparked meaningful dialogue with a handful of non-Natives, for Jordan, this was not enough. So, when she ran the Boston Marathon, she painted a red handprint on her face to symbolize the silence surrounding the violence inflicted on Indigenous women and girls. While the bib change created a small ripple, she hoped the red handprint would create a swelling wave.

Runners attest to feeling high from endorphins, but when Jordan runs, she often feels emotionally and mentally embattled. That she even has a list of 26 names to pray for during the miles of her race is sobering. Despite the downtrodden mood that can dull her morale as she carries this spiritually heavy load and reflects upon these names, she urges herself to connect her feet to the ground and proceed. Her run is about her ties to the lands, her stolen sisters, and demanding policy change and accountability for her missing and murdered relatives.

During the races she has run, while many may claim unawareness of the 5,596 missing Native women, a woman running a race with a red hand painted on her face is hard to turn away from.

As a runner, Jordan relies on meals that are high in protein and carbs to sustain her energy and give her endurance. The Fry Bread + Bison Tarts, made with scrambled eggs, ground bison, peppers, and sweet potatoes all cushioned by a slightly sweet, chewy fried dough base, are inspired by Jordan's childhood home on the Lower Brulé reservation in South Dakota.

There is some controversy within Indian Country about fry bread. The fluffy delicacy was born from ingredients provided to Indians as part of the United States Commodity Supplemental Food Program, which included rations that consisted mostly of canned goods, salt, sugar, flour, and lard. The cruel intention of the "commodity box" was to separate Indians from their native ancestral diet of corn, elk, deer, and grains that they were used to.

Some view fry bread as a symbol of the genocide of Native Americans as well as the erasure of the cultural traditions of Indigenous people. Jordan recognizes the ills behind fry bread's history, but she also expresses that "fry bread is life." This open-faced tart not only symbolizes the cultural significance behind the fried treat but also provides healthy indigenous ingredients to fuel the body.

FRY BREAD + BISON TARTS

MAKES EIGHT 7-INCH TARTS

FRY BREAD

4 cups (544g) all-purpose flour (preferably Blue Bird flour)

3 tablespoons baking powder

1 teaspoon kosher salt

1½ cups (355g) warm water

3 tablespoons vegetable oil

BLACK BEANS

2 tablespoons extra-virgin olive oil

1 medium vine-ripened tomato, cored and diced

½ large sweet onion, finely diced

1 large jalapeño, finely diced (about 2 tablespoons)

2 (15 oz/425g) cans black beans, drained

2 garlic cloves, finely diced

1 teaspoon chili powder

1 teaspoon ground cumin

1 teaspoon dried oregano

1 teaspoon smoked paprika

2 teaspoons kosher salt

BISON FILLING

2 tablespoons extra-virgin olive oil

2 tablespoons unsalted butter

1 large sweet onion, diced

1 pound (455g) ground bison

4 garlic cloves, crushed

¼ cup chipotle peppers in adobo sauce, drained and roughly chopped

2 teaspoons chili powder

1 teaspoon ground cumin

1 teaspoon kosher salt

½ teaspoon red pepper flakes

½ teaspoon freshly ground black pepper

SCRAMBLED EGGS

8 large eggs

½ cup (120g) whole milk

3 tablespoons unsalted butter

1 teaspoon kosher salt

ASSEMBLY

Vegetable oil, for frying

Flour, for dusting

2 cups (225g) grated sharp cheddar cheese

4 medium vine-ripened tomatoes, cored and diced

4 avocados, sliced ¼ inch thick

MAKE THE FRY BREAD: In a large bowl, whisk together the flour, baking powder, and salt. Create a well in the center of the mixture and add ¾ cup (180g) of the warm water to the well. Use your hand to mix the flour and water together, gradually adding more water as needed (you may not use all of it) while combining. Mix until the flour mixture is no longer dry and then knead the dough until it is soft and a slightly sticky ball forms. Lift the ball of dough up with one hand and pour 2 tablespoons (18g) of the oil into the bowl. Place the ball of dough back in the bowl, pour the remaining 1 tablespoon (9g) oil on top of the dough, and roll the dough around in the bowl to fully coat. Make indentations in the dough with your fingers, then place a kitchen towel over the bowl and allow it to rest for 2 hours.

MAKE THE BLACK BEANS: In a medium saucepan, heat the olive oil over medium-high heat. Add the tomatoes, onion, and jalapeño and cook, stirring occasionally, until the onions are translucent, about 10 minutes. Stir in the beans, garlic, chili powder, cumin, oregano, smoked paprika, and salt. Allow the filling to cook until it steams, then reduce the heat to low and simmer for 10 to 12 minutes to meld the flavors. Remove from the heat and set aside.

MAKE THE BISON FILLING: In a Dutch oven or large heavy-bottomed pot, combine the olive oil and butter and heat over medium heat. Once the butter melts, add the onion and cook, stirring occasionally, until tender, 15 to 20 minutes.

RECIPE CONTINUES >>

Add the ground bison, breaking up the meat with a spatula or fork, and brown, stirring often, until cooked through, about 15 minutes.

Add the garlic and continue to cook, stirring often, until fragrant, about 5 more minutes. Stir in the chipotle peppers, chili powder, cumin, salt, pepper flakes, and black pepper. Reduce the heat to low and simmer, stirring occasionally, until fragrant, 3 to 5 minutes.

MAKE THE SCRAMBLED EGGS: In a large bowl, whisk together the eggs, milk, and salt and set aside. In a large skillet, melt the butter over medium-low heat. Add the egg mixture and cook undisturbed until the edges of the egg mixture begin to dry slightly, about 30 seconds. Using a silicone spatula, scrape the sides and the bottom of the skillet to form soft curds. Continue cooking while stirring and folding every few seconds. For soft, creamy scrambled eggs, stop stirring and cooking once the eggs are mostly set but very soft. For harder set eggs, continue to stir and fold until the desired texture is reached.

ASSEMBLE THE TARTS: In a 10-inch cast-iron skillet, heat 2 inches of vegetable oil over medium-high heat until it reaches 380°F (190°C).

While the oil heats, shape the fry bread. Turn the dough out onto a lightly floured surface. Divide the dough into 8 equal pieces (each should be about ½ cup). Shape each piece into a ball and then flatten into a disk. Use a rolling pin (preferably a small one if you have it) to roll the dough into a 6- to 7-inch round that is ⅛ inch thick (you can also just stretch the dough using your hands), adding more flour to prevent sticking to the surface or the rolling pin as needed. Using your finger or a small paring knife, poke a small hole in the middle of each dough round (this helps the fry bread remain flat as it cooks; it's perfectly fine if the fry bread has several holes throughout).

Line a plate with paper towels. When the oil reaches 380°F (190°C), carefully slide one round of dough into the oil and fry for 10 seconds. Using a fork or metal tongs, carefully flip the fry bread over and cook on the other side for 10 seconds. Remove the fry bread from the skillet and place on the paper towels. Repeat with the remaining rounds of dough.

To serve, set a piece of fry bread on a plate. Top with about ¼ cup of beans, ¼ cup of bison filling, and some scrambled eggs. Finish with ¼ cup of cheese, ¼ cup diced tomatoes, and a few avocado slices. Serve immediately.

ROASTED BRUSSELS SPROUTS + CHERRY TART

MAKES ONE 10-INCH TART

One evening when I was a kid, I was having dinner at my aunt Pat's house with my older twin cousins (whom I idolized), Jason and Justin. That night's vegetable was steamed Brussels sprouts. I had never had them and didn't know what to make of them, but they looked like baby cabbages, and I didn't like cabbage.

My aunt announced that no one could leave their seats until we'd finished our plates.

We sat at a round wooden table held up by a large, singular leg. The area between the top of the leg and under the tabletop had a groove with some spacing. I watched, wide-eyed, as my cousins stuffed Brussels sprouts into the spacing under the table.

I nudged Justin and asked him to make my Brussels sprouts magically disappear, too. We finished the remainder of our dinner, put our plates in the sink, and quickly ran off to the bedroom to get as far away as possible from the scene of our sneaky act.

As an adult, I told my aunt Pat about what the boys and I had done years before. She replied, "Do you know I found those Brussels sprouts two years later!" and we all roared with laughter!

I have since learned that roasting Brussels sprouts brings out their sweetness, and pairing them with other ingredients such as Parmesan cheese and a sweetener—in this case plump cherries, sugar, and apple cider vinegar—makes them so damn delicious. The end result is a mildly sweet, nutty, and crispy tart that no one would ever stuff under a table!

2 cups pitted dark cherries, frozen or fresh

½ cup (100g) granulated sugar, plus 1½ tablespoons (18g)

2 tablespoons fresh lemon juice

Flour, for rolling out

All-Butter Pie Dough (page 220)

6 tablespoons (82g) extra-virgin olive oil

4 tablespoons (½ stick/57g) unsalted butter

3 large sweet onions, diced

3 teaspoons kosher salt, plus more for finishing

2 teaspoons freshly ground black pepper, plus more for finishing

¼ cup (60g) apple cider (or Mexican Coca-Cola)

4 cups trimmed and halved Brussels sprouts

1 cup (128g) bread crumbs

½ cup (60g) grated or shaved Parmesan cheese

¼ cup Cherry Balsamic Vinaigrette (page 216)

In a small saucepan, combine the cherries, ½ cup (100g) of the granulated sugar, and the lemon juice. Set over medium-high heat and cook, stirring, until the liquid reduces by half, about 30 minutes. Remove from the heat, drain the cherries in a sieve set over a bowl (save the juice for making the vinaigrette), and place the cherries in a bowl.

Lightly dust the countertop with flour and roll out the dough to about 12 inches in diameter. Carefully transfer the dough to a 2-inch-deep 10-inch tart pan with a removable bottom. Gently mold the dough into the tart pan. Use your fingers to mend any tears, lines, holes, or cracks so that there are no gaps in the dough. Make sure the dough is flush to the corners and grooves of the tart pan. Trim the overhanging dough in one of two ways: Use a paring knife and trim off the dough following the edge of the tart pan. Or use the rolling pin and gently roll it on top of the tart pan's edge. (You can use the excess dough to patch cracks or add to create thicker sides if needed.)

In a heavy-bottomed pot or Dutch oven, heat 3 tablespoons of the olive oil and the butter over medium heat until the butter melts. Add the onions and cook until they are tender and begin to brown, about 20 minutes.

Meanwhile, adjust an oven rack to the middle position and preheat the oven to 350°F (175°C).

Prick the bottom of the tart shell with the tines of a fork. Line the tart shell with parchment paper and add pie weights or dried beans to weight down the paper and the dough.

RECIPE CONTINUES >>

Transfer to the oven and bake until the crust is lightly golden around the edges, about 15 minutes. Remove the crust from the oven and remove the pie weights and parchment paper. Return to the oven and bake until golden brown, about 15 minutes longer. Set aside. Leave the oven on and increase the oven temperature to 425°F (220°C).

Meanwhile, add the remaining 1½ tablespoons granulated sugar, 1½ teaspoons of the salt, and 1 teaspoon of the pepper to the onions. Allow the onions to stick to the pan to brown, but stir occasionally so they don't burn. If the onions start to dry out a little bit, add 2 tablespoons of water to the pot and stir. Using a metal spatula is recommended for scraping up the browned bits on the bottom of the pan and mixing it with the onions. Continue to cook the onions until they are a deep golden brown, 25 to 30 minutes. Add the apple cider and cook until the liquid has evaporated, 7 to 10 minutes.

Place the Brussels sprouts in a medium bowl. Add the remaining 3 tablespoons of olive oil, 1½ teaspoons of salt, and 1 teaspoon of pepper and toss to coat. Transfer the Brussels sprouts to a baking sheet and roast until the sprouts are tender, deeply browned, and slightly charred, about 25 minutes. Remove from the oven and set aside. Leave the oven on.

Spread the bread crumbs out evenly across the bottom of the tart shell. Add half of the Brussels sprouts, half of the caramelized onions, and half of the Parmesan. Repeat the layering, ending with the Parmesan.

Place the tart on a baking sheet, transfer to the oven, and bake until the cheese melts, about 15 minutes.

Remove the tart from the oven and set aside to cool slightly.

Drizzle the vinaigrette over the tart and finish with a pinch of salt and pepper.

To remove the tart from the pan, place the tart pan on top of an upturned bowl and gently press down on the outer ring to release the tart crust from the pan. Place the tart (still on the bottom of the pan) on a serving plate. Enjoy the tart warm.

To store the tart, cover with plastic wrap and refrigerate for up to 3 days.

MARGARITA TART

MAKES ONE 9-INCH TART

This tart is inspired by an occasion on which I had one-too-many margaritas with one of my best friends and our moms (all I'll say is that by the end of lunch they were very happy and slightly tipsy). I decided to create a margarita tart so that our mothers could enjoy all the sweet-tart-citrusy flavors with none of the boozy aftereffects. The shortbread crust is sweet and buttery, and the filling is tart and tangy. After baking, the tequila in the tart retains only about 25 percent of its alcohol content—it is the perfect treat that won't put you down for a nap after indulging in it.

Shortbread Crust (page 241)

3 tablespoons (25g) unbleached all-purpose flour

1 cup (200g) sugar

3 large eggs

Grated zest of 1 lime

¼ cup (59g) fresh lime juice (2 or 3 limes)

¼ cup (55g) blanco tequila

Vanilla Bean Chantilly Cream (page 214), for serving

Lime slices, for garnish

Prepare the crust, remove from the oven, set aside, and leave the oven on at 350°F (175°C).

In a large bowl, whisk together the flour and sugar. Add the eggs and whisk until well combined, about 1 minute. Whisk in the lime zest, lime juice, and tequila.

Place the tart shell on a baking sheet, place the baking sheet on a pulled-out oven rack, and pour the filling into the tart shell. (Placing the baking sheet on the rack before filling the pie helps avoid spillage.)

Bake until the tart is set and the center only jiggles slightly, about 22 minutes. Remove the tart from the oven and allow it to cool to room temperature, about 1½ hours.

Refrigerate the tart uncovered for at least 2 hours. To remove the tart from the pan, place the tart pan on top of an upturned bowl and gently press down on the outer ring to release the tart crust from the pan. Place the tart (still on the bottom of the pan) on a serving plate.

Serve with Chantilly cream and garnish with lime slices.

To store the tart, cover with plastic wrap and refrigerate for up to 7 days or freeze for up to 2 months.

NOTE: To make individual tarts, evenly press ¼ cup of dough into 4-inch mini tart pans. Press the dough across the bottom and up the fluted sides so it's about ¼-inch thick. Pinch off excess dough to create a clean edge.

CHOCOLATE-PEANUT BUTTER + PRETZEL TART

MAKES ONE 10-INCH TART

Flour, for rolling out

Pâte Sucrée (page 225)

8 tablespoons (1 stick/113g) unsalted butter, at room temperature

1½ cups (402g) creamy peanut butter, plus 2 tablespoons (33g)

1 cup (117g) confectioners' sugar

½ teaspoon pure vanilla extract

1 cup (173g) semisweet chocolate chips

½ cup (118g) heavy cream

¼ teaspoon kosher salt

¾ cup (50g) salted miniature pretzels

I met pastry chef Christina Tosi, the founder of the Milk Bar bakery chain, during the summer of 2020 when we recorded a segment for her series of baking collaborations called "Bake Club."

Her laid-back, casual demeanor, paired with her whimsical, quirky creative spirit, made the experience so enjoyable and unintimidating—plus, her desserts are nonconventional and unorthodoxly creative like my own. I immediately felt a deep, culinary connection with her.

A couple of months after recording "Bake Club," I was handpicked by Chef Tosi to be a part of a new show that would stream on Netflix called *Bake Squad*. As one of four *Bake Squad* members, I'd be charged with baking massive desserts for individuals who were celebrating milestone events in their lives. Each guest could pick only one of the desserts from the four members of *Bake Squad* as the one to be showcased at their special event. The experience allowed me to expand my creativity and really push myself in all ways.

I've always admired Chef Tosi's ability to think outside of the box when creating new desserts—she even calls the inspiration behind many of her sweets "happy mistakes."

So, when a Justice of the Pies client once requested a chocolate pecan pie, but without any pecans, I channeled Chef Tosi's "happy mistakes" philosophy and created this tart as an alternative. It has the same fudgy filling as the pie the client requested, but the pecans were switched out for slightly salty pretzels that balance really well with the sweet pastry crust.

Lightly dust the countertop with flour and roll out the pâte sucrée to 12 to 13 inches in diameter. Carefully transfer the dough to a 1-inch-deep 10-inch tart pan with a removable bottom. Gently mold the dough into the tart pan, leaving an overhang. Use your fingers to mend any tears, lines, holes, or cracks so that there are no gaps in the dough. Make sure the dough is flush to the corners and grooves of the tart pan. Trim the overhanging dough in one of two ways: Use a paring knife and trim off the dough following the edge of the tart pan. Or use the rolling pin and gently roll it on top of the tart pan's edge. (You can use the excess dough to patch cracks or add to create thicker sides if needed.)

Cover the tart pan with plastic wrap and chill for 30 minutes.

Position an oven rack in the middle position and preheat the oven to 335°F (170°C).

Remove the tart pan from the refrigerator and discard the plastic wrap. Prick the bottom of the crust with the tines of a fork. Line the tart shell with parchment paper and add pie weights or dried beans to weight down the paper and the dough.

Transfer to the oven and bake the tart shell until golden brown, 30 to 35 minutes. Remove the parchment and pie weights and set the tart shell aside to cool.

In a medium bowl, whisk the butter and 1½ cups (402g) of the peanut butter until well combined, about 1 minute. Add the confectioners' sugar and continue to mix until it is incorporated. Mix in the vanilla.

Pour the peanut butter mixture into the tart shell and use a silicone spatula to evenly spread the filling in the crust. Place the tart in the refrigerator, uncovered, for 15 minutes.

Place the chocolate chips and remaining 2 tablespoons of peanut butter in a small heatproof bowl. In a small saucepan, heat the cream over medium heat until it steams, about 5 minutes. Pour the hot cream directly over the chocolate chips and peanut butter. Cover with plastic wrap and let it stand until the chocolate chips are melted, about 5 minutes. Stir the salt into the mixture until smooth and there are no visible chunks of chocolate chips. Remove and discard the plastic wrap. Pour the chocolate/peanut butter ganache over the chilled peanut butter filling in the tart. Using an offset spatula or a silicone spatula, spread the ganache evenly on top of the peanut butter filling. Carefully place the pretzels on top of the ganache until they fully cover the tart.

Return the tart to the refrigerator and chill, uncovered, for at least 2 hours before serving. To remove the tart from the pan, place the tart pan on top of an upturned bowl and gently press down on the outer ring to release the tart crust from the pan. Place the tart (still on the bottom of the pan) on a serving plate.

To store the tart, cover with plastic wrap and refrigerate for up to 7 days or freeze for up to 2 months.

MANGO + COCONUT MACAROON TART

MAKES ONE 10-INCH TART

The flavor of a mango reminds me of a pineapple, an orange, and a peach all rolled into one. When ripe, a mango is so extremely sweet; and since it is a tropical fruit, it of course pairs well with another tropical ingredient: coconut. So, I take the two and combine them into this bright and slightly chewy tart that has coconut in the crust and filling, and mango in the crust and laid across the finished pie, too. The macaroon crust browns so nicely at the edges, and its crispness makes it an ideal tart base, especially filled with a creamy coconut custard that is topped with fresh mango slices.

Macaroon Crust mixture (page 240)

3 or 4 large mangoes, peeled and fruit sliced away from the pit

2 cups (500g) canned full-fat coconut milk

4 tablespoons (½ stick/57g) unsalted butter

¾ cup (150g) granulated sugar

¾ cup (90g) cornstarch

2 large eggs

3 large egg yolks

1 tablespoon pure vanilla extract

Adjust an oven rack to the middle position and preheat the oven to 325°F (165°C).

Make the macaroon crust mixture as directed and keep the uncooked mixture in the bowl it was mixed in.

Finely dice enough mango to get ⅔ cup and then thinly slice the remaining mango. Refrigerate until serving.

Fold the diced mango into the macaroon crust mixture and then press the mixture into and up the sides of a 1-inch-deep 10-inch tart pan with a removable bottom. Use your fingers to mend any gaps and make sure the crust is flush to the corners and grooves.

Transfer the tart shell to the oven and bake until the edges are toasty and golden brown, about 45 minutes. (The crust does not need to be weighted down.) Remove from the oven and set aside to cool slightly, 15 to 20 minutes.

Meanwhile, in a medium saucepan, combine the coconut milk, butter, and sugar and set over medium heat. Stir, allowing the butter to melt, and continue to cook, stirring occasionally, until the mixture steams, about 10 minutes.

In a medium bowl, whisk together the cornstarch, whole eggs, and egg yolks. While whisking, very slowly pour the warm coconut milk mixture into the egg mixture (pouring too quickly may cook the eggs). Once the mixture in the bowl is well combined, return the entire contents of the bowl to the saucepan. Return the saucepan to medium heat and gently simmer while whisking constantly (make sure to get into the corners of the pan), until the mixture thickens, 4 to 5 minutes. Using a fine-mesh sieve, strain the filling into a clean medium bowl. Stir the vanilla into the filling and pour the filling into the slightly cooled tart shell, using an offset spatula to spread it out evenly. Cover with plastic wrap and refrigerate until the filling is firm to the touch, at least 3 hours.

Remove the tart from the refrigerator and discard the plastic. To remove the tart from the pan, place the tart pan on top of an upturned bowl and gently press down on the outer ring to release the tart crust from the pan. Place the tart (still on the bottom of the pan) on a serving plate. Layer mango slices on top of the tart, slice, and serve.

To store the tart, cover with plastic wrap and refrigerate for up to 3 days.

LAVENDER WHOOPIE PIES

MAKES NINE OR TEN 1½-INCH WHOOPIE PIES

I have extremely poor sleeping habits. I generally spend between 14 and 16 hours a day in the kitchen, and I come home exhausted, but often find that I cannot fall asleep. My close friend Asha, a Reiki master and herbalist, suggested that I sleep with a small satchel of dried lavender flowers near my pillow and rub some lavender oil on the soles of my feet before going to sleep.

Her suggestion worked and now I get a much better night's rest. I shared with her how much I loved lavender and she said, "Why don't you try baking something with lavender in it?"

And here we are! Thanks to Asha for helping birth the idea for these floral whoopie pies. When baking, they fill the room with such a botanical bliss and they are absolute delectation when sandwiched with buttery, sweet cream cheese filling.

WHOOPIE COOKIES

8 tablespoons (1 stick/113g) unsalted butter, at room temperature

1½ cups (300g) granulated sugar

1 large egg, at room temperature

½ cup (126g) buttermilk

1 teaspoon pure vanilla extract

2½ cups (340g) unbleached all-purpose flour

2 tablespoons (3g) dried lavender flowers

1½ teaspoons baking powder

FILLING

4 ounces (113g) cream cheese, at room temperature

4 tablespoons (½ stick; 57g) unsalted butter, at room temperature

1½ cups (176g) confectioners' sugar

1 teaspoon pure vanilla extract

Pinch of kosher salt

Adjust an oven rack to the middle position and preheat the oven to 350°F (175°C).

MAKE THE WHOOPIE COOKIES: In a large bowl, use a silicone spatula to cream together the butter and granulated sugar until well blended. Add the egg and stir until completely combined. Mix in the buttermilk and vanilla.

In a separate bowl, whisk together the flour, lavender, and baking powder. Add half of the flour mixture to the wet ingredients and use the spatula to fold together. Once well combined, add the remaining flour and blend until just combined. Do not overmix.

Line two baking sheets with parchment paper. Using a 1-ounce cookie scoop or two large spoons, drop 2-tablespoon amounts of batter onto the prepared sheets 1½ inches apart.

Bake the whoopie cookies until they are pale in color and look slightly underbaked, 15 to 17 minutes. The bottoms should be a light golden brown and the edges should remain pale. (If overbaked, they will be hard, rather than fluffy.) Remove from the oven and cool on the pan for about 5 minutes.

MEANWHILE, MAKE THE FILLING: In a large bowl, use a silicone spatula to mix the cream cheese and butter together until well blended. Gradually stir in the confectioners' sugar until combined. Stir in the vanilla and salt.

Using a small offset spatula or a butter knife, spread about 1½ tablespoons of cream cheese filling on the flat side of one whoopie cookie and sandwich with the flat side of another whoopie cookie. Repeat with the remaining filling and cookies.

The unfilled whoopie cookies can be stored in an airtight container at room temperature for up to 5 days. The filling can be stored in an airtight container in the refrigerator for up to 5 days. Remove the filling from the refrigerator and allow it to come to room temperature before spreading on the whoopie cookies.

CARROT CAKE WHOOPIE PIES

MAKES EIGHT OR NINE 3-INCH WHOOPIE PIES

A few times a year, my father would shuffle me into our car around ten o'clock at night and we'd drive to a twenty-four-hour seafood haven called Lawrence's Fisheries. Whether you walked in at two o'clock in the afternoon or two o'clock in the morning, there'd always be a line of people waiting for their piping-hot fried fish and shrimp served in a grease-stained brown paper bag with small containers of homemade hot sauce. As much as I loved fried shrimp, my favorite memory of the fishery was their carrot cake, which was served in a thick slab with plenty of rich cream cheese frosting. Now, whenever I eat something hot and spicy or anything dipped in hot sauce, I am always looking for a sweet and creamy dessert to follow it up. In addition to how good they are, one of the best things about these carrot cake whoopie pies is that you can make them in about a quarter of the time it takes to make a good carrot cake.

WHOOPIE COOKIES

8 tablespoons (1 stick/113g) unsalted butter, at room temperature

½ cup (110g) packed light brown sugar

½ cup (100g) granulated sugar

2 large eggs, at room temperature

½ cup (126g) buttermilk

1 teaspoon pure vanilla extract

1½ teaspoons ground cinnamon

½ teaspoon ground cloves

½ teaspoon ground ginger

½ teaspoon ground nutmeg

1½ cups (1 or 2 large) carrots, peeled and finely grated

2 cups (272g) unbleached all-purpose flour

1½ teaspoons baking soda

1 teaspoon baking powder

½ teaspoon kosher salt

½ cup drained canned crushed pineapple

½ cup golden raisins

FILLING

4 ounces (113g) cream cheese, at room temperature

4 tablespoons (½ stick/57g) unsalted butter, at room temperature

1½ cups (176g) confectioners' sugar

1 teaspoon pure vanilla extract

Pinch of kosher salt

Adjust an oven rack to the middle position and preheat the oven to 350°F (175°C).

MAKE THE WHOOPIE COOKIES: In a large bowl, with a silicone spatula or a hand mixer, cream together the butter, brown sugar, and granulated sugar. Add 1 egg and mix until fully combined before adding the second egg. Stir in the buttermilk, vanilla, cinnamon, cloves, ginger, and nutmeg. Stir in the grated carrots.

In a separate bowl, whisk together the flour, baking soda, baking powder, and salt. Add half of the flour mixture to the wet ingredients and use a silicone spatula to fold together. Once the flour has fully incorporated into the filling, add the remaining flour. Mix until just combined (do not overmix). Fold in the crushed pineapple and golden raisins until they are evenly distributed.

Line two baking sheets with parchment paper. Using a 1-ounce cookie scoop or two large spoons, drop 2-tablespoon amounts of batter onto the prepared sheets 1½ inches apart.

Bake until the whoopie pie cookies have puffed and are golden brown, 15 to 17 minutes. Remove from the oven and let the whoopie cookies cool, about 5 minutes.

RECIPE CONTINUES >>

MEANWHILE, MAKE THE FILLING: In a large bowl, use a silicone spatula to mix the cream cheese and butter together until well blended. Gradually stir in the confectioners' sugar until combined. Stir in the vanilla and salt.

Using a small offset spatula or a butter knife, spread about 1½ tablespoons of cream cheese filling on the flat side of one whoopie cookie and sandwich with the flat side of another whoopie cookie. Repeat with the remaining filling and cookies.

The unfilled whoopie cookies can be stored in an airtight container at room temperature for up to 5 days. The filling can be stored in an airtight container in the refrigerator for up to 5 days. Remove the filling from the refrigerator and allow it to come to room temperature before spreading on the whoopie cookies.

BONUS: For a bit of a crunch, add ¼ cup chopped walnuts to the carrot cake batter.

RUM PUNCH WHOOPIE PIES

MAKES TEN TO TWELVE 1½-INCH WHOOPIE PIES

Rum cake is often served at celebrations in the Caribbean—be it a wedding or a holiday like Christmas or New Year's. The slightly boozy cake has often been said to be derived from the English steamed puddings that were brought to the islands by British colonists during the eighteenth century. Dark rum is added to the batter to give the cake a smoky, intense flavor, and a rum sauce is poured on the cake after it cools, leaving the cake with a deliciously moist texture.

A few years ago, I received a request for a rum cake without the alcohol. I thought it was a peculiar request. "So, you'd like a rum cake . . . but without the rum?" Where would the flavor come from? I turned to the rum punch cocktail for inspiration—the punch is typically made with light and dark rums, pineapple and orange juice, and a bit of grenadine. In an effort to retain the same moisture in a traditional rum cake without the rum-infused sauce, I added crushed pineapple and orange zest to the batter.

These whoopie pies are derived from that rum punch cake. They're super moist with a bright boost from the orange zest. Here, I add real rum into the creamy filling, but you can replace it with rum extract to keep these treats alcohol-free.

WHOOPIE COOKIES

8 tablespoons (1 stick/113g) unsalted butter, at room temperature

½ cup (110g) packed light brown sugar

½ cup (100g) granulated sugar

2 large eggs, at room temperature

½ cup (126g) buttermilk

Grated zest of 1 orange

1 teaspoon rum extract

½ teaspoon pure vanilla extract

2½ cups (340g) unbleached all-purpose flour

1 teaspoon baking powder

½ teaspoon baking soda

½ teaspoon kosher salt

½ cup drained canned crushed pineapple

FILLING

4 ounces (113g) cream cheese, at room temperature

4 tablespoons (½ stick/57g) unsalted butter, at room temperature

2 cups (234g) confectioners' sugar

1 teaspoon pure vanilla extract

Pinch of kosher salt

1 tablespoon coconut-flavored rum (optional)

¼ cup maraschino cherries, finely diced (optional)

Adjust an oven rack to the middle position and preheat the oven to 350°F (175°C).

MAKE THE WHOOPIE COOKIES: In a large bowl, use a silicone spatula to cream together the butter, brown sugar, and granulated sugar. Add the eggs and mix until completely combined with the butter and sugars. Stir in the buttermilk, orange zest, rum extract, and vanilla.

In a separate bowl, whisk together the flour, baking powder, baking soda, and salt. Add half of the flour mixture to the wet ingredients and use a silicone spatula to fold together. Once the flour has fully combined with the wet ingredients, add the remaining flour mixture to the bowl. Mix until just combined. Do not overmix. Fold in the crushed pineapple until it is distributed throughout the batter.

Line two baking sheets with parchment paper. Using a 1-ounce cookie scoop or two large spoons, drop 2-tablespoon amounts of batter onto the prepared sheets 1½ inches apart.

Bake until the whoopie cookies have puffed and are golden brown, 15 to 17 minutes. Remove from the oven and let the whoopie cookies cool, about 5 minutes.

MEANWHILE, MAKE THE FILLING: In a large bowl, use a silicone spatula to mix the cream cheese and butter together until well blended. Gradually stir in the

RECIPE CONTINUES >>

confectioners' sugar until combined. Stir in the vanilla, salt, and coconut rum (if using). If desired, add the maraschino cherries for color and texture.

Using a small offset spatula or a butter knife, spread about 1½ tablespoons of cream cheese filling on the flat side of one whoopie cookie and sandwich with the flat side of another whoopie cookie. Repeat with the remaining filling and cookies.

The unfilled whoopie cookies can be stored in an airtight container at room temperature for up to 5 days. The filling can be stored in an airtight container in the refrigerator for up to 5 days. Remove the filling from the refrigerator and allow it to come to room temperature before spreading on the whoopie cookies.

BONUS: For my rum punch cocktail, combine 1 ounce coconut rum, 1 ounce dark rum, 1 ounce Caribbean rum, 1 ounce pineapple juice, 1 ounce orange juice, the juice of ½ lime, and a dash of grenadine. Shake all of the ingredients in a cocktail shaker filled with ice for 10 seconds. Pour into a tall glass, kick back, relax, and enjoy!

CRANBERRY-ORANGE WHOOPIE PIES

MAKES TEN TO TWELVE 1½-INCH WHOOPIE PIES

Dried cranberries are excellent as a snack with salted sunflower seeds, added to tuna salad, baked into muffins, or stirred into a bowl of piping hot oatmeal. I love to indulge in their chewy tanginess especially when partnered with the bright, citrusy orange. Many may consider cranberries a winter ingredient to be used in holiday dishes, but these Cranberry-Orange Whoopie Pies are a favorite 365 days a year.

WHOOPIE COOKIES

8 tablespoons (1 stick/113g) unsalted butter, at room temperature

1½ cups (300g) granulated sugar

1 large egg, at room temperature

Grated zest of 1 orange

½ cup (126g) buttermilk

½ teaspoon orange extract

½ teaspoon pure vanilla extract

2½ cups (340g) unbleached all-purpose flour

1 teaspoon baking powder

½ teaspoon baking soda

½ teaspoon kosher salt

1½ cups dried cranberries

FILLING

4 ounces (113g) cream cheese, at room temperature

4 tablespoons (½ stick/57g) unsalted butter, at room temperature

1½ cups (176g) confectioners' sugar

1 teaspoon pure vanilla extract

Pinch of kosher salt

Adjust an oven rack to the middle position and preheat the oven to 350°F (175°C).

MAKE THE WHOOPIE COOKIES: In a large bowl, use a silicone spatula to cream together the butter and granulated sugar. Add the egg and mix until completely combined with the butter. Stir in the orange zest, buttermilk, orange extract, and vanilla.

In a separate bowl, whisk together the flour, baking powder, baking soda, and salt. Add half of the flour mixture to the wet ingredients and use a silicone spatula to fold together. Once the flour has fully combined with the wet ingredients, add the remaining flour mixture to the bowl. Mix until just combined. Do not overmix. Gently fold in the dried cranberries until they are well distributed throughout the batter.

Line two baking sheets with parchment paper. Using a 1-ounce cookie scoop or two large spoons, drop 2-tablespoon amounts of batter onto the prepared sheets 1½ inches apart.

Bake until the whoopie cookies have puffed up and are slightly golden brown, 15 to 17 minutes. Remove from the oven and let the whoopie cookies cool, about 5 minutes.

MEANWHILE, MAKE THE FILLING: In a large mixing bowl, use a silicone spatula to mix the cream cheese and butter together until well blended. Gradually stir in the confectioners' sugar until combined. Stir in the vanilla and salt.

Using a small offset spatula or a butter knife, spread about 1½ tablespoons of cream cheese filling on the flat side of one whoopie cookie and sandwich with the flat side of another whoopie cookie. Repeat with the remaining filling and cookies.

The unfilled whoopie cookies can be stored in an airtight container at room temperature for up to 5 days. The filling can be stored in an airtight container in the refrigerator for up to 5 days. Remove the filling from the refrigerator and allow it to come to room temperature before spreading on the whoopie cookies.

LEMON-BLUEBERRY WHOOPIE PIES

MAKES NINE OR TEN 1½-INCH WHOOPIE PIES

By the fourth grade, I was cooking in the kitchen unsupervised. I started out making relatively basic dishes such as cheese omelets, cupcakes, pudding, and drop biscuits, but blueberry muffins were my favorite. I would use Jiffy mix, and after making the batter I'd pick out the tiny balls of imitation blueberries and pop them in my mouth. My dad would yell at me to stop—"The actual muffins won't have any blueberries!" Along with my muffin, I'd always eat a lemon yogurt on the side, my favorite flavor. Lemon and blueberries are still one of my most beloved pairings. In these whoopie pies, the slightly tart lemon accentuates the blueberries with their brightness.

WHOOPIE COOKIES

8 tablespoons (1 stick/113g) unsalted butter, at room temperature

1 cup (200g) granulated sugar

1 large egg, at room temperature

½ cup (126g) buttermilk

Grated zest of 2 lemons

½ teaspoon pure lemon extract

½ teaspoon pure vanilla extract

2½ cups (340g) unbleached all-purpose flour

½ teaspoon baking soda

1 teaspoon baking powder

½ teaspoon kosher salt

1½ cups blueberries

FILLING

4 ounces (113g) cream cheese, at room temperature

4 tablespoons (½ stick/57g) unsalted butter, at room temperature

1½ cups (176g) confectioners' sugar

1 teaspoon pure vanilla extract

Pinch of kosher salt

Adjust an oven rack to the middle position and preheat the oven to 350°F (175°C).

MAKE THE WHOOPIE COOKIES: In a large bowl, use a silicone spatula to cream together the butter and granulated sugar. Add the egg and mix until completely combined. Stir in the buttermilk, lemon zest, lemon extract, and vanilla.

In a separate bowl, whisk together the flour, baking soda, baking powder, and salt. Add half of the flour mixture to the wet ingredients and use the spatula to fold together. Once combined, add the remaining flour mixture and mix until just combined. Do not overmix. Gently fold in the blueberries until well distributed.

Line two baking sheets with parchment paper. Using a 1-ounce cookie scoop or two large spoons, drop 2-tablespoon amounts of batter onto the prepared sheets 1½ inches apart.

Bake until the whoopie cookies have puffed and the center is dry, 15 to 17 minutes. Remove from the oven and let the whoopie cookies cool, about 5 minutes.

MEANWHILE, MAKE THE FILLING: In a large bowl, use a silicone spatula to mix the cream cheese and butter together until well blended. Gradually stir in the confectioners' sugar until combined. Stir in the vanilla and salt.

Using a small offset spatula or a butter knife, spread about 1½ tablespoons of cream cheese filling on the flat side of one whoopie cookie and sandwich with the flat side of another whoopie cookie. Repeat with the remaining filling and cookies.

The unfilled whoopie cookies can be stored in an airtight container at room temperature for up to 5 days. The filling can be stored in an airtight container in the refrigerator for up to 5 days. Remove the filling from the refrigerator and allow it to come to room temperature before spreading on the whoopie cookies.

SEEMA R. HINGORANI

GIRLS WHO INVEST

As a kid growing up in Norwalk, Connecticut, one of Seema's favorite shows was *Perry Mason* on TV.

She loved the idea of strutting about a courtroom and arguing cases, and resolved to become a lawyer. She entered Yale as a psychology and philosophy major with the end goal of graduating from law school and practicing corporate law. She figured that since she was interested in corporate law, she should take a year off between undergrad and law school to work on Wall Street.

Seema landed a job at a small boutique investment outfit on Wall Street and quickly realized that the number crunching wasn't for her. She felt as though she were at an impasse and asked her mentor for guidance. They sat down and created a pros and cons list and, after examining it, they realized that what she really enjoyed was writing and presenting research reports that determined the value of a company. It seemed that her psychology and philosophy degrees came in handy for recognizing investment patterns.

The market changes daily and Seema loved waking up and solving a new puzzle in the stock market as a junior investment analyst. Two years later, she entered the Wharton School at the University of Pennsylvania, where she earned her MBA in finance. She was doing what she loved and it showed—after grad school, she built an impressive career as an equity analyst with T. Rowe Price before moving on as a partner, portfolio manager, and senior equity analyst at several hedge funds. Then in 2010, Seema moved from the private sector to the public sector and ultimately became the chief investment officer for the New York City Retirement Systems. Asset managers and investment firms from all over would fly to New York to meet with Seema in an attempt to pitch their firm to help manage that money. She'd meet with the firms, listen to their presentations, and inevitably ask, "Where are all the women on your investment team?"

Every single firm told Seema that they never, ever receive résumés from women. She did not completely judge or blame these firms because she knew it was a pipeline problem, but she also knew that investment firms had a culture that was not so welcoming to women—less than 5 percent of industry assets are managed by women.

In September of 2014, she wrote an op-ed piece for Bloomberg News, in which she talked about the challenges of recruiting more women into the investment business and proposed a program that would offer four weeks of intensive training for college sophomores immediately followed by a six-week paid internship at leading investment firms. If they wanted to continue their investing journey, they could return to school and have enough time to enroll in finance-related courses. She called the idea "Girls Who Invest." Here, young women could be trained, mentored, educated, prepared, guided, and set off into the industry—and, most important, these women would never need to feel alone in this historically male-dominated space.

Seema wrote the article and thought that she was done. But after the article was released, she received hundreds of letters and emails from college professors and firms asking her to please activate a program like this.

So, in 2015, she started the tuition-free pilot program at her alma mater, Wharton, with thirty women from different colleges across the United States. Girls Who Invest quickly expanded and also started offering online programs to other colleges across the country and, since 2016, fourteen hundred women have come through her programs. Seventy percent of the participants are women of color, 22 percent of the women come from economically disadvantaged backgrounds, and over 70 different majors were represented, not just finance, economics, or business. Most impressive, 75 percent of the women who complete the Girls Who Invest ten-week intensive remain in the investment industry after their first internship postgraduation.

The recipe Wealthy Whoopie Pies celebrates Seema's efforts to create and maintain gender diversity in asset management. The ingredients in the whoopie pies include rich cashews, cardamom, and chocolate, all inspired by kaju katli, a popular fudge-like Indian dessert traditionally gifted during Diwali, the festival of lights. As it is the most expensive of mithai (sweets), receiving the gift of kaju katli is a significant measure of one's social standing. These whoopie pies are perfect for celebrating the wealth of knowledge and resources that Girls Who Invest provides for many young women who wish to thrive in the world of investments.

WEALTHY WHOOPIE PIES

MAKES TEN TO TWELVE 1½-INCH WHOOPIE PIES

WHOOPIE COOKIES

12 tablespoons (1½ sticks/127g) unsalted butter, at room temperature

1½ cups (300g) granulated sugar

2 large eggs, at room temperature

1½ cups (385g) buttermilk

1 teaspoon vanilla extract

3 cups (605g) unbleached all-purpose flour

¾ cup (64g) Dutch process cocoa powder

1 teaspoon baking powder

1 teaspoon baking soda

1 teaspoon ground cardamom

1 teaspoon kosher salt

FILLING

¾ cup (180g) creamy cashew butter, at room temperature

4 tablespoons (½ stick/57g) unsalted butter, at room temperature

2 cups (235g) confectioners' sugar

½ teaspoon ground cardamom

1 teaspoon vanilla extract

Pinch of kosher salt

GARNISH

1 cup (137g) cashews, finely chopped

Adjust the rack to the middle position and preheat the oven to 350°F (175°C).

MAKE THE WHOOPIE COOKIES: In a large bowl, use a silicone spatula to cream together the butter and granulated sugar. Add the eggs and mix until completely combined. Beat until the mixture is fluffy, about 4 minutes. Pour in the buttermilk and vanilla extract and mix until well combined.

In a separate bowl, whisk together the flour, cocoa powder, baking powder, baking soda, cardamom, and salt. Add half of the flour mixture to the wet ingredients and use a silicone spatula to fold together. Once the flour has fully combined with the wet ingredients, add the remaining flour mixture to the bowl and mix until just combined (do not overmix).

Line two baking sheets with parchment paper. Using a 1-ounce cookie scoop or two large spoons, drop 2-tablespoon amounts of batter onto the prepared sheets 1½ inches apart.

Bake until the whoopie pie cookies have puffed and are set, 15 to 17 minutes. Remove from the oven and let the whoopie pies cool, about 5 minutes.

MEANWHILE, MAKE THE FILLING: In a large bowl, use a silicone spatula to mix the cashew butter and butter together until well blended. Gradually stir in the confectioners' sugar until combined. Stir in the cardamom, vanilla, and salt.

Using a small offset spatula or a butter knife, spread about 1½ tablespoons of cashew butter filling on the flat side of one whoopie cookie and sandwich with the flat side of another whoopie cookie. Repeat with the remaining filling and cookies.

Place the chopped cashews in a small bowl. Roll each whoopie pie in the cashews until the nuts adhere to the frosting between pies. The whoopie pies are best eaten the day of assembling.

You can make the whoopie pie cookies up to 5 days ahead and store them in an airtight container at room temperature. The filling can be refrigerated in a covered container for up to 5 days as well. Remove the filling from the refrigerator and allow it to come to room temperature before spreading on the whoopie pie cookies.

CHURRO WHOOPIE PIES

MAKES TEN TO TWELVE 1½-INCH WHOOPIE PIES

My mom and I frequent chef Rick Bayless's XOCO, a casual-modern Mexican restaurant in Chicago, for their *tortas*. We always call my brother, Mazi, and ask what he wants—and it's always (and only) an order of churros. That's it. Probably because XOCO makes some of the freshest and best churros in the city. Crispy and covered in cinnamon and sugar on the outside and tender and eggy on the inside, this deep-fried pastry is usually served with a small bowl of hot chocolate for dipping or is sometimes filled with cream or fruit jams. These whoopie pies retain all of the cinnamon-sugary elements of a classic churro in a pillowy-soft package for bites of goodness that will make you fall in love.

WHOOPIE COOKIES

8 tablespoons (1 stick/113g) unsalted butter, at room temperature

1½ cups (300g) granulated sugar

1 large egg, at room temperature

½ cup (126g) buttermilk

Grated zest of 1 orange

1 teaspoon pure vanilla extract

2½ cups (340g) unbleached all-purpose flour

2½ teaspoons ground cinnamon

1 teaspoon baking powder

½ teaspoon baking soda

½ teaspoon kosher salt

TOPPING

3 tablespoons granulated sugar

2 teaspoons ground cinnamon

Juice of 1 orange

FILLING

4 ounces (113g) cream cheese, at room temperature

4 tablespoons (½ stick/57g) unsalted butter, at room temperature

1½ cups (176g) confectioners' sugar

1 teaspoon pure vanilla extract

Pinch of kosher salt

Adjust an oven rack to the middle position and preheat the oven to 350°F (175°C).

MAKE THE WHOOPIE COOKIES: In a large bowl, use a silicone spatula to cream the butter and granulated sugar. Add the egg and stir until completely combined with the butter and sugar. Stir in the buttermilk, orange zest, and vanilla.

In a separate bowl, whisk together the flour, cinnamon, baking powder, baking soda, and salt. Add half of the flour mixture to the wet ingredients and use a silicone spatula to fold together. Once the flour has fully combined with the wet ingredients, add the remaining flour mixture to the bowl. Mix until just combined. Do not overmix.

Line two baking sheets with parchment paper. Using a 1-ounce cookie scoop or two large spoons, drop 2-tablespoon amounts of batter onto the prepared sheets 1½ inches apart.

Bake until the whoopie cookies have puffed up and are slightly golden brown, 15 to 17 minutes. Remove from the oven and let the whoopie cookies cool, about 5 minutes.

WHILE THE COOKIES BAKE, MAKE THE TOPPING: In a small bowl, whisk together the sugar and cinnamon.

RECIPE CONTINUES >>

CHURRO WHOOPIE PIES *continued*

While the cookies are still warm, use a pastry brush to dab the tops of the cookies with orange juice and then sprinkle with the cinnamon-sugar so they are generously coated.

WHILE THE WHOOPIE COOKIES COOL, MAKE THE FILLING: In a large bowl, use a silicone spatula to mix the cream cheese and butter together until well blended. Gradually stir in the confectioners' sugar until combined. Stir in the vanilla and salt.

Using a small offset spatula or a butter knife, spread about 1½ tablespoons of cream cheese filling on the flat side of one whoopie cookie and sandwich with the flat side of another whoopie cookie. Repeat with the remaining filling and cookies.

The unfilled whoopie cookies can be stored in an airtight container at room temperature for up to 5 days. The filling can be stored in an airtight container in the refrigerator for up to 5 days. Remove the filling from the refrigerator and allow it to come to room temperature before spreading on the whoopie cookies.

BONUS: Warm up some Hot Fudge Sauce (page 217) or dulce de leche topping to dip your churro whoopie pies into. It might get messy, but when you're eating something this good, who cares?

CHOCOLATE-RASPBERRY WHOOPIE PIES

MAKES TEN TO TWELVE 1½-INCH WHOOPIE PIES

Chocolate whoopie pies are a New England classic. The dessert was named Maine's state treat, where they are known to be paired with another Maine delicacy: lobster rolls!

Chocolate and raspberries are an ultimate match. The raspberries cut through the rich chocolate and add a fresh brightness to the whoopie pies.

WHOOPIE COOKIES

12 tablespoons (1½ sticks/170g) unsalted butter, at room temperature

1½ cups (300g) granulated sugar

2 large eggs, at room temperature

1½ cups (378g) buttermilk

1 teaspoon pure vanilla extract

3 cups (408g) unbleached all-purpose flour

¾ cup (60g) Dutch process cocoa powder

1 teaspoon baking powder

1 teaspoon baking soda

1 teaspoon kosher salt

FILLING

4 ounces (113g) cream cheese, at room temperature

4 tablespoons (½ stick/57g) unsalted butter, at room temperature

2 cups (234g) confectioners' sugar

1 teaspoon pure vanilla extract

Pinch of kosher salt

1 cup raspberries

Adjust an oven rack to the middle position and preheat the oven to 350°F (175°C).

MAKE THE WHOOPIE COOKIES: In a large bowl, use a silicone spatula to cream together the butter and granulated sugar. Add the eggs and mix until completely combined. Mix in the buttermilk and vanilla until well combined.

In a separate bowl, whisk together the flour, cocoa powder, baking powder, baking soda, and salt. Add half of the flour mixture to the wet ingredients and fold together until well combined, then add the remaining flour mixture to the bowl. Mix until just combined. Do not overmix.

Line two baking sheets with parchment paper. Using a 1-ounce cookie scoop or two large spoons, drop 2-tablespoon amounts of batter onto the prepared sheets 1½ inches apart.

Bake until the whoopie cookies have puffed and are set, 15 to 17 minutes. Remove from the oven and cool for about 5 minutes.

MEANWHILE, MAKE THE FILLING: In a large bowl, use a silicone spatula to mix the cream cheese and butter together until well blended. Gradually stir in the confectioners' sugar until combined. Stir in the vanilla and salt. Add the raspberries and mix until the filling turns deep pink.

Using a small offset spatula or a butter knife, spread about 1½ tablespoons of filling on the flat side of one whoopie cookie and sandwich with the flat side of another. Repeat with the remaining filling and cookies.

The unfilled whoopie cookies can be stored in an airtight container at room temperature for up to 5 days. The filling can be stored in an airtight container in the refrigerator for up to 5 days. Remove the filling from the refrigerator and allow it to come to room temperature before spreading on the whoopie cookies.

TEQUILA LIME WHOOPIE PIES

MAKES NINE OR TEN 1½-INCH WHOOPIE PIES

Baking with booze always makes a treat better. These whoopie pies pack a punch with the addition of the lime zest and tequila. They're the perfect sweet finish to enjoy after eating the Deep-Dish Chilaquiles Quiche (page 123).

WHOOPIE COOKIES

8 tablespoons (1 stick/113g) unsalted butter, at room temperature

1½ cups (300g) granulated sugar

1 large egg, at room temperature

½ cup (126g) buttermilk

Grated zest of 1 lime

1 teaspoon pure vanilla extract

2½ cups (340g) all-purpose flour

1½ teaspoons baking powder

FILLING

4 ounces (113g) cream cheese, at room temperature

4 tablespoons (½ stick/57g) unsalted butter, at room temperature

Grated zest of 2 limes

3 cups (352g) confectioners' sugar

¼ cup (60g) blanco tequila

1 teaspoon pure vanilla extract

Pinch of kosher salt

Adjust an oven rack to the middle position and preheat the oven to 350°F (175°C).

MAKE THE WHOOPIE COOKIES: In a large bowl, use a silicone spatula to cream together the butter and granulated sugar. Add the egg and stir until completely combined. Mix in the buttermilk, lime zest, and vanilla.

In a separate bowl, whisk together the flour and baking powder. Add half of the flour mixture to the wet ingredients and use a silicone spatula to fold together until fully combined. Add the remaining flour mixture to the bowl and mix until just combined. Do not overmix.

Line two baking sheets with parchment. Using a 1-ounce scoop or a large spoon, drop 2-tablespoon amounts of batter onto the prepared sheets 1½ inches apart.

Bake the whoopie cookies until they are pale in color and look slightly underbaked, 15 to 17 minutes. If the whoopie cookies are overbaked, the whoopie pies will be hard and chewy. We want fluffy and airy whoopie pies! Remove from the oven and let cool for about 5 minutes.

MAKE THE FILLING: In a large bowl, mix the cream cheese, butter, and lime zest together until well blended. Gradually stir in the confectioners' sugar until combined. Mix in the tequila, vanilla, and salt.

Using a small offset spatula or a butter knife, spread about 1½ tablespoons of the filling on the flat side of each cookie and sandwich with the flat side of another. Repeat with the remaining filling and cookies.

The unfilled whoopie cookies can be stored in an airtight container at room temperature for up to 5 days. The filling can be refrigerated in an airtight container for up to 5 days. Let the filling come to room temperature before spreading on the whoopie cookies.

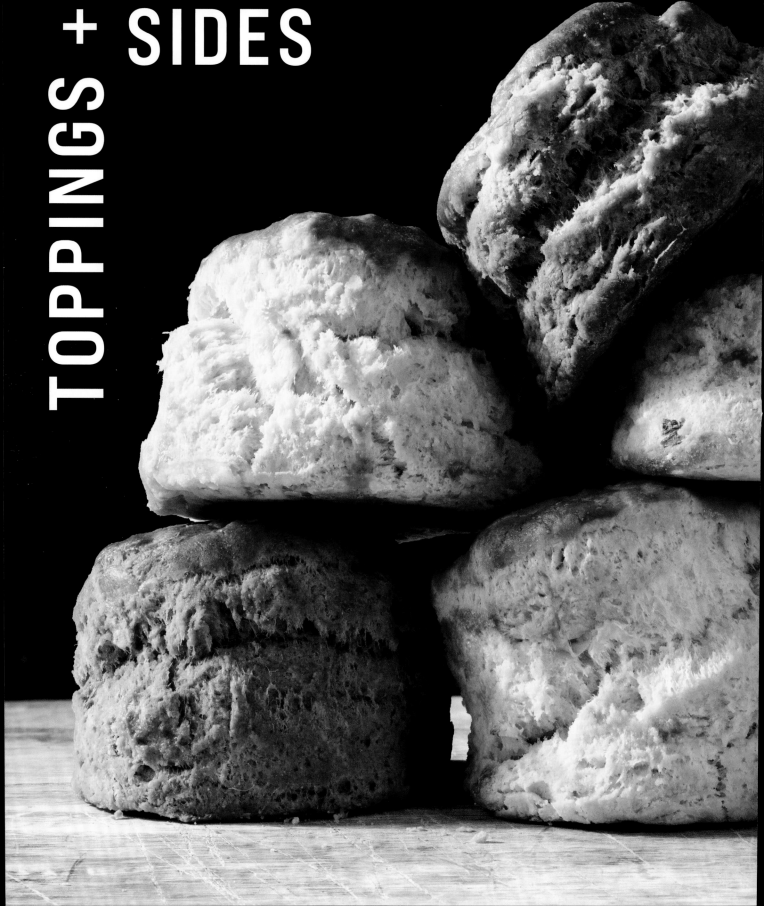

BILLOWY BISCUITS

MAKES 12 TO 14 BISCUITS

4 cups (544g) unbleached all-purpose flour

2 tablespoons baking powder

2 teaspoons kosher salt

1 teaspoon baking soda

24 tablespoons (3 sticks/336g) very cold unsalted butter, cut into ½-inch pieces

8 ounces (225g) very cold cream cheese, cut into 2-inch pieces

1½ cups (378g) buttermilk

1 large egg

Flour, for rolling out

I occasionally cater for film crews. On one shoot, the guy running the craft services trailer asked me, "Chef! What else do you make? I know you actually make more than pies and quiches."

I slowly turned my head toward him, "Well, actually, I . . . umm . . ."—then I chuckled, knowing he wasn't ready for this deliciousness—"I make biscuits."

"Word!" he exclaimed. "Bet! Bring four dozen of 'em tomorrow . . . matter of fact—make it six. And bring something to go with them."

The next morning I placed several trays of biscuits along with my Lemon-Ginger Honey (page 199) and Blueberry-Mint Preserves (page 213) on the serving table just outside of the show's set.

Later that day I received a text: "Chef. Those biscuits."

I smiled.

"Can you bring some more tomorrow?"

I showed up to set the next day with a fresh batch of biscuits. A few crew members were there waiting for me to make the drop.

One crew member announced into his walkie-talkie, "The Biscuit Lady just got here. Hurry up before they're gone." That's it. I had them hooked.

These biscuits are *the* business! The secret is the cream cheese. It helps the biscuits retain their moisture and bake up a crunchy exterior and a soft, melt-in-your-mouth interior. If you have a convection option for your oven, I recommend using it. The fan circulating the air inside the oven allows the biscuits to brown more easily and rise high. That said, note that the baking time for the convection oven version here is nearly double the time it takes for the conventional oven version, as the oven is set to a lower temperature.

Adjust an oven rack to the middle position and preheat the oven to 400°F (205°C). If your oven has a convection option, preheat to 325°F (165°C). Line a baking sheet with parchment paper.

In a large bowl, whisk together the flour, baking powder, salt, and baking soda. Add the butter and cream cheese. Use a pastry cutter, a fork, or your fingers to cut the butter and cream cheese into the flour until the pieces are no bigger than a pea.

Pour in the buttermilk and, using your hands, combine the flour and buttermilk together until the mixture is no longer dry. With the dough still in the bowl, turn and fold the dough over onto itself until the dough is sticky and the flour is fully incorporated with the dough. If the dough is too dry or if there is a bit of flour in the bottom of the bowl that won't mix with the dough, add ½ tablespoon of buttermilk to the bottom of the bowl to help the flour get incorporated.

Generously flour your work surface with 1 to 2 tablespoons of flour. Place the biscuit dough on the work surface and, using your hands, knead the dough together while pinching any tears or lines in the dough. Add another dash of flour if your work surface becomes sticky.

Flour a rolling pin and your hands. Set a small bowl of flour near your work surface. Roll out the dough until it is 1 inch thick. Using a 3-inch round biscuit cutter (or a similar size of overturned drinking glass), dip the biscuit cutter into the bowl of flour and then cut out a biscuit round. Repeat, dipping the cutter in the flour between the cuts and cutting biscuits as close together as possible to minimize the amount of scraps.

Collect the scraps and knead them together, then press 1 inch thick and cut a few more biscuits (discard any remaining scraps). Transfer the biscuits to the prepared baking sheet.

RECIPE CONTINUES >>

In a small bowl, whisk together the egg and 1 tablespoon water. Using a pastry brush, apply the egg wash onto the tops of the biscuits.

In a conventional oven at 400°F (205°C): Bake the biscuits for 20 minutes. Reduce the oven temperature to 350°F (175°C) and continue baking until the center of the biscuit is set, 10 to 12 minutes.

In a convection oven at 325°F (165°C): Bake without reducing the oven temperature until golden brown, about 1 hour.

Store in an airtight container or zip-top bag at room temperature for up to 4 days.

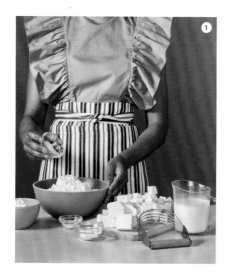

GOAT CHEESE + CHIVE BISCUITS

MAKES 12 TO 14 BISCUITS

Billowy Biscuits (page 193) are my favorite for both sweet and savory dishes, but sometimes I want biscuits with a savoriness that also offers a more aromatic experience. Adding chives and goat cheese to the biscuits does just that while retaining the crunchy exterior and light, airy interior.

4 cups (544g) unbleached all-purpose flour

½ cup (16g) finely chopped fresh chives

2 tablespoons (27g) baking powder

2 teaspoons kosher salt

1 teaspoon baking soda

24 tablespoons (3 sticks/339g) very cold unsalted butter, cut into ½-inch pieces

4 ounces (113g) very cold cream cheese, cut into 2-inch pieces

4 ounces (113g) goat cheese

1½ cups (315g) buttermilk, plus more as needed

1 large egg

Flour, for rolling out

Adjust an oven rack to the middle position and preheat the oven to 400°F (205°C). If your oven has a convection option, preheat to 325°F (165°C). Line a baking sheet with parchment paper.

In a large bowl, whisk together the flour, chives, baking powder, salt, and baking soda. Add the butter, cream cheese, and goat cheese. Use a pastry cutter, a fork, or your fingers to cut the butter and cheeses into the flour until the pieces are no bigger than a pea.

Pour in the buttermilk and, using your hands, combine the flour and buttermilk until the mixture is no longer dry. With the dough still in the bowl, turn and fold the dough over onto itself until the dough is sticky and the flour is fully incorporated with the dough. If the dough is too dry or if there is a bit of flour in the bottom of the bowl that won't mix with the dough, add ½ tablespoon of buttermilk to the bottom of the bowl to help the flour get incorporated.

Generously flour your work surface with 1 to 2 tablespoons of flour. Place the biscuit dough on the work surface and, using your hands, knead the dough together while pinching any tears or lines in the dough. Add another dash of flour if your work surface becomes sticky.

Flour a rolling pin and your hands. Set a small bowl of flour near your work surface. Roll out the dough until it is 1 inch thick. Using a 3-inch round biscuit cutter (or a similar size of overturned drinking glass), dip the biscuit cutter in the flour and then cut out a biscuit round. Repeat, dipping the cutter in the flour between the cuts and cutting biscuits as close together as possible to minimize the number of scraps.

Collect the scraps and knead them together, then press 1 inch thick and cut a few more biscuits (discard any remaining scraps). Transfer the biscuits to the prepared baking sheet.

In a small bowl, whisk together the egg and 1 tablespoon water. Using a pastry brush, apply the egg wash onto the tops of the biscuits.

In a conventional oven at 400°F (205°C): Bake the biscuits for 20 minutes. Reduce the oven temperature to 350°F (175°C) and continue baking until the center of the biscuit is set, 10 to 12 minutes.

In a convection oven at 325°F (165°C): Bake without reducing the oven temperature until golden brown, about 1 hour.

Store in an airtight container or zip-top bag at room temperature for up to 4 days.

SWEET POTATO BISCUITS

MAKES 7 OR 8 INDIVIDUAL SERVINGS

I began making drop biscuits from a Bisquick box when I was in the fourth grade. They were not very aesthetically pleasing—but it didn't matter. I made them, and I was damn proud.

My dad would warm up a little syrup in the microwave and pour it into a bowl. I would saturate the biscuits in the thick, sweet brown liquid. A part of me did that because I loved the sweetness, but a part of me also did that because my little drop biscuits were *dry*, baby!

Thank goodness for growth, because my biscuit-making skills have clearly evolved with age and experience. Although my biscuits are now extremely moist, there is still a yearning for a bit of sweetness.

Now, instead of dipping my biscuits in syrup, I make them sweet the natural way—by adding sweet potatoes (well, a couple tablespoons of brown sugar helps, too!). These biscuits are extra tender, soft, and slightly sweet.

1½ cups (204g) unbleached all-purpose flour

2 tablespoons packed light brown sugar

1 tablespoon baking powder

1 teaspoon baking soda

½ teaspoon ground cinnamon

8 tablespoons (1 stick/113g) very cold salted butter, cut into ½-inch cubes

¾ cup mashed, cooked, and peeled sweet potato

½ cup (126g) buttermilk, plus more as needed

1 large egg

Flour, for shaping

Adjust an oven rack to the middle position and preheat to 425°F (220°C).

In a large bowl, whisk together the flour, brown sugar, baking powder, baking soda, and cinnamon. Add the butter. Use a pastry cutter or your fingers to cut the butter into the flour until the pieces are the size of peas. Add the mashed sweet potatoes and use your hands to mix until well combined.

Make a well in the center of the dough and add the buttermilk. Still using your hands, combine the buttermilk and sweet potato mixture. Turn and fold the dough over onto itself until it comes together and the flour is fully incorporated with the buttermilk. If the dough is too dry or if there is a bit of flour in the bottom of the bowl that won't mix with the dough, add ½ tablespoon of buttermilk to the bottom of the bowl until the flour dissolves into the dough.

Knead the dough on a generously floured work surface, pinching together any tears until the dough is smooth. Reflour the surface as needed.

Set a small bowl of flour near your work surface. Pat the dough with floured hands (don't use a rolling pin—the dough is tender, and it could create tears) for a 1-inch-thick and 5-inch-wide rectangle. Using a 3-inch round biscuit cutter (or a similar size of overturned drinking glass), cut out biscuits by dipping your biscuit cutter in the cup of flour and then cutting out a round, dipping the cutter in the flour in between the cuts.

Collect and knead any scrap dough pieces together and form a 1-inch slab of dough. Continue cutting biscuits. Discard any remaining scraps. Transfer the biscuits to a parchment paper-lined baking sheet.

In a small bowl, whisk together the egg and 1 tablespoon of water. Use a pastry brush to egg wash the biscuit tops.

Bake until the biscuits are golden brown and firm to the touch, 12 to 14 minutes. Remove from the oven and cool slightly before serving.

The biscuits will keep in an airtight container or zip-top bag at room temperature for up to 4 days.

LEMON-GINGER HONEY

MAKES 2 CUPS

This topping is so easy to make and is a favorite at Justice of the Pies. The combination comes directly from my grandma Billingslea, who would give it to me when I was sick: warmed lemon juice infused with ginger stirred into a mug of straight honey. Now I use this trio as a spread that goes beautifully with Billowy Biscuits (page 193) and is also excellent as a topping for pancakes and crêpes; served alongside cheese and crackers, grilled fruit, or root vegetables; used as a base marinade for meat and fish; and of course for stirring into hot tea.

2 cups (680g) raw unfiltered honey

5 tablespoons (48g) finely grated fresh ginger

Grated zest of 2 large lemons

Juice of ½ lemon (optional)

In a small bowl, stir together the honey, ginger, and lemon zest until well blended. If the honey is especially thick, thin it out with the lemon juice, if desired. Store in a covered glass jar in the refrigerator for up to 6 months.

BONUS: If the honey crystallizes, place a small pot filled halfway with water on a burner set over medium-high heat. When the water boils, turn off the heat and set the jar containing the honey in the water (with the lid on) Allow it to sit until liquefied, 15 to 20 minutes. Remove from the water and stir the honey.

BROWN SUGAR + OAT CRUMBLE

MAKES 1½ CUPS (ENOUGH TO TOP ONE 9-INCH PIE)

This crumble is intended to replace the top crust of a pie. You can also add dried fruits and nuts to the crumble if you like—or turn the crumble into granola! See Customize Your Crumble and Make Granola (below) for some fun and delicious variations.

1 cup (85g) rolled oats (not instant or quick-cooking)

¼ cup (55g) packed light brown sugar

⅓ cup (45g) unbleached all-purpose flour

4 tablespoons (½ stick/57g) unsalted butter, melted

In a medium bowl, stir together the rolled oats, brown sugar, and flour with a silicone spatula. Pour in the melted butter and toss together until the mixture is no longer dry. Use immediately after making.

Place the crumble on top of a pie and bake until the topping is browned. Follow the directions in each recipe that calls for this topping.

CUSTOMIZE YOUR CRUMBLE AND MAKE GRANOLA

Here are my favorite ways to turn your crumble into granola.
    For all granola: Preheat the oven to 350°F (176°C). For each version, mix all the dry ingredients (oats, light brown sugar, flour, plus your choice of nuts, spices, and dried fruit) together, then stir in the melted butter and honey until the mixture is no longer dry and you have large and small clusters. Sprinkle evenly on a parchment-lined baking sheet and bake until browned, 20 to 25 minutes.

ORANGE + CRANBERRY SPICE

4 cups (340g) rolled oats

2¾ cups (374g) unbleached all-purpose flour

1 cup (220g) packed light brown sugar

1 cup dried cranberries

1 cup (100g) pecans, chopped

Grated zest of 1 orange

1 teaspoon ground cinnamon

1 teaspoon ground ginger

16 tablespoons (2 sticks/227g) unsalted butter, melted

½ cup (178g) honey

TROPICAL DREAM

4 cups (340g) rolled oats

2¾ cups (374g) unbleached all-purpose flour

1 cup golden raisins

1 cup (220g) packed light brown sugar

1 cup (116g) sweetened coconut flakes

1 teaspoon ground allspice

16 tablespoons (2 sticks/227g) unsalted butter, melted

½ cup (178g) honey

Mix in after baking and while the mixture is still warm:

½ cup dried banana slices

½ cup dried pineapple, diced

YOU'RE SUCH A NUT

4 cups (340g) rolled oats

2¾ cups (374g) unbleached all-purpose flour

1 cup (108g) slivered almonds

1 cup (150g) cashews

1 cup (220g) packed light brown sugar

½ cup dried apricots, chopped

½ cup dried cranberries

1 teaspoon ground cinnamon

1 teaspoon ground nutmeg

16 tablespoons (2 sticks/227g) unsalted butter, melted

½ cup (178g) honey

Mix in after baking and while the mixture is still warm:

1 cup (173g) mini semisweet chocolate chips

MORNING PERSON

4 cups (340g) rolled oats

2¾ cups (374g) unbleached all-purpose flour

1 cup (220g) packed light brown sugar

1 cup (100g) pecans, chopped

1 cup raisins

1 cup (117g) walnuts, chopped

1 tablespoon (4g) ground espresso beans

16 tablespoons (2 sticks/227g) unsalted butter, melted

½ cup (178g) honey

Mix in after baking and while the mixture is still warm:

½ cup (86g) butterscotch chips

½ cup (86g) mini semisweet chocolate chips

BROUSSARD PRALINE SAUCE

MAKES 1¼ CUPS

2 tablespoons unsalted butter

¼ cup (50g) granulated sugar

1¼ cups (295g) heavy cream

Every year for Fat Tuesday, my dad would have a king cake and a tin of pralines shipped to our house from New Orleans. I don't recall us ever actually eating the cake. His reasons for purchasing a king cake were merely so that *he* could find the baby—you see, there is always a plastic baby baked into a king cake and whoever finds it is crowned "king" for the day. Dad always wanted to be king.

I was never in the mood to play these king cake games. I never desired the cake either. Instead, I always had my eyes set on the tin of pralines.

Pralines are a confection that consists of sugar, milk, butter, and pecans, but there are other praline fillings that are amazing as well: They can include coconut, chocolate, and coffee and milk (café au lait). To me, the taste and the consistency of a pecan praline are similar to those of nutty fudge, but so much better. So, I turned it into a sauce that's not quite as sweet as caramel but rather has a deep caramel and toffee-like favor that's so good over the Bleu Cheese Praline Pear Pie (page 18), with Billowy Biscuits (page 193), or on waffles or pancakes instead of maple syrup.

In a large heavy-bottomed pot or Dutch oven, melt the butter over medium heat. Stir in the sugar until it's fully coated in butter. Continue cooking the sugar, stirring every 2 to 3 minutes, until it reaches deep amber brown, 15 to 20 minutes.

Stir in the heavy cream—the browned sugar will get hard once the cold cream hits it—just trust and continue to stir until the sugar dissolves. Reduce the heat to low and allow the mixture to simmer. The sauce along the sides of the pot will start to form a thicker film. Keep whisking and scraping along the sides of the pot, whisking the thick parts back into the center of the filling, until the mixture is an amber color, 30 to 45 minutes.

Remove from the heat and allow the mixture to cool for 20 minutes. Pour the mixture into a glass jar with a lid (a mason jar or something similar works best). Once it comes to room temperature, the consistency of the praline sauce is spreadable. You can leave it at room temperature for up to 3 days—or refrigerate for up to 1 month. To quickly bring the praline sauce back to room temperature, fill a saucepan with a few inches of water, bring to a boil, then turn off the heat and set the jar (with the lid on) in the water for 15 to 20 minutes. For a pourable consistency, leave the jar in the water for 25 to 30 minutes. Stir (it's normal for some butter to separate) before serving.

BONUS: Broussard Praline Sauce is amazing with vanilla ice cream. For an extra-fancy à la mode experience, top a slice of pie with a scoop of vanilla ice cream, drizzle with even more praline sauce, and add chopped walnuts as a crunchy garnish.

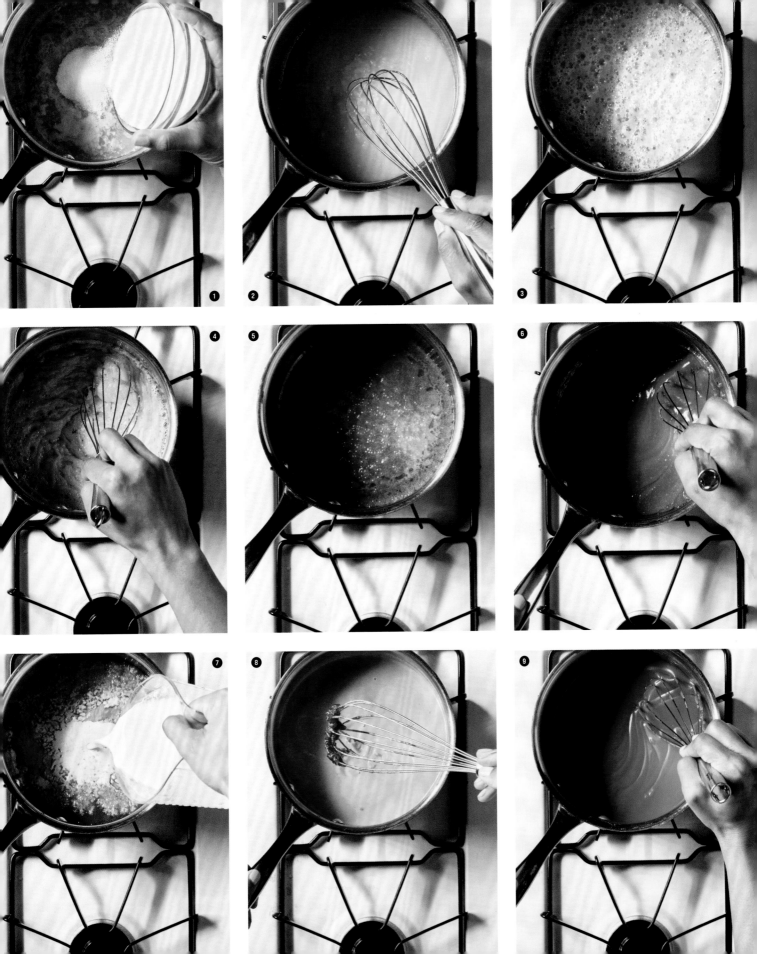

LEMON CURD

MAKES ½ CUP

4 large egg yolks

⅔ cup (134g) sugar

⅓ cup (76g) fresh lemon juice (2 or 3 lemons)

¼ teaspoon kosher salt

6 tablespoons (¾ stick/85g) unsalted butter

Finely grated zest of 2 medium lemons

Tart and sweet. I think that's how my dad once described me. Oh, wait, no—it was sugar and spice. Eh—same difference! Either way, we're talking about a study in sublime balance—that's how I think of lemon curd. I love it as a spread for Billowy Biscuits (page 193), as a pie filling, like the Lemon Espresso Pie (page 44), or over vanilla ice cream with a dash of herbes de Provence.

The key to making curd is using a double boiler, which is a heatproof bowl placed over a pot filled with softly simmering water to prevent direct heat from scorching the mixture and curdling the eggs.

I add lemon zest to brighten the curd and focus on its citrus infusion.

Fill a pot halfway with water and set over medium-high heat.

In a medium glass bowl, whisk together the egg yolks, sugar, lemon juice, and salt. Once the water boils, place the glass bowl on top of the pot and turn the heat down to low. Whisk the curd constantly until running a spoon across the top of the curd leaves a trail (even a loose one), 10 to 12 minutes.

Carefully remove the glass bowl from the pot and set aside. If the curd has any cooked egg bits (or looks lumpy), strain the filling through a fine-mesh sieve and into a medium bowl. Immediately whisk in the butter and lemon zest until the butter melts. Cover with plastic wrap so that it touches the top of the curd (this will prevent a film from forming as the curd cools). Don't worry if the curd looks thin—it will continue to thicken as it cools. Once the custard is cooled, transfer it to an airtight glass jar or container. Store in the refrigerator for up to 12 days.

SWEET POTATO CORNBREAD

MAKES ONE 10-INCH ROUND

My love for sweet potatoes is long-standing and as such I have a sweet potato recipe to suit all my moods. On a cold winter day in Chicago, I'll make the Sweet Potato + Lentil Pot Pie (page 95). When people ask me what is my favorite pie, Sweet Potato Praline (page 38) has always been my answer. When I want a touch of sweetness with a bit of savory, flaky bite, I head straight for the Sweet Potato Biscuits (page 198). And when I want something ultramoist and comforting, this sweet potato cornbread delivers.

2 large sweet potatoes (2 to 2½ pounds)

2 cups (272g) unbleached all-purpose flour

1 cup (145g) yellow cornmeal

1 cup (220g) packed light brown sugar

1 tablespoon baking powder

1 teaspoon ground cinnamon

1 teaspoon kosher salt

½ teaspoon ground nutmeg

4 large eggs

1½ cups (378g) buttermilk

1 teaspoon pure vanilla extract

12 tablespoons (1½ sticks/170g) unsalted butter, melted

Adjust an oven rack to the middle position and preheat the oven to 350°F (175°C).

Wrap the sweet potatoes with foil and place them on a baking sheet. Bake until the sweet potatoes are extremely soft and a knife inserted into each meets no resistance, about 2 hours.

Remove from the oven and cool for 20 minutes. Halve each potato lengthwise and use a spoon to scoop the potato flesh into a medium bowl. Using a potato masher, fork, or spoon, mash the potatoes until the flesh is completely creamy and there are no lumps. Discard any visible fibrous sweet potato strings. Cover the bowl with plastic wrap and refrigerate for 1 hour.

In a stand mixer fitted with the whisk attachment (or in a large bowl with a hand mixer), whisk together the flour, cornmeal, brown sugar, baking powder, cinnamon, salt, and nutmeg.

Add the eggs to the dry ingredients and whisk until well blended. Pour in the buttermilk and vanilla and mix until just combined. Measure out 2 cups of the mashed sweet potatoes (save the rest for another use, like Sweet Potato Biscuits, page 198). Add the sweet potatoes to the batter and mix until just combined. Add the melted butter and mix until well combined. Do not overmix.

Mist a 10-inch cast-iron skillet or a 7½ × 10½-inch baking dish with cooking spray. Scrape in the batter and use a spatula to smooth out the top.

Bake until the cornbread is golden brown, the center resists light pressure, and a cake tester inserted in the center comes out clean, 25 to 30 minutes.

Store in an airtight container in the refrigerator for up to 5 days.

BONUS: You can also bake this cornbread as muffins: Mist a 12-cup muffin tin or an extra-large/jumbo 6-cup muffin tin (or 6 ramekins) with cooking spray or line with muffin liners. Fill each cup until it's halfway full. Bake until golden brown and a cake tester inserted in the center comes out clean, 12 to 18 minutes (jumbo muffins may take a bit longer).

SALTED CARAMEL SAUCE

MAKES 2½ CUPS

A good caramel is both easy and hard to make. The ingredients are fairly simple, but the recipe requires considerable patience and attentiveness. This is my go-to sauce to top the Salted Caramel Peach Pie (page 21). I also drizzle it over vanilla ice cream, crème brûlée French toast, or even some fresh popcorn that has been topped with cheddar cheese powder—which is my take on the legendary "Chicago mix."

1 cup (235g) heavy cream
2 cups (400g) sugar
12 tablespoons (1½ sticks/170g) unsalted butter, cut into 12 pieces

1 teaspoon pure vanilla extract
1 teaspoon kosher salt

In a small saucepan, warm the heavy cream over medium-high heat until it is steaming, 3 to 5 minutes. Remove from the heat.

Set a medium saucepan over medium-high heat. Add the sugar and allow it to caramelize while constantly stirring with a silicone spatula. The sugar will become clumpy; continue to stir until the sugar turns deep amber, 10 to 12 minutes.

Add the butter to the caramelized sugar (it will hiss violently—that's okay) and whisk until the butter melts.

Remove from the heat and, while whisking, pour in the warmed heavy cream until the caramel is well blended and smooth, about 3 minutes. Whisk in the vanilla and salt.

Allow the caramel sauce to cool slightly before using.

Store in a jar at room temperature for up to 3 days or refrigerate for up to 1 month.

BUTTERMILK CORNBREAD

MAKES ONE 10-INCH ROUND

Sugar is a hotly debated topic when it comes to certain dishes: Should you add a pinch to spaghetti sauce? Do you stir a little in your grits, or are only butter, salt, and pepper acceptable? And then there is cornbread. Some argue that cornbread is supposed to be completely void of sweetness and many others insist that cornbread be made with a touch of sugar. As a Chicagoan and a Northerner, I like mine to be fluffy and sweet, so I use buttermilk, baking powder, and, yes, sugar *and* vanilla.

While the debate on cornbread will always remain, there is one thing that both parties can agree on: The best way to make it is in a cast-iron skillet. And don't forget to check out Sweet Potato Cornbread (page 207)—it's one of my favorite ways to enjoy one of my favorite vegetables.

2 cups (272g) unbleached all-purpose flour

1 cup (145g) yellow cornmeal

1½ cups (300g) granulated sugar

1 tablespoon baking powder

1 teaspoon salt

4 large eggs

1 cup (252g) buttermilk

1 teaspoon pure vanilla extract

12 tablespoons (1½ sticks/170g) unsalted butter, melted

Adjust an oven rack to the middle position and preheat the oven to 350°F (175°C).

In a stand mixer fitted with the whisk attachment (or in a large bowl with a hand mixer), whisk together the flour, cornmeal, sugar, baking powder, and salt.

Add the eggs to the dry ingredients and whisk until well blended. Pour in the buttermilk and vanilla and mix until just combined. Add the melted butter and mix until well combined, but do not overmix the batter.

Mist a 10-inch cast-iron skillet or a 7½ × 10½-inch baking dish with cooking spray. Scrape in the batter and use a spatula to smooth out the top.

Bake until the cornbread is golden brown and the center resists light pressure and is dry when a cake tester is inserted, 25 to 30 minutes.

Store in an airtight container in the refrigerator for up to 5 days.

PILLOW-SOFT MARSHMALLOWS

Biting into a fresh homemade marshmallow is like sinking yourself into its softness—I like to roll the fluffiness around in my mouth and then let the marshmallow melt away on my tongue. I use these marshmallows to top my Petite S'mores Pies (page 49); they also make for some excellent crispy rice treats and are so good floating on top of hot chocolate. I like to add them to the top of a pan of straight-out-of-the-oven brownies that I will *then* drizzle with Salted Caramel Sauce (page 208), too.

These marshmallows feature classic vanilla flavor, but you can experiment by adding different flavorings, extracts, food colorings, and fillings such as champagne, raspberries, peppermint, or chocolate.

0.75 ounce (23g) unflavored powdered gelatin

2 cups (400g) granulated sugar

⅔ cup (222g) light corn syrup

¼ teaspoon kosher salt

1 tablespoon pure vanilla extract

½ cup (65g) confectioners' sugar, plus more for dusting

In the bowl of a stand mixer, sprinkle the gelatin over ½ cup of water. Using the whisk attachment, whip the gelatin at low speed until it dissolves, about 5 seconds. Turn off the mixer and let the mixture stand to bloom.

In a medium saucepan, combine the granulated sugar, corn syrup, salt, and ½ cup of water. Clip a candy thermometer to the side of the pan and set it over medium-high heat. Let the mixture come to a boil. Once the mixture boils and reaches 240°F (115°C), remove the saucepan from the heat.

Turn the mixer back on to low speed and slowly pour the hot sugar syrup mixture into the bowl. Once all the syrup is added, increase the speed to high and whip until the mixture becomes thick and voluminous, 13 to 16 minutes.

Decrease the speed to medium and slowly pour in the vanilla. Turn the mixer off and remove the bowl from the stand. Using a silicone spatula, scrape down the sides of the bowl and fold the mixture into the center to make sure the vanilla is well combined. Parts of the mixture may have streaks of stark white (compared with the mixture that has already combined with the vanilla and is slightly off-white).

Lightly mist a 7½ × 10½-inch baking dish with cooking spray. Using a wire-mesh sieve or a sifter, dust the dish with confectioners' sugar. Tip the baking dish as needed to ensure that the bottom, sides, and the corners are well coated. Tap out any excess confectioners' sugar back into the sieve or sifter. Pour or scrape the marshmallow into the baking dish. Lightly mist a silicone spatula with cooking spray and use the spatula to evenly spread out the sticky mixture in the dish. Dust the top of the marshmallow with the remainder of the confectioners' sugar. Set aside, uncovered and at room temperature, for 24 hours to firm up.

Once firm, cut the marshmallows into 1-inch squares. Remove the squares and set them on a large sheet of parchment, leaving space between them. Place some confectioners' sugar in a small bowl. Lightly dust all sides of each square with confectioners' sugar and set aside.

Store in a zip-top bag or an airtight container for up to 3 months.

BUTTERY MASHED POTATOES

MAKES 4 TO 6 SERVINGS

Mashed potatoes have always been my guilty pleasure—but not so guilty that I refrain from giving myself a heaping double serving on my dinner plate. While I started making them using potato flakes from a box (see page 55), now I've graduated to real, smooth, delightful, mashed potatoes because they're really not that much more work to make and are so much better.

Using Yukon Gold potatoes ensures a naturally buttery and slightly sweet taste. To prevent the mashed potatoes from becoming "gluey," avoid overworking the potatoes when mashing them. The more you mash, the more starch is released, and the starchier the mash, the more gummy the texture becomes.

1 tablespoon plus 2 teaspoons kosher salt

3 pounds Yukon Gold potatoes, peeled and cut into 2-inch chunks

4 tablespoons (½ stick/57g) unsalted butter

1 teaspoon ground white pepper

¼ cup (58g) sour cream

¼ cup (60g) heavy cream

Fill a large pot halfway with water, add 1 tablespoon of the kosher salt, and set over medium-high heat. Add the potatoes and bring to a boil. Boil the potatoes until they are fork-tender, 18 to 20 minutes.

Drain the potatoes and transfer them to a stand mixer fitted with the paddle attachment (or to a large bowl if using a hand mixer). Cream the potatoes until the segments are broken up, 2 to 3 minutes. Add the butter, white pepper, and the remaining 2 teaspoons of salt and continue to cream until well blended, about 2 minutes. While mixing, pour in the sour cream and heavy cream and continue to blend until the cream has dissolved into the mashed potatoes.

Remove from the mixer and serve immediately.

Refrigerate in an airtight container for up to 3 days.

BLUEBERRY-MINT PRESERVES

MAKES 1½ CUPS

When purchasing ingredients to bake in bulk for Justice of the Pies, I try to avoid waste as much as possible. So, when I have a small bit of fruit or filling remaining after making a pie or quiche to sell, I challenge myself to come up with new ways to use the leftover ingredients. Whenever I find myself with a few extra containers of blueberries, I always know how I'm using them: this simple blueberry preserve, which relies on the berries' natural pectin to form a jam-like consistency as it cools. I add fresh mint leaves to the mixture while it simmers for an unexpected fresh note. I highly recommend you slather these preserves onto freshly baked Billowy Biscuits (page 193) or use to top a cheesecake, serve with waffles, or just spread onto good toast.

2½ cups blueberries

¼ cup (50g) sugar

2 teaspoons fresh lemon juice

¼ teaspoon kosher salt

4 sprigs fresh mint

In a saucepan, combine the blueberries, sugar, lemon juice, and salt. Stir until combined, then add the mint sprigs. Cover and bring to a boil over medium heat. Uncover, stir, reduce the heat to low, and simmer until the liquid has evaporated, about 15 more minutes.

Remove from the heat. Set the mixture aside to cool for 1½ to 2 hours; the preserves will thicken and gel. Discard the mint sprigs.

Now you have the option to purée the blueberries with a hand blender so the preserves are smooth, or leave the preserve as is, a bit rough and chunky.

Transfer the preserves to a jar with an airtight lid and refrigerate to chill. Once the preserves have chilled sufficiently, after about 6 hours, they will reach a spreadable consistency.

The preserves will keep in the refrigerator for up to 10 days or in the freezer for up to 6 months.

VANILLA BEAN CHANTILLY CREAM

MAKES 1½ TO 2 CUPS

When my mother and I go to the Pancake House in Hyde Park for breakfast, these are the things that will remain unchanged: My mom will always order a Western omelet. I will always order pancakes. Mom will order coffee. I will order hot chocolate.

I will tell the waitress to leave the whipped cream off my hot cocoa, then my mom will interrupt me and tell the waitress to leave the whipped cream on my hot chocolate.

Our beverages will arrive, and without a word I will push my mug toward my mom, and she will take the whipped cream off my hot chocolate and put it in her coffee, then she will dip and scoop her spoon in my mug two or three more times, and I will say, "Hey, hey, hey . . . now you're just taking hot chocolate."

Whenever I make whipped cream, I always smile to myself as I recall this scene. This vanilla bean Chantilly cream is a doubly sweet, silkier version of a classic whipped cream thanks to the confectioners' sugar, which gives it some body and also helps it hold its shape (and allows you to make the whipped cream ahead of time without it weeping). It's perfect for topping cakes, layered pastry desserts, fruits, pies, tarts, and, yes, even hot chocolate.

1 cup (235g) heavy cream (with at least 35% butterfat)

½ vanilla bean

2 tablespoons confectioners' sugar

½ teaspoon pure vanilla extract

Place a stand mixer bowl and the whisk attachment (or a medium mixing bowl and beaters if using a hand mixer) in the freezer for 15 to 20 minutes.

While the equipment chills, pour the heavy cream into a measuring cup. Using a sharp paring knife, slice the vanilla bean lengthwise down the center of the pod. Gently scrape the seeds from each half of the pod into the heavy cream. (Try not to apply too much pressure or you may actually scrape up some of the skin.) Discard the vanilla pod.

Remove the mixing bowl and beaters from the freezer and pour the heavy cream into the bowl (make sure to scrape out any seeds that stick to the measuring cup). Whip the heavy cream on medium-high speed until it thickens slightly, 3 to 5 minutes. Once the cream has thickened slightly, pour in the confectioners' sugar and continue beating until soft peaks form, about 3 more minutes (a soft peak will form at the tip of the whisk attachment). Turn off the mixer and pour in the vanilla extract. Fold in the vanilla using a silicone spatula.

Cover the bowl with plastic wrap and chill in the refrigerator until ready to use (you may need to give it a quick whisk before using). Chantilly cream is best used within 1 day of making.

CHERRY BALSAMIC VINAIGRETTE

MAKES 1¾ CUPS

I used to buy salad dressing at the grocery store. I'd stand there as if I was playing Russian roulette with my taste buds, faced with scores of bottles and trying to imagine what each dressing would taste like while I carefully read the details and ingredients.

I always ended up grabbing two bottles, figuring if I didn't love one of them then I would love the other. Most often, I hated them both.

Then a friend hosted a casual dinner party where salad was being served. I had one forkful of lettuce and my eyes widened—you could literally see the stars shooting out from them.

I got up and asked her where she bought the dressing. She looked at me confused, and with a slight wave of her hand said, "Oh, honey . . . I made that."

"WHAT!?" I gave her a look that let her know that I would be asking her for the recipe later.

Well, I never did get her recipe, but I fully understood that sometimes the best recipes are the simplest ones—and this cherry balsamic vinaigrette is just that. I start with the cherry juice created when I simmer a batch of tart cherries in sugar, which I then mix with oil, seasonings, sweetener, and vinegar. Yes, it is amazing for salads, and it is also the perfect drizzle for the Roasted Brussels Sprouts + Cherry Tart (page 147, watermelon with feta cheese and mint, roasted string beans, or even the Heirloom Tomato Tart (page 138).

I've made this vinaigrette and given it away as gifts; it's that exquisite.

½ cup (139g) balsamic vinegar

½ cup (125g) cherry juice (preferably from fresh cherries)

½ cup (100g) olive oil

¼ cup (89g) honey

1 tablespoon crushed garlic

1 teaspoon dried basil

1 teaspoon dried thyme

1 teaspoon kosher salt

1 teaspoon freshly ground black pepper

½ teaspoon onion salt

In a small bowl, whisk together the balsamic vinegar, cherry juice, olive oil, and honey until the honey loosens and combines with the other ingredients.

Pour the mixture into a glass jar and add the garlic, basil, thyme, salt, pepper, and onion salt. Close the jar with an airtight lid, shake well, and use as desired or refrigerate for up to 12 days.

The ingredients may separate—so always shake before using.

HOT FUDGE SAUCE

MAKES 4 CUPS

Homemade hot fudge sauce is one of my favorite toppings. It's richer than chocolate sauce, thanks to the addition of heavy cream and butter, and the consistency is so pleasantly thick. This sauce is perfect to pair with the Lemon Espresso Pie (page 44), to use in the Chocolate + Bacon Bourbon Pecan Pie (page 28), or to top ice cream—especially when enjoying with a slice of pie.

1 cup (235g) evaporated milk

1 cup (235g) heavy cream

1 cup (200g) granulated sugar

¼ cup (55g) packed light brown sugar

½ teaspoon kosher salt

4 tablespoons (½ stick/57g) unsalted butter

2 ounces (57g) unsweetened baking chocolate, broken into smaller pieces

1 cup (80g) Dutch process cocoa powder

1 teaspoon pure vanilla extract

In a small saucepan, combine the evaporated milk, heavy cream, granulated sugar, light brown sugar, salt, and butter. Bring to a simmer over medium heat, about 10 minutes. Add the chocolate and whisk until it dissolves, about 3 minutes. Remove from the heat and, while whisking, sift in the cocoa powder. Return to low heat and constantly whisk until a sheen is formed, about 1 minute. Remove the saucepan from the heat and whisk in the vanilla.

Allow the fudge sauce to cool slightly before using.

Store in a jar at room temperature for up to 3 days or refrigerate for up to 1 month.

CRUSTS

ALL-BUTTER PIE DOUGH

MAKES ENOUGH FOR 1 SINGLE-CRUST 9-INCH PIE

A good pie dough recipe is imperative if you want to bake a pie (obviously). When you serve a slice of pie to someone, you definitely want them to exclaim, "That crust!" Some bakers are loyal to using lard or shortening, as these fats may seem to offer more flakiness, but I believe that when the dough is handled correctly, an all-butter crust can achieve equal flakiness—plus it offers more flavor!

For this recipe, while you may use a food processor or a stand mixer to make the dough, in my opinion the best way to achieve peak flakiness is to make it by hand. This will lessen the likelihood of the butter and flour being overworked. And with most things made with your hands, practice is the road to a place called perfection.

8 tablespoons (1 stick/113g) unsalted butter, preferably European-style, cut into 1-inch cubes

1½ cups (204g) unbleached all-purpose flour

1 tablespoon plus 1 teaspoon granulated sugar

½ tablespoon kosher salt

Flour, for rolling out

Pour ½ cup of water into a measuring cup filled with ice cubes. Set aside.

Place the cubes of butter on a parchment-lined baking sheet and place it in the freezer for about 15 minutes to quickly chill.

In a large bowl, whisk together the flour, sugar, and salt. Add the chilled butter to the flour mixture and, using a pastry cutter, fork, food processor, or stand mixer, cut the butter into the flour until there are no visible bits of butter that are larger than a pea (about ½-inch pieces). This will allow the crust to be marbled with butter so it melts in the oven while it bakes, and the steam from the butter will separate the crust into multiple layers—resulting in a flaky crust.

Pour ¼ cup of the ice water into the flour and butter mixture. Using your hands, gently work the water into the flour mixture until the dough comes together. If the dough is still very crumbly and dry, add ice water 1 tablespoon at a time until the dough comes together.

Lightly flour your work surface and set the dough on top. Gently knead the dough into a ball. Do not overwork the dough or else you may activate the gluten. Having too much water or overworking the dough may mean that your pie dough will contract while you roll it out and will not hold its shape.

Use your hands to press the dough into a disk 1½ inches thick. Wrap the dough well in plastic wrap and refrigerate for at least 1 hour and up to 3 days. (If refrigerating for more than 1 hour, let the dough sit on the countertop for 20 to 30 minutes before rolling; you can also freeze the dough for up to 6 months; if freezing, thaw in the refrigerator overnight before using.)

While the dough chills, fill a large bowl or a large baking dish with ice cubes. Place the bowl or baking dish on the countertop to chill your work area. (This is especially helpful to do on a hot day; chilling the countertop helps prevent the butter in your pie dough from melting while you roll it out.)

Remove the chilled dough from the refrigerator and discard the plastic wrap. Pat the countertop dry if you used ice cubes to chill it and lightly flour the surface. Set your dough on the countertop, then lightly flour the top of your dough.

When rolling the pie dough, start rolling from the center of the dough and roll away from your body. Slightly turn the dough with each roll, forming a round shape as you go. Turning the dough as you roll also ensures that your dough does not stick to your countertop. If any part of the dough tears along the outer edges while you are rolling it out, simply mend it back together using your fingertips.

Once the dough has been rolled out to the diameter called for in the recipe, pick up the dough by rolling it over the rolling pin, and transfer it to your pie pan or baking dish, unrolling the dough and draping it over the baking vessel. Follow the recipe instructions for fitting the dough into the pie pan and crimping.

VARIATION: LAVENDER ALL-BUTTER PIE DOUGH

Add 2 tablespoons dried lavender flowers to the other dry ingredients. The rest of the recipe is the same.

Making a lattice top crust is the perfect way to make a double-crust pie look extra special.

On a lightly floured surface, roll out one disk of All-Butter Pie Dough (opposite). The dough should exceed the diameter of your pie plate's rim by 3 inches (so for a 9-inch pie plate, roll the dough to 12 inches). Using a knife or pastry wheel, cut the dough into even strips about ½-inch to ¾-inch wide. You may freehand your cuts or use a ruler for straighter lines.

Lay strips of the pie dough on top of the filling in parallel lines, with about ½ to ¾ inches between each. The number of strips used depends on how thick your strips are. Fold back every other strip, with the fold being in the center of the pie.

Place one long strip of dough perpendicular to the parallel strips, then unfold the folded strips over the perpendicular strip.

Next, take the parallel strips that are running underneath the perpendicular strip and fold them back over the perpendicular strip. Place a second perpendicular strip of dough next to the first strip, keeping ½ to ¾ inch of space between strips. Unfold the folded parallel strips over the second strip.

Continue folding strips underneath the perpendicular strip and placing another strip of dough next to it until the weaving is complete.

The overhanging strips can be trimmed so they are even with the rim and bottom crust. Roll the edges of the crust together and crimp.

Brush the lattice with egg wash and bake according to the recipe's instructions.

RECIPE CONTINUES >>

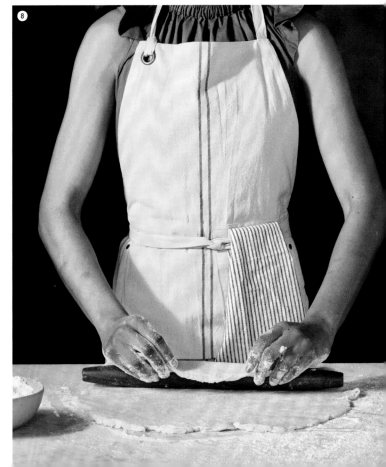

PÂTE SUCRÉE

MAKES ENOUGH FOR ONE 9-INCH TART

This French dough, also referred to as a short-crust pastry since it tastes similar to a shortbread, is sweet, crisp, and perfect for tarts like the Margarita Tart (page 157). Using confectioners' sugar instead of granulated sugar gives the crust a more tender texture, while also providing it with the strength of a traditional pie crust. Feel free to flavor it by adding cinnamon, ginger, lemon zest, or cocoa powder.

8 tablespoons (1 stick/113g) unsalted butter

⅔ cup (88g) confectioners' sugar

1 large egg

1 teaspoon pure vanilla extract

½ teaspoon kosher salt

1¾ cups (238g) unbleached all-purpose flour

In a stand mixer fitted with the paddle attachment (or a large bowl with a hand mixer), blend together the butter and confectioners' sugar until well mixed. Add the egg, vanilla, and salt and mix until well combined. Add the flour and continue to mix until a dough ball forms.

Remove the dough from the bowl and use your hands to press it into a disk 1½ inches thick. Wrap in plastic wrap and refrigerate for at least 30 minutes or up to 3 days.

VEGAN PIE DOUGH

MAKES ENOUGH FOR 1 SINGLE-CRUST 9-INCH PIE

Many of my friends are vegans and many of them have a serious sweet tooth! I always want to make sure they feel included in dessert, so I developed a crust that is free of dairy while still offering both flavor and flakiness. To do so, I use a combination of vegan butter and vegan shortening: the butter offers flavor and the shortening helps give the pie crust a flaky texture.

This vegan pie crust is also a perfect alternative crust to use for any sweet pie recipe that has a vegan filling or for savory pies such as the Vegetarian Chili Pot Pie (page 86) or the Sweet Potato + Lentil Pot Pie (page 95).

8 tablespoons (113g) vegan butter

8 tablespoons (113g) vegetable shortening

1½ cups (204g) unbleached all-purpose flour

1 tablespoon plus 1 teaspoon granulated sugar

½ tablespoon kosher salt

Flour, for rolling out

Place the entire containers of both vegan butter and shortening in the freezer to firm them up for about 1 hour before cutting.

Remove the butter and shortening from the freezer. If using a stick of butter, cut it into 1-inch cubes. If using tub butter, scoop into 1-tablespoon amounts. Do the same for the shortening.

Pour ¾ cup of water into a measuring cup filled with ice cubes. Set aside.

In a large mixing bowl, whisk together the flour, sugar, and salt. Add the butter to the flour mixture. With a pastry cutter, fork, or food processor, cut the butter into the flour until there are no bits of butter larger than a pea (about ½-inch pieces). Next, lightly add the shortening and lightly cut into the flour until it is coated in flour. Shortening is very soft, so you want to take care to not overwork the mixture.

Pour ¼ cup of the ice water into the flour mixture. Using your hands, gently work the water into the flour mixture until the dough comes together. If the dough is still very crumbly and dry, then add ice water 1 tablespoon at a time until the dough comes together.

Roll the dough out of the bowl and onto a lightly floured work surface. Gently knead the dough into a ball. (Do not overwork the dough or else you may activate the gluten, which could cause the dough to contract when you roll it.)

Press the dough into a 1½-inch-thick disk with your hands and wrap the dough in plastic wrap and refrigerate for at least 1 hour or up to 3 days.

While the dough chills, fill a large bowl or a large baking dish with ice cubes. Place the bowl or baking dish on the countertop to chill your work area. (This is especially helpful to do on a hot day; chilling the countertop helps prevent the butter in your pie dough from melting while you roll it out.)

Remove the chilled dough from the refrigerator and discard the plastic wrap. Pat the countertop dry if you used ice cubes to chill it and lightly flour your surface. Set your dough on the countertop, then lightly flour the top of your dough.

When rolling the pie dough, start rolling from the center of the dough and roll away from your body. Slightly turn the dough with each roll, forming a round shape as you go. Turning the dough as you roll also ensures that your dough does not stick to your countertop. If any part of the dough tears along the outer edges while you are rolling it out, simply mend it back together using your fingertips.

Once the dough has been rolled out to the diameter called for in the recipe, pick up the dough by rolling it over the rolling pin, and transfer it to your pie pan or baking dish, unrolling the dough and draping it over the baking vessel. Follow the recipe instructions for fitting the dough into the pie pan and crimping the crust.

The dough can be stored in the refrigerator for up to 3 days and in the freezer for up to 6 months.

CURRY DOUGH

MAKES ENOUGH FOR 1 DOUBLE-CRUST OR 2 SINGLE-CRUST PIES

One of the more challenging doughs to make is a Jamaican-style curry dough for patties. I begged all my friends from the West Indies to please, just *please*, ask their mothers to teach me how to make a good dough for patties. Their mothers all responded with "No." When I asked, "But why?" they each said, "Too hard."

Not willing to give up, I devised a dough that is similar to an empanada dough, but with a touch of Jamaican hot curry in it. It's pliable and easy to work with and, when baked, it's crispy on the outside and slightly chewy on the inside. It's really delicious used in place of a butter dough for making savory pies like Chili-Roasted Sweet Potato + Goat Cheese Quiche (page 113), Brazilian Fish Pot Pie (page 77), or Salmon Wellington (page 81). Or cut out the dough into small rounds to make hand pies (see Bonus, opposite).

12 tablespoons (1½ sticks/170g) very cold unsalted butter, cut into 1-inch cubes

3 cups (408g) unbleached all-purpose flour

1 tablespoon curry powder (preferably Jamaican hot curry powder)

½ teaspoon kosher salt

1 large egg

Flour, for rolling out

Place the cubes of butter on a parchment-lined baking sheet and place it in the freezer to quickly chill it, about 15 minutes.

In a large bowl, whisk together the flour, curry powder, and salt. Add the chilled butter to the flour and use a pastry cutter, fork, or food processor to cut the butter into the flour until there are no pieces larger than a pea (about ½-inch pieces). These marbles of butter will melt in the dough while it bakes and the steam from the butter will separate the crust into multiple layers, resulting in a flaky crust.

Pour ¾ cup of water into a measuring cup and add a few ice cubes. Set aside.

Add the egg and knead it into the dough until well incorporated. Pour ½ cup of the ice water into the flour and butter mixture. Using your hands, gently work the water into the flour mixture until the dough comes together. If the dough is still very crumbly and dry, then add ice water 1 tablespoon at a time until the dough comes together.

Roll the dough out of the bowl and onto a lightly floured countertop. Gently knead the dough into a ball. Do not overwork the dough or else you may activate the gluten. Having too much water or overworking the dough may mean that your pie dough will contract while you roll it out and will not hold its shape.

Once the dough is formed into a ball, pick it up and form a disk with your hands. Wrap the dough well in plastic wrap and place it in the refrigerator to chill and allow the butter in the dough to firm up, 1 to 2 hours.

While the dough chills, fill a large bowl or a large baking dish with ice cubes. Place the bowl or baking dish on the countertop to chill your work area. This is especially helpful to do on a hot day; chilling the countertop will prevent the butter in your pie dough from melting while you roll it out.

Remove the chilled dough from the refrigerator and discard the plastic wrap. Pat the countertop dry if you used ice cubes to cool it down, then lightly flour your surface. Place your dough disk on the countertop and lightly flour the top of the dough.

When rolling the dough, start rolling from the center of the disk of dough and roll away from your body. Slightly turn the dough with each roll to forming a circular shape as you go. Turning the dough as you roll also ensures that your crust does not stick to your countertop. If any part of the dough tears along the outer edges while you are rolling it out, simply meld it back together using your fingertips. Fit the dough into the pie pan as instructed in the recipe.

The dough can be stored in the refrigerator for up to 2 days or in the freezer for up to 6 months.

BONUS: For hand pies, after rolling the dough, use an empanada cutter, a small plate, or a large cookie cutter to cut out 3-inch rounds from the dough as close together as possible to minimize scraps. Use a small metal offset spatula to transfer the dough rounds to a parchment-lined baking sheet. Add 2 to 3 tablespoons of filling—such as the filling from Sweet Potato + Lentil Pot Pie (page 95), Brazilian Fish Pot Pie (page 77), or Cauliflower Patties (page 90)—to the center of each round of dough. Fold the dough over and pinch the edges to seal. Refrigerate while the oven heats to 425°F (220°C), then bake until golden brown, 25 to 30 minutes. Remove from the oven and cool slightly before eating.

GLUTEN-FREE DOUGH

MAKES ENOUGH FOR 2 SINGLE-CRUST 9-INCH PIES

As a baker, I live and breathe flour. Even though flour has such an important place in my work, I also want people who have a gluten intolerance to feel included because everyone deserves to enjoy our pies and quiches!

There are many brands of gluten-free flour on the market. It is important to find a brand that works best for achieving the perfect gluten-free crust.

16 tablespoons (2 sticks/227g) unsalted butter, cut into 1-inch cubes

1½ cups (222g) gluten-free flour

1½ cups (240) rice flour

2 tablespoons granulated sugar

2 teaspoons xanthan gum

1 teaspoon kosher salt

½ cup plain Greek yogurt (3.25% milkfat)

Flour, for rolling out

Pour ½ cup of water into a cup and add a few ice cubes. Set aside.

Place the cubes of butter on a parchment-lined baking sheet and place in the freezer for 15 minutes to quickly chill.

In a large bowl, whisk together the gluten-free flour, rice flour, sugar, xanthan gum, and salt. Add the cold butter. Use a pastry cutter, fork, or food processor to cut the butter into the flour until there are no visible bits of butter than are larger than the size of peas (about ½-inch pieces). This will help ensure a butter-marbled crust after rolling the dough—in the oven, the steam from the marbled butter melting will result in a flaky crust.

Add the yogurt and, using your hands, gently work the yogurt into the flour mixture until the dough comes together and resembles a ball. If the dough is still very crumbly and dry, add ice water 1 tablespoon at a time until the dough comes together.

Set the dough on a lightly floured countertop. Gently knead the dough into a ball. Do not overwork the dough. (Having too much water or overworking the dough may mean that your pie dough will contract while you roll it out and will not hold its shape.) Press the dough into a disk 2 inches thick. Wrap the dough well with plastic wrap and refrigerate for at least 1 hour or up to 3 days (or freeze for up to 6 months and thaw overnight in the refrigerator).

Remove the chilled dough from the refrigerator and discard the plastic wrap. Allow the dough to sit out for 20 to 30 minutes to return to room temperature. Since the crust does not have gluten in it, it will be difficult to overwork the dough, meaning you can let it come to room temp for easier rolling.

Lightly flour your work surface. Start rolling the dough from the center of the disk and roll away from your body. Slightly turn the dough with each roll, forming a round shape as you go. Turning the dough as you roll also ensures that your dough does not stick to your countertop. If any part of the dough tears along the outer edges while you are rolling it out, simply mend it back together using your fingertips.

Once the dough has been rolled out to the proper diameter called for in the recipe, gently roll the dough over the rolling pin, transfer it to your baking vessel, and unroll the dough over the baking vessel.

PUFF PASTRY

MAKES THREE 1-POUND SHEETS

There may be no crust more buttery than puff pastry, a flaky light sheet of dough with layers of butter inside the dough. The key to making it is to create a "brick" of dough made with mostly butter (and some flour) called a *beurrage* in French, and then fold it into a more traditional butter-speckled dough called the *détrempe*. The rolling and folding process is called lamination, and it requires considerably more time and patience than a traditional pie crust pastry. The extra-flaky results that come from the rolling, folding, and chilling of the dough are so worth it.

When the dough bakes, the butter melts and the water in the butter creates a steam. That steam puffs up the dough and produces light and flaky layers, like heavenly pastry clouds.

BEURRAGE

3 sticks (12 oz/340g) unsalted butter, at room temperature

1 cup (136g) unbleached all-purpose flour

DÉTREMPE

4 cups (544g) unbleached all-purpose flour

1 cup (237g) cold water

1 tablespoon granulated sugar

1 tablespoon fresh lemon juice

2 teaspoons kosher salt

9 tablespoons (126g) unsalted butter, cut into 9 pieces

Flour, for rolling out

MAKE THE BEURRAGE: In a stand mixer fitted with the paddle attachment (or in a large bowl with a hand mixer), blend the butter and flour until the butter is creamed and the flour is well combined, about 2 minutes. Place two long sheets of plastic wrap over an 8-inch square cake pan that covers all the corners of the pan with a little bit of an overhang. Add the beurrage to the pan, cover the top with the plastic wrap, and use your hands to pat down the beurrage to make it as even as possible. Place the cake pan in the refrigerator to chill for 2 hours.

MAKE THE DÉTREMPE: In a stand mixer fitted with the dough hook, mix together the flour, cold water, sugar, lemon juice, and salt. Blend to slightly mix the water and lemon juice with the flour, about 30 seconds—the mixture will be slightly wet in the center, but still dry with flour on the sides of the bowl. Add the butter pieces and turn the mixer to medium-low speed to continue mixing the dough until the it forms a cohesive ball, about 4 minutes.

Transfer the dough ball to a countertop and shape the dough into an 8-inch square. Enclose the détrempe in plastic wrap and refrigerate for 1 hour to rest.

Generously flour your countertop. Uncover the beurrage and use the plastic wrap to lift it out of the pan. Set it on a work surface and roll into a 16 × 9-inch rectangle. Unwrap the détrempe and set it on the center of the rolled-out butter, with the long side of the détrempe parallel to the long side of the beurrage. Fold the two ends of the butter over the dough to meet in the middle (they shouldn't overlap). Pinch the sides to seal the dough.

Using a large rolling pin with handles on the end (not the handleless, French-style rolling pin), roll the dough into a 16 × 20-inch rectangle. If the dough is still really hard, gently whack the dough with your rolling pin to widen it and soften it a bit and then continue rolling.

Once the dough is 16 × 20 inches, make a trifold by folding the left side of the dough to the center. Use a pastry brush to remove any excess flour. Then fold the right side of the dough over the center and overlap the other end of the dough—the edge of the right side of the dough should fold neatly over and be flush with the new left side of the dough.

For the second fold, roll the dough into an 18 × 20-inch rectangle. Repeat **STEPS 9 TO 14** as shown on the following spread. Dust off the excess flour using a pastry brush and fold the dough into a trifold again. If the dough becomes hard to handle—either it bucks back when you try to roll it (this means the dough needs to rest) or the butter gets too soft and starts to ooze/leak out—transfer the dough to a plate or sheet pan, cover with plastic wrap, and refrigerate for 20 minutes before continuing.

After the second fold is complete, wrap the dough in plastic wrap and refrigerate for at least 2 hours to chill.

Once chilled, remove the dough from the refrigerator, roll out into an 18 × 20-inch rectangle and fold once more. Evenly divide the dough into thirds, using a knife or a pastry scraper to cut 1-pound sections of dough.

The dough is now ready to use. It can also be wrapped in plastic and stored in the refrigerator for up to 3 days or stored in the freezer for up to 6 months. To thaw, remove from the freezer and let sit in the refrigerator for up to 4 hours.

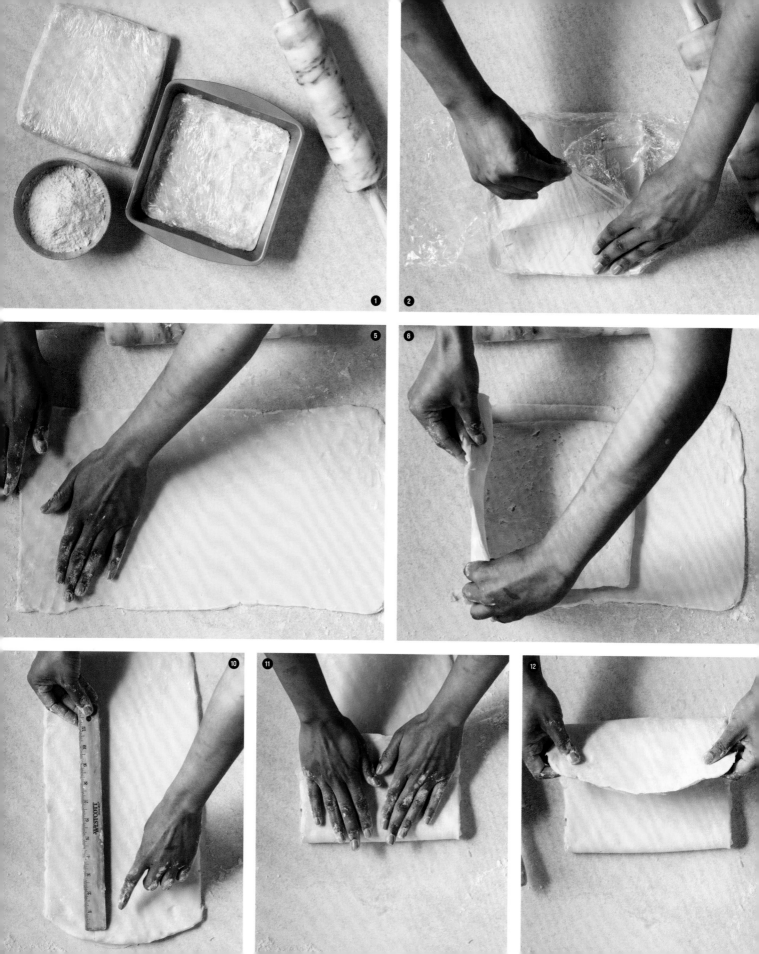

CHOCOLATE COOKIE CRUST

MAKES ONE 9-INCH CRUST

Chocolate sandwich cookies are delicious and can be revealing; some people like to eat only the cookies and not the filling; some like the whole cookie, while others twist open the cookie, lick the creme filling off, and then either eat the cookies or dunk them into a tall glass of milk.

I'm a cookie-only person all the way, which is why I love this chocolate cookie crust.

You can either use store-bought cookies in the crust or make homemade cookies (opposite). Both methods will produce an amazing crust, so use whichever one suits your mood and time frame (note that if using store-bought cookies, you do not need to make the Cream Cheese Filling since the cookies are already sandwiched with it). If you're a whole-cookie person, be sure to make the Cream Cheese Filling (at right) to make sandwich cookies! (You're welcome.)

CREAM CHEESE FILLING

4 tablespoons (57g) unsalted butter

4 ounces (113g) cream cheese

2 cups (234g) confectioners' sugar

2 teaspoons pure vanilla extract

2 tablespoons whole milk

COOKIE CRUST

2 cups (315g) chocolate sandwich cookies, either store-bought (with filling) or homemade (recipe follows)

3 tablespoons unsalted butter, melted

3 tablespoons Cream Cheese Filling (only needed if using homemade cookies)

MAKE THE CREAM CHEESE FILLING (SKIP THIS STEP IF USING STORE-BOUGHT COOKIES): In a large bowl, use a silicone spatula to cream together the butter and cream cheese until well combined. Sift in the confectioners' sugar and mix until well combined and the sugar is incorporated. Stir in vanilla extract and milk. Set 3 tablespoons aside for the crust and refrigerate the rest for 15 minutes.

MAKE THE COOKIE CRUST: Place the cookies in a blender or food processor and pulse until crumbs are formed. Transfer the crumbs to a medium bowl, pour in the melted butter and 3 tablespoons of the cream cheese filling (if using store-bought cookies, additional cream cheese is not needed). Using a silicone spatula, stir the butter and cream cheese filling into the chocolate cookie crumbs until the crumbs are well moistened and the crumbs hold a shape when pressed.

Transfer the crumbs to a 9-inch pie pan or or a 9-inch tart pan with a removable bottom and press the crumb mixture into the bottom and up the sides of the pan. Bake or fill the pie crust as directed in the individual recipe.

VARIATION: ESPRESSO CHOCOLATE COOKIE CRUST

Add 1 tablespoon ground espresso to the food processor with the cookies and continue as instructed.

BONUS: The remainder of the cream cheese can be used to fill the leftover homemade cookies to make 8 to 10 sandwich cookies, or use the cream cheese to pipe cream cheese filling on top of the pie for a tasty and decorative flair!

CHOCOLATE COOKIES

MAKES 30 COOKIES (15 COOKIE SANDWICHES)

1½ cups (204g) unbleached all-purpose flour

¾ cup (70g) black cocoa (see Note)

¼ teaspoon baking powder

¼ teaspoon baking soda

¼ teaspoon kosher salt

18 tablespoons (2¼ sticks/227g) unsalted butter

1 cup (170g) semisweet chocolate chips

¾ cup granulated sugar

1 large egg

2 teaspoons pure vanilla extract

Flour, for rolling out

In a large bowl, whisk together the flour, black cocoa, baking powder, baking soda, and salt. Set aside.

Bring 2 inches of water to a simmer in a small saucepan. Set a shallow glass or stainless steel bowl on the saucepan to create a double boiler (the bottom of the bowl shouldn't touch the water). Add the butter and chocolate chips to the bowl and stir constantly until the chocolate has melted and the mixture is smooth. Remove the saucepan from the heat and set aside. Allow the filling to cool until slightly warm, about 10 minutes.

Using a silicone spatula, stir the sugar into the chocolate mixture. Then whisk in the egg and vanilla. Pour the melted chocolate mixture into the bowl with the flour mixture and stir to combine until the batter is well blended and without any flour streaks. Cover the bowl with plastic wrap and allow the dough to cool to room temperature, 1 to 1½ hours.

Line three or four baking sheets with parchment paper. Divide the chilled dough in half. Roll one piece on a lightly floured work surface until it is ¼ inch thick. Using a 2-inch round cookie cutter, stamp out the cookie dough as close together as possible (to minimize scraps), then use a small metal spatula to transfer the cookies to the prepared baking sheets. Cover the baking sheet with plastic wrap and chill in the refrigerator for at least 4 hours or up to 3 days. Repeat with the remaining dough.

Adjust an oven rack to the middle position and preheat the oven to 325°F (165°C).

Discard the plastic wrap and bake the cookies until the edges are dry, 18 to 22 minutes. Remove from the oven and allow them to cool.

NOTE: You can find black cocoa (the extra-dark and alkalized cocoa used to make chocolate sandwich cookies) online and in some specialty baking stores.

VARIATION: HOMEMADE SANDWICH COOKIES

Place the Cream Cheese Filling (opposite) in a pastry bag (or use a very small cookie scoop) and pipe 1 tablespoon of filling on the flat half of the baked cookies. Top the filling with another cookie and gently press together. The cookies can be kept at room temperature, in a cookie jar, for up to 3 days, refrigerate for up to 1 week (they will soften over time), or freeze for up to 6 months.

GRAHAM CRACKER CRUST

MAKES ONE 10-INCH PIE CRUST

Graham crackers are such a nostalgic snack for me that I keep a box in my pantry at all times. During school and at summer camp, we were served peanut butter and jelly sandwiches made with graham crackers instead of bread and, if I was home sick, my mom would give me graham crackers to snack on while I sipped on ginger ale. So, of course I have a soft spot for pie crust made from graham crackers—and especially homemade graham crackers. It's a crust that makes many of the custard-based pies sing a sweet, buttery song. Of course you can skip the homemade crackers and use store-bought instead—you'll still get the delicious taste of nostalgia.

1¾ cups (227g) graham cracker crumbs, store-bought or homemade (recipe follows)

1 tablespoon packed light brown sugar

8 tablespoons (1 stick/113g) unsalted butter, melted

In a medium bowl, stir together the graham cracker crumbs, brown sugar, and melted butter until the crumbs are well combined with the butter and there are no dry crumbs visible. Transfer the crumbs to a pie pan or baking dish and tamp down so that the crumbs form a solid layer across the bottom and up the sides of the pan or baking dish. Consult the recipe for how to bake the crust.

GRAHAM CRACKERS

MAKES 24 CRACKERS

1¼ cups (170g) unbleached all-purpose flour

1¼ cups (170g) whole wheat flour

¼ cup plus 2 tablespoons (85g) dark brown sugar

¾ teaspoon baking powder

½ teaspoon baking soda

½ teaspoon ground cinnamon

½ teaspoon kosher salt

6 tablespoons (¾ stick/85g) unsalted butter, cut into ¼-inch cubes and chilled

¼ cup (89g) honey

2 tablespoons molasses

2 tablespoons whole milk

1 teaspoon pure vanilla extract

Flour, for rolling out

In a food processor, pulse together the all-purpose flour, whole wheat flour, brown sugar, baking powder, baking soda, cinnamon, and salt. Add the butter and pulse until the mixture is mealy. Add the honey, molasses, milk, and vanilla and continue to pulse until combined and the dough forms a ball.

Remove the dough from the bowl and divide it in half. Form each half into a disk, tightly cover with plastic wrap, and chill for at least 1 hour.

Adjust an oven rack to the middle position and preheat the oven to 350°F (175°C). Line two baking sheets with parchment paper.

Remove the chilled dough from the refrigerator and discard the plastic wrap. Lightly flour your countertop. Roll out one piece of dough until it is about ⅛ inch thick. Transfer the rolled-out dough to the baking sheet and use a cookie cutter (or a pastry wheel and a ruler) to cut the crackers into 2-inch squares. Place the crackers on the prepared baking sheet. Prick the crackers with the tines of a fork. Repeat the process for the second half of the dough, placing it on the second baking sheet.

Bake the dough one sheet at a time (unless you can fit them side by side on the middle rack) until the crackers are golden brown, 10 to 15 minutes.

Remove from the oven and allow to cool, 20 to 25 minutes.

MACAROON CRUST

MAKES ONE 10-INCH CRUST

A macaroon is a cookie that was originally (and traditionally) made using almond paste or ground nuts.

Different countries have their own variations and ingredients that make up a macaroon. In India, cashews are used; in Spain, hazelnuts are preferred; and in Scotland, macaroons are often made with a paste of potato and sugar. In the Dominican Republic and in Puerto Rico, coconut is the preferred way to make the macaroons, and that's how I make my macaroon crust.

Sweetened coconut makes for a candied, sweet, and crunchy base that toasts and browns quite nicely as it bakes. I loved this paired with the filling for Mango + Coconut Macaroon Tart (page 163) and as an alternative crust for the Chocolate Pear Tart (page 132).

1½ cups (145g) sweetened shredded coconut

2 tablespoons unbleached all-purpose flour

⅓ cup (67g) granulated sugar

½ teaspoon kosher salt

2 large egg whites, at room temperature

½ teaspoon vanilla extract (or any other flavored extract)

Flour, for forming the crust

Adjust an oven rack to the middle position and preheat the oven to 325°F (165°C).

In a large bowl, whisk together the shredded coconut, flour, sugar, and salt. In a small bowl, whisk together the egg whites and vanilla. Add the egg whites to the coconut and flour mixture and stir with a silicone spatula.

Place the entire mixture in a 9-inch or 10-inch tart pan. Dip two fingers into a small cup of flour and use your floured fingers to mold the crust to the pan. Dip your fingers in the flour each time you press a new section of the mixture onto the pan.

Bake until the edges are crispy and golden brown, 20 to 25 minutes.

Remove from the oven and cool before adding the pie filling.

SHORTBREAD CRUST

MAKES ENOUGH FOR 1 SINGLE-CRUST 9-INCH PIE

I used to be obsessed with dresses. I insisted on wearing a dress during my first trip to Disneyland. And I'm not talking about a casual sundress: I wore my Easter dress, complete with ribbon-lined frilly socks, lace gloves, and a white crocheted shawl. I probably looked like a ghost from the Victorian era as I walked over to meet Minnie Mouse. This is the same outfit I would wear when my mom would take my grandma Billingslea and me to the Walnut Room in the Marshall Field's department store. We went for high tea, but I was there only for the shortbread cookies.

Shortbread cookies are so dense and crumbly. The way they melt in your mouth is close-your-eyes-and-tilt-your-head-to-the-ceiling good. It's a treat that is always worth getting dressed up for.

The shortbread crust, with its balance of butter and sugar, is the perfect base for tarts that are, well, tart. The acidity of a citrus filling offers a nice juxtaposition to the crust's buttery flavor.

2 cups (272g) unbleached all-purpose flour

½ cup (100g) granulated sugar

½ teaspoon kosher salt

2 teaspoons pure vanilla extract

16 tablespoons (2 sticks/227g) unsalted butter, melted

Adjust an oven rack to the middle position and preheat the oven to 350°F (175°C).

In a large bowl, whisk together the flour, sugar, and salt. Add the vanilla to the melted butter and stir, then pour the butter into the flour mixture. Using a silicone spatula, stir the flour mixture until it is well combined with the butter.

Scrape the shortbread dough into a 9-inch tart pan with a removable bottom and spread it evenly using a silicone spatula or a large spoon. Tamp the dough down so it forms a solid layer across the bottom and up the sides of the pan.

Bake until the edges are lightly golden brown, about 15 minutes.

Remove from the oven. Using the tines of a fork, poke shallow holes on the bottom of the crust. Set aside until called for in the recipe.

VARIATION: LAVENDER SHORTBREAD CRUST

Add 2 tablespoons dried lavender flowers to the flour mixture before adding the vanilla and melted butter. Proceed with the recipe as instructed.

VANILLA WAFER CRUST

MAKES ONE 9-INCH CRUST

Vanilla wafer cookies are crispy and light and make for a wonderfully crispy and tasty pie crust, especially when paired with custard-based pies like the Blueberry Banana Pudding Pie (page 33) or the Strawberry Basil Key Lime Pie (page 37) and Margarita Tart (page 157). The use of confectioners' sugar rather than granulated sugar in the cookie dough makes it very tender and the ideal pie crust.

1½ cups (118g) vanilla wafer crumbs, either from store-bought (Nilla Wafers) or homemade cookies (recipe follows)

1 tablespoon light brown sugar

8 tablespoons (1 stick/113g) unsalted butter, melted

In a medium bowl, whisk together the wafer crumbs and brown sugar. Pour in the melted butter and, using a silicone spatula, stir the butter into the crumb mixture until the crumbs are well combined with the butter and there are no dry crumbs visible. Transfer the crumbs to a pie pan or baking dish and tamp down so that the crumbs firmly adhere to the baking dish.

VANILLA WAFERS

MAKES 36 TO 40 COOKIES

8 tablespoons (1 stick/113g) unsalted butter, at room temperature

¾ cup (97g) confectioners' sugar

3 large egg whites, at room temperature

1 large egg, at room temperature

1 tablespoon pure vanilla extract

1⅓ cups (180g) unbleached all-purpose flour

¼ teaspoon kosher salt

Adjust an oven rack to the middle position and preheat the oven to 350°F (175°C). Line a baking sheet with parchment paper.

In a stand mixer fitted with the paddle attachment (or in a large bowl with a hand mixer), cream together the butter and confectioners' sugar on medium speed until light and fluffy, 3 to 4 minutes. Add the egg whites and mix until the batter is smooth. In a small bowl, whisk the whole egg and vanilla together and then add it to the mixing bowl. Mix until well blended.

In a separate bowl, whisk together the flour and salt. Reduce the speed of the mixer to low, add half of the flour mixture, and blend until just combined and the mixture begins to thicken. Add the remaining flour mixture and continue to mix until combined. Do not overmix.

Using a ½-ounce small cookie scoop, scoop out batter and place it on the prepared baking sheet, leaving about 1 inch between mounds.

Bake until the wafers are golden brown, about 20 minutes. Remove the wafers from the oven and allow them to cool completely, 15 to 20 minutes.

GINGERSNAP COOKIE CRUST

MAKES ONE 10-INCH CRUST

Gingersnap cookies are one of the sturdiest cookies around. Flavored with cinnamon and ginger, they have not only a slight chewiness to them but also a great crunch or *snap*. I rely on gingersnaps to provide me with a dependable pie crust with a touch of gingery heat that I love paired with pies like Petite S'mores Pies (page 49), Brandied Banana Butterscotch Pie (page 24), and Cherry Amaretto Tart (page 131).

1¾ cups (270g) gingersnap cookie crumbs, either from store-bought or homemade cookies (recipe follows)

1 tablespoon light brown sugar

8 tablespoons (1 stick/113g) unsalted butter, melted

In a medium bowl, whisk together the cookie crumbs and brown sugar. Pour in the melted butter and, using a silicone spatula, stir the butter into the cookie mixture until the crumbs are well combined with the butter and there are no dry crumbs visible. Pour the crumbs into a pie pan and tamp down so that the crumbs firmly adhere to the bottom and sides of the pan.

GINGERSNAP COOKIES

MAKES 18 TO 20 COOKIES

2½ cups (340g) unbleached all-purpose flour

1 tablespoon ground ginger

2 teaspoons baking soda

1 teaspoon ground cinnamon

½ teaspoon ground cardamom

½ teaspoon ground cloves

¾ teaspoon kosher salt

¾ cup (165g) packed dark brown sugar

6 tablespoons (¾ stick/84g) unsalted butter

¼ cup (89g) dark molasses

2 large eggs

2 teaspoons pure vanilla extract

Adjust an oven rack to the middle position and preheat the oven to 350°F (175°C). Line a baking sheet with parchment paper.

In a large bowl, whisk together the flour, ginger, baking soda, cinnamon, cardamom, cloves, and salt. Set aside.

In a stand mixer fitted with the paddle attachment (or in a large bowl with a hand mixer), cream together the brown sugar, butter, and molasses on medium speed until light and fluffy, 3 to 4 minutes. Add the eggs and vanilla extract and mix until well blended.

Reduce the speed of the mixer to low, add half of the flour mixture, and blend until just combined. Add the remaining flour mixture and continue to mix until just combined. Do not overmix.

Using a medium cookie scoop, scoop out cookie batter and place the scoops about 1½ inches apart on the prepared baking sheet.

Bake until the cookies puff up, 13 to 15 minutes. Remove the cookies from the oven and allow them to cool completely, 25 to 30 minutes.

ACKNOWLEDGMENTS

To my mama, Dr. Camille Billingslea, thank you for lifting me up and holding me down. I love you *deep* deep.

To my agent, Cherise Fisher, thank you for being the gin to my tonic, the candy to my yam, the boom to my sonic, and the Gina to my Pam.

To my editor, Raquel Pelzel, thank you for keeping an eye on me over the years and for reaching out to me at just the right time. I appreciate your dedication to this book and your support for my vision.

To my creative director, Marysarah Quinn, thank you for your insightful opinions and sensitive eye for great design.

To my photographer, Dan Goldberg, thank you for having a genuine vested interest in the aesthetic integrity of this book. To my food stylist, Maria del Mar Cuadra, pero like, you made my food look so damn good. To my bonus food stylist, Jane Katte, thank you for having the prettiest hands when working with pastry. To my prop stylist, Andrea Kuhn, thank you for your effortlessly cool style. To the studio pup, Finley, thank you for being the sweetest doggy ever and a natural-born model. Thank you to Bodhi, the other studio pup, with your sweet, icy-blue eyes. To Andrew Kusznir, Brian Eaves, Elaine Miller, and Travas Machel, thank you for your contributions to this project—you all have made the experience one of the more enjoyable elements of this project. I will miss my lunches and end-of-the-day cocktails with the entire photography team.

To my illustrator, Noa Denmon, your work makes me smile with such satisfaction every time I see it.

Thank you to my bestie, Asha Dickens, and my forever bae, Keewa Nurullah, for your love and support. I'm so glad that your pretty smiles and beautiful souls are reflected on these pages.

Thank you to Bianca Cruz, Windy Dorresteyn, Kate Tyler, Allison Renzulli, Monica Stanton, Erica Gelbard, Stasia Whalen, Carisa Hayes, and everyone at Penguin Random House and Clarkson Potter who have supported me, the Justice of the Pies brand, and this book.

Thank you to my team at Justice of the Pies who held it down for me so that I could divert more energy to this project: Ermina Veljacic, Suejung Hong, Paige Carter, Lindsay Eberly, Claudette Soto, and Docia Buffington.

Thank you to my Fairy Bakemother, Chef Christina Tosi, and to Shannon Salzano for opening up your NYC kitchen to me and for putting me in touch with some amazing individuals who made this book even more special. I am grateful to you both.

Thank you to my Chicago Urban League IMPACT Fellows—the Untouchables—and to my Sorors of Alpha Chapter, Delta Sigma Theta Sorority, Inc. (and most especially to my linesisters of Atavistic 52), for testing all of my recipes.

Thank you to the individuals who were willing to open up to me and share the intimate details of your journeys: Christopher LeMark, Claudia Gordon, Grace Bonney, Jordan Marie Brings Three White Horses Daniel, Julia Turshen, Kika Keith + Kika Jr., Kleaver Cruz, Lauren Bush Lauren, Paige Chenault, Seema Hingorani, and Tanya Lozano.

Thank you to my ancestors who constantly surround me, propel me, and protect me. Thank you to the spirit of Aunt Sandy Boo, for loving me so deeply and nurturing all of my creative explorations. Thank you to the spirit of my dad, Stephen J. Broussard—I know you are beaming because I can see your face right now.

INDEX

Library of Congress Cataloging-in-Publication Data
Names: Broussard, Maya-Camille, author. | Goldberg, Dan,
other. Title: Justice of the pies : sweet and savory pies,
quiches, and tarts plus inspirational stories from exceptional
people / Maya-Camille Broussard ; photographs by Dan
Goldberg. Description: First edition. | New York : Clarkson
Potter/Publishers, [2022] | Includes index. | Identifiers:
LCCN 2022016143 (print) | LCCN 2022016144 (ebook) | ISBN
9780593234440 (hardcover) | ISBN 9780593234457 (ebook)
Subjects: LCSH: Pies. | Baking. | Desserts. | LCGFT: Cook-
books. Classification: LCC TX773 .B85 2022 (print) | LCC
TX773 (ebook) | DDC 641.86/52—dc23/eng/20220426
LC record available at https://lccn.loc.gov/2022016143
LC ebook record available at https://lccn.loc.gov/
2022016144

ISBN 978-0-593-23444-0
eBook ISBN 978-0-593-23445-7

Photographer: Dan Goldberg
Photography Assistant: Travas Machel
Illustrator: Noa Denmon
Production Assistants: Elaine Miller and Brian Eaves

Food Stylists: Maria del Mar Cuadra and Jane Katte
Prop Stylist: Andrea Kuhn
Editor: Raquel Pelzel
Editorial Assistant: Bianca Cruz
Book and cover designer: Marysarah Quinn
Production Editor: Patricia Shaw
Production Manager: Jessica Heim
Compositor: Merri Ann Morrell
Copy Editor: Kate Slate
Indexer: Elizabeth T. Parson
Marketer: Monica Stanton
Publicist: Erica Gelbard
Cover photographs: Dan Goldberg

Printed in China

10 9 8 7 6 5 4 3 2 1

First Edition